Study Edition

my REFLECTIONS on WORLD HISTORY

re•flec'tion (ri-FLEK-shuhn) ▶ noun

1. a thought, idea, or opinion formed or a remark made as a result of meditation **2.** consideration of some subject matter, idea, or purpose **3.** an instance of reflecting; especially: the return of light or sound waves from a surface **4.** the production of an image by or as if by a mirror **5.** something produced by reflecting, as **a:** an image given back by a reflecting surface **b:** an effect produced by an influence

Use the study edition to record your thoughts, ideas, and opinions and make connections between the essential questions and yourself, your community, and the world.

McGraw-Hill **networks**™
A Social Studies Learning System

Cover Photo Credit: Nefertiti, Getty Images

www.mheonline.com

ISBN: 978-0-07-661726-5
MHID: 0-07-661726-2

Printed in the United States of America.

4 5 6 7 8 9 ROV 16 15 14 13 12

How will YOU use *My Reflections on World History?*

The *My Reflections on World History: Florida Study Edition* was created as a study edition just for you. Using this interactive textbook along with your full student edition and **netw⊙rks** will empower you to learn world history in a whole new way.

You will be able to write directly in this book! You can take notes, interact with what you read, and reflect on what you learn.

As a result, you will be able to make connections between world history and your life, your community, and your world today.

Show Your Skill

1. Identify Cause and Effect
What effect did healthier food have on people?

> Dig into the text and show what you know!

Think Critically

2. Analyze Why did early people form governments?

> Analyze what you read!

Mark the Text

3. Underline two ways that Paleolithic people adapted.

> Finally—a book you can write in!

Take the Challenge

4. Create your own pictograph that shows characteristics shared by early river valley civilizations. Be creative!

> Create a unique project or do some learning on your own!

Keep Going! ➤➤

TO THE STUDENT

Make the Most of the *My Reflections* Activities!

Does world history matter to you today? Is it relevant to your daily life? Yes, it is!

The ideas and events you learn about in world history help you understand people and the past. As a result, you are better equipped to understand your life and the world today.

The "My Reflections" activities at the end of each chapter were created to help you make connections between the past and the present. Each activity allows you to reflect on what you have learned and how that relates to you, your community, and even the world.

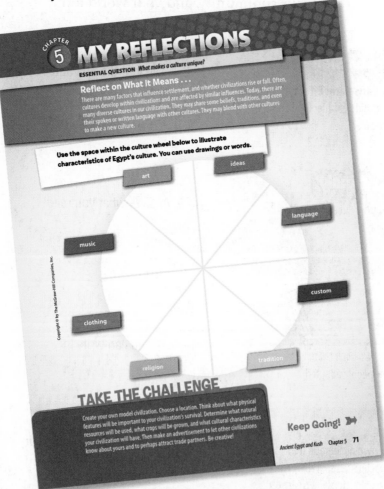

Have fun with *My Reflections on World History: Florida Study Edition!* You never know . . . you might just love world history by the time you're finished.

FLORIDA *Study Edition*

Contents

page 1

page 64

page 91

networks
*Interact with your
Florida Study Edition Online!*

page 149

page 184

page 230

netw⊙rks
Interact with your
Florida Study Edition Online!

Copyright © by The McGraw-Hill Companies, Inc.

PHOTO: (t) Indian School/The Bridgeman Art Library/Getty Images; (c) DEA/G. DAGLI ORTI/De Agostini Picture Library/Getty Images; (b) Burstein Collection/CORBIS

WHAT DOES A HISTORIAN DO?

NGSSS

SS.6.W.1.6 Describe how history transmits culture and heritage and provides models of human character.

ESSENTIAL QUESTIONS *Why is history important? How do we learn about the past? How do you research history?*

Historians use the work of archaeologists to study the past. Francis Bacon (1561–1626) was an English philosopher who wrote a great deal about science and learning. He was interested in education. This excerpt is from *Essays or Counsels, Civil and Moral.*

"Histories make men wise; poets, witty; the mathematics, subtle; natural philosophy, deep, moral, grave; logic and rhetoric, able to contend."

FRANCIS BACON

Write down any words in the excerpt for which you do not know the meaning. Use a dictionary to find the meanings.

_____

_____

PHOTO: Lynsey Addario/VII Network/Corbis

Copyright © by The McGraw-Hill Companies, Inc.

DBQ BREAKING IT DOWN

Contend can mean to struggle, argue, or assert. Why do you think Bacon says that history makes men "able to contend"?

_____

_____

_____

_____

What is Francis Bacon saying about history?

_____

_____

_____

_____

McGraw-Hill
networks™
There's More Online!

NGSSS

SS.6.W.1.1 Use time lines to identify chronological order of historical events.

SS.6.W.1.2 Identify terms (decade, century, epoch, era, millennium, B.C./B.C.E, A.D./C.E.) and designations of time periods.

SS.6.W.1.5 Describe the roles of historians and recognize varying historical interpretations (historiography).

SS.6.W.1.6 Describe how history transmits culture and heritage and provides models of human character.

Essential Question
Why is history important?

Guiding Questions
1. What types of things can history reveal about the past?
2. What are historical periods?
3. What do students of prehistory look for?

Terms to Know

era
a large division of time

archaeology
the study of the past by looking at what people left behind

artifact
an object made by people

paleontology
the study of the past using fossils

fossil
plant or animal remains that have been preserved from an earlier time

anthropology
the study of human culture and how it develops over time

species
a class of individuals with similar physical characteristics

What Do You Know?

Directions: In the photographs below, circle the tools that archaeologists use to study the past.

networks Read Chapter 1 Lesson 1 in your textbook or online.

Why Study History?

People who study history are called historians. Historians study causes and effects of historical events. A cause is a reason that something happened. An effect is what happened after an event. Historians try to figure out why things happened. They use their understanding to think about how those things make a difference today.

Learning about the past helps us understand the present. It helps us decide what to do in the future. We can learn from the choices people made long ago. Knowing what went wrong in the past can help us make better decisions today.

Measuring Time

A group of 10 years is called a *decade*. A group of 100 years is called a *century*. Ten centuries grouped together is called a *millennium,* which is a period of 1,000 years.

A period of several centuries is sometimes called an **era.** The earliest era is called *prehistory*. Prehistory is the time before people invented writing. The next period is called *Ancient History.* Then come the *Middle Ages.* Sometimes the Middle Ages are called the medieval period. The era after the Middle Ages is *Modern History.* We live in the era of Modern History.

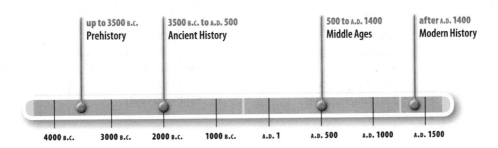

up to 3500 B.C. **Prehistory** | 3500 B.C. to A.D. 500 **Ancient History** | 500 to A.D. 1400 **Middle Ages** | after A.D. 1400 **Modern History**

4000 B.C.   3000 B.C.   2000 B.C.   1000 B.C.   A.D. 1   A.D. 500   A.D. 1000   A.D. 1500

To keep track of days and months, we use a calendar. Some cultures use calendars that are different from ours. Some calendars are arranged according to nature or the position of the moon.

Our modern calendar is based on one that started in ancient Rome. Julius Caesar invented it. We call it the Julian calendar. It started counting years from the time that Rome began. It was created with 365 days each year and one extra day every fourth year, called a leap year. However, there was a problem with the

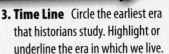

Mark the Text

1. Underline the sentence that explains what historians look for when they study history.

Think Critically

2. **Sequence** Put these words in order from largest number of years to smallest number of years: *century, decade, millennium*

_____

Mark the Text

3. **Time Line** Circle the earliest era that historians study. Highlight or underline the era in which we live.

Copyright © by The McGraw-Hill Companies, Inc.

What Is History?   Lesson 1   **3**

_____

_____

_____

Think Critically

5. **Explain** What do the letters A.D. and B.C. mean?

_____

_____

_____

_____

_____

_____

Take the Challenge

6. Make a parallel time line. Create a time line that shows events in your lifetime. Make a second time line below it and include important historic events in your community, the nation, and the world.

Julian calendar. After many years, the calendar did not follow the seasons correctly. It needed to be fixed.

Pope Gregory XIII decided to create a new calendar. Pope Gregory changed the starting date of his calendar. He began counting years on his calendar with what he thought was the birth of Jesus. He also fixed the mistake from the Julian calendar. Pope Gregory included leap years in his calendar, too. He made a plan so that the calendar will always be accurate. We call Pope Gregory's calendar the Gregorian calendar. Although there are other calendars, many people throughout the world use the Gregorian calendar today.

The Gregorian calendar has a special way to mark the years. Years that happened after the birth of Jesus are marked A.D. The letters stand for the words _anno domini_. Those are the Latin words for "in the year of the Lord." The years before the birth of Jesus have different letters. They are marked as B.C., which means "before Christ."

To date events before the birth of Jesus, or B.C., historians count backwards from A.D. 1. There is no year 0. The year before A.D. 1 is 1 B.C.

Sometimes when historians write, they use a different way to explain the years. Instead of B.C., they use B.C.E., which means "before the common era." Instead of A.D., they use C.E., which means "common era." The years are still numbered the same way.

Julian Calendar

- by Julius Caesar
- started with founding of Rome
- included leap years
- did not follow seasons correctly

Gregorian Calendar

- by Pope Gregory XIII
- started with birth of Jesus
- included leap years
- used A.D. and B.C.
- still used today

A time line shows the order of events in a period of time. Most time lines are divided into even sections of time. They have labels that tell when something happened. Sometimes a time line cannot show all the events in a long period. In this case, a time line might have a slanted or jagged line in the middle. That means that some years are left out of the time line. A multilevel time line is one that has two or more lines stacked on top of each other.

Digging Up the Past

Archaeology is the study of the past by looking at what people left behind. An archaeologist is someone who digs in the earth for artifacts. An **artifact** is an object made by people. Tools, pottery, weapons, and jewelry are artifacts. They help archaeologists learn what life was like in the past.

Paleontology is another study of the past. Paleontologists study fossils. **Fossils** are the remains of plant and animal life that have been preserved from an earlier time.

Anthropology is the study of human culture. Anthropologists study artifacts and fossils, too. They look for clues about what people valued and believed.

A paleontologist named Donald Johanson made an important discovery. He found the skeleton of an early human who lived more than 3.2 million years ago. He called the skeleton Lucy. Lucy belonged to a new species of early human. A **species** is a group of living beings. The members of a species are alike in some way. Lucy is the oldest human species that scientists have ever found. Lucy can help us learn more about how humans developed.

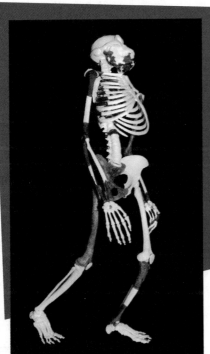

Often, archaeologists find only parts of an object from the past, and they need to guess what makes up the other parts. This skeleton is a recreation of what Lucy's entire skeleton might have looked like.

NGSSS Check How do archaeologists use artifacts and fossils? SS.6.W.1.5

_____

_____

_____

Think Critically

7. Analyze What do paleontologists look for in fossils when they dig in the earth?

_____

_____

_____

_____

Show Your Skill

8. Draw Conclusions How are archaeologists, paleontologists, and anthropologists like detectives?

_____

_____

_____

Think Critically

9. Conclude What can we learn from the discovery of Lucy or other fossils and artifacts?

_____

_____

_____

_____

PHOTO: Adam Gault/OJO Images/Getty Images

LESSON **2**

HOW DOES A HISTORIAN WORK?

NGSSS

SS.6.W.1.4 Describe the methods of historical inquiry and how history relates to other social sciences.

SS.6.W.1.5 Describe the roles of historians and recognize varying historical interpretations (historiography).

Essential Question
How do we learn about the past?

Guiding Questions
1. What types of evidence do historians use to understand the past?
2. How do we write about history?

Terms to Know

evidence
something that shows proof or an indication that something is true

primary source
firsthand evidence of an event in history

secondary source
a document or written work created after an event

point of view
a general attitude about people or life

bias
an unreasoned, emotional judgment about people and events

scholarly
concerned with academic learning or research

conclusion
a final decision reached by reasoning

It Matters Because

Knowing how historians work helps us understand historical information.

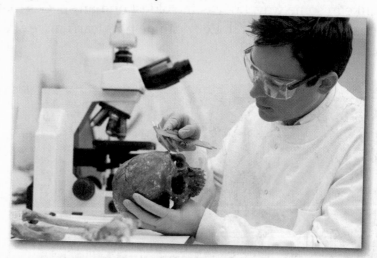

Discuss with a partner what this man is doing, and how his research might reveal information about the past.

What Do You Know?

Directions: In the *K* column, list what you already know about how a historian works. In the *W* column, list what you want to know. After reading the lesson, fill in the *L* column with the information that you learned.

K	W	L

What Is the Evidence?

Historians look at **evidence** to find out about the past. Evidence is proof that something is true. Evidence might be an object, such as a soldier's uniform or a scrap of pottery. Evidence might also be a document or book that was written long ago.

A **primary source** is a kind of evidence. Primary sources are created by people who saw or were part of an event. Letters and diaries are primary sources. Tools and clothing are also primary sources. Historians use primary sources to learn what people were thinking at the time of the event.

A **secondary source** is also evidence. Secondary sources are created after an event. They are created by people who were not part of the event. Your history textbook is a secondary source. Encyclopedias are also secondary sources.

Historians analyze the information in their sources. They look for reasons that the source was created. Then historians decide if they can trust the source. Each source was written with a particular **point of view,** or attitude about people or life. The author of a source uses his or her point of view to decide what to include in the document. Sometimes a point of view is based on feelings and not on facts. A judgment based only on feelings is called a **bias.** Sources with a bias cannot always be trusted.

Sources That Historians Use

Primary Sources
- Written at the time of the event
- Eyewitness to history
- Reliable source for historians
- Includes letters, diaries, tools, clothing

Secondary Sources
- Written after an event
- Author did not witness the event
- Contains facts about an event
- Includes textbooks and encyclopedias

Writing About History

Historians analyze what they read. They make inferences about the information. Making an inference means choosing the most likely explanation for the facts. Sometimes the inference is simple. When you see someone with a wet umbrella, you can make the inference that it is raining. Making inferences about historical events is sometimes not that easy.

Show Your Skill

1. **Compare and Contrast** Which kind of source is more trustworthy: a primary source or a secondary source? Why?

_____

_____

_____

_____

Mark the Text

2. Underline the definition of *bias*. Then write an example.

_____

_____

_____

_____

Think Critically

3. **Paraphrase** In your own words, explain how to make an inference.

_____

_____

_____

_____

_____

_____

Think Critically

5. Explain How could historians disagree about something that happened in the past?

_____

_____

_____

_____

_____

_____

_____

Take the Challenge

6. In a small group, research an event in the past. Then follow the steps in the graphic organizer. Give each group member a task. Write a conclusion together based on what you have learned.

To make an inference, historians start with primary sources. Then they use facts they already know are true. Next, they read secondary sources. They think about the different points of view. Finally, they make an inference to explain what happened.

Many historians write articles about their inferences. Most articles are published in **scholarly** journals, or magazines. Scholarly magazines are concerned with learning. Usually, other historians read the articles to make sure the facts are correct. They decide whether they agree with the inferences in the article. Historians must be careful to make inferences based on facts. They do not want to show a bias in their writing.

A **conclusion** is a final decision that is reached by reasoning. It is like an inference. Historians draw conclusions about events of the past. They look for facts and evidence in their sources. Then they use reasoning to draw a conclusion.

Sometimes historians disagree in their conclusions. For example, many historians disagree about Genghis Khan. Some say that Genghis Khan was a brutal leader. They tell how he would destroy cities and kill people when he came to a new land. Other historians disagree. They say that Genghis Khan was a good ruler. His empire had a time of peace. Traders were safe to trade goods. People were protected by good laws.

Which conclusion is correct? Was Genghis Khan a terrible or a good leader? A historian must use evidence to explain his or her conclusions. If both conclusions are supported by evidence, they both can be correct.

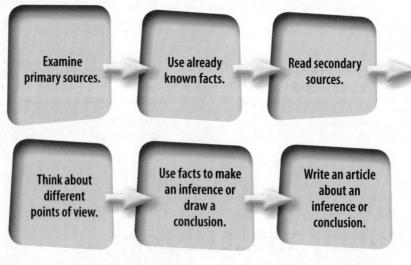

Examine primary sources. → Use already known facts. → Read secondary sources. →

Think about different points of view. → Use facts to make an inference or draw a conclusion. → Write an article about an inference or conclusion.

 NGSSS Check Explain how historians use different sources to draw conclusions. **SS.6.W.1.5**

_____

_____

NGSSS

SS.6.W.1.4 Describe the methods of historical inquiry and how history relates to the other social sciences.

SS.6.W.1.5 Describe the roles of historians and recognize varying historical interpretations (historiography).

LESSON 3 RESEARCHING HISTORY

Essential Question
How do you research history?

Guiding Questions
1. How do you begin a research project?
2. How do you safely research on the Internet?
3. How do you interpret historical events accurately?

Terms to Know

credentials
qualifications or something that gives confidence

URL
abbreviation for *uniform resource locator;* the address of an online resource

.gov
the ending of a URL for a government Web site

.edu
the ending of a URL for a Web site of an educational institution

.org
the ending of a URL for a Web site of an organization

plagiarize
to present someone's work as your own without giving that person credit

It Matters Because

Knowing where to find information about your subject will make it easier to complete research projects and other schoolwork.

Choose a topic to research. After you have finished the lesson, write down the steps you learned to show how you will research the topic.

_____

_____

_____

_____

What Do You Know?

Read the list of words that relate to the Internet. Circle the words you know. Write something you know about each circled word.

URL

_____

Web site

_____

blog or blogger

_____

search engine

_____

Show Your Skill

1. **Identify the Main Ideas** Circle the research topics that are too broad for a short research paper.

   World War II

   Swimming the Backstroke

   Trees

   Vampire Bats

Mark the Text

2. Underline the sentences that tell the meanings of *fact* and *opinion*.

Think Critically

3. **Explain** Why would you want to know the credentials of an author?

   _____

   _____

   _____

Show Your Skill

4. **Compare and Contrast** What is the difference between the endings .gov and .edu at the end of a URL?

   _____

   _____

   _____

   _____

   _____

Planning Your Project

The first step in researching a history topic is to choose a topic. Your topic should not be too broad or too narrow. To test your topic, look it up in an encyclopedia. If there is no entry for your topic, it may be too small. If there are many entries, or a very long entry, the topic may be too large.

After you choose a topic, the next step is to collect your research materials. Start with an encyclopedia. Then visit the library to find a book about your subject. Finally, look for articles on the Internet. Look at each book and article to make sure it is trustworthy. A source that has too many opinions could be biased or untrustworthy. A good source will be full of facts. Remember, a fact is something that can be proven by evidence. An opinion is an attitude toward something. It cannot be proven true or false.

Starting Historical Research

Choose a topic. → Collect sources. → Decide if each source can be trusted.

Researching on the Internet

Looking for information on the Internet can be quick. However, finding sources you can trust can be tricky. Many articles on Web sites do not name the author. The reader cannot tell whether the author is an expert on the subject. A trustworthy article will include the author's name and **credentials.** Credentials are evidence that someone is an expert.

The home page of the Web site can give more clues about the trustworthiness of the article. If the article is on the Web site of a university, government office, or museum, it is probably reliable.

A good clue to find out about a Web site is its online address, or **URL.** Look at the end of the URL. A URL that ends in **.gov** is a government site. This site probably has good information about the government. A URL that ends in **.edu** is the site of a school or college. Most .edu sites pride themselves on accuracy.

Nonprofit organizations usually end their URLs in **.org.** These sites may be very accurate. However, they often contain opinions.

Internet Tips

If you answer NO to any of the questions below, the Web site is probably not a good source.

- **Can you tell who wrote the article?**
- **Can you easily find out who is responsible for the Web site?**
- **Has the page been updated recently?**
- **Does the writing show a bias toward one point of view?**

Writing Without Bias

Putting all the facts of your research together can be hard work. You should watch out for some easy mistakes.

The first one to watch out for is **plagiarism.** Plagiarism happens when a writer uses the exact words or ideas from another person without giving credit. Copying someone else's work is wrong, and it is against the law. Students who plagiarize are likely to get a failing grade.

To avoid plagiarism, follow these rules:

- **Put the ideas you read in your own words.**
- **When you restate an opinion from something you read, include a reference to the author: "According to Smith and Jones . . ."**
- **Always include a footnote when you use a direct quotation from one of your sources.**

Something else to watch out for is when you write about history, be careful that you do not use values from today to make a judgment about what happened in the past. For example, long ago, women had different rights than women have today. A historian should use evidence to draw conclusions. He or she should not use modern ideas about how women work and live in today's society.

 NGSSS Check List three rules for doing historical research. SS.6.W.1.4

_____

_____

_____

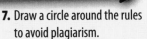

Think Critically

5. Analyze Why is plagiarism wrong?

_____

_____

_____

6. Explain What are two important mistakes to avoid when you are writing about history?

_____

_____

_____

_____

_____

Mark the Text

7. Draw a circle around the rules to avoid plagiarism.

Take the Challenge

8. Go back to the research topic you chose at the beginning of the lesson. Write down the steps you have learned to research it. Use those steps as a guide to help you. Gather enough information to deliver a short speech about your topic.

CHAPTER 1 MY REFLECTIONS

ESSENTIAL QUESTION *Why is history important?*

Reflect on What It Means . . .

History is not just something that happened in the past. It happens every day in places in your community and around the world. Knowing the *history* of an event or the *story* behind something can provide a wealth of information to knowing the big picture. In other words, smaller events over a period of time can lead to a major event, one that can affect your life, your community, and your world—all in one.

Research an event that took place in the distant or recent past, either in your community or around the world. Make sure the event made an impact on you, your community, and on the world.

On the map below, label where the event took place, write a brief description of the event and date, and then write on a separate piece of paper about how it affected you, your community, and the world.

TAKE THE CHALLENGE

Make a time capsule with items that you would want a future civilization to uncover. Place objects in the shoebox that will reveal how you live today, such as what you eat, the games that you play, the music that you listen to, and the clothes and accessories that you wear. Share your time capsule with the class.

Copyright © by The McGraw-Hill Companies, Inc.

STUDYING GEOGRAPHY, ECONOMICS, AND CITIZENSHIP

NGSSS

SS.6.G.1.4 Utilize tools geographers use to study the world.

ESSENTIAL QUESTIONS *How does geography influence the way people live? Why do people trade? Why do people form governments?*

Arne Duncan was nominated as U.S. Secretary of Education by President-elect Barack Obama in 2009. In a speech in June 2010, Duncan made the following statement:

" The study of history and civics helps provide that sense of time beyond the here and now. The study of geography and culture helps build a sense of space and place. "

ARNE DUNCAN

In Your Own Words

What is Arne Duncan saying about the importance of geography?

_____

_____

What does Arne Duncan mean by "beyond the here and now"?

_____

_____

DBQ BREAKING IT DOWN

Why do you think that the study of geography, history, civics, and culture is important?

_____

_____

_____

McGraw-Hill
netw⊙rks™
There's More Online!

PHOTO: B2M Productions/
Photographer's Choice/Getty Images

STUDYING GEOGRAPHY

NGSSS

SS.6.G.1.2 Analyze the purposes of map projections (political, physical, special purpose) and explain the applications of various types of maps.

SS.6.G.1.4 Utilize tools geographers use to study the world.

SS.6.G.6.1 Describe the Six Essential Elements of Geography (The World in Spatial Terms, Places and Regions, Physical Systems, Human Systems, Environment, The Uses of Geography) as the organizing framework for understanding the world and its people.

Terms to Know

hemisphere
a "half sphere," used to refer to one-half of the globe

latitude
imaginary lines that circle the Earth parallel to the Equator

longitude
imaginary lines that circle the Earth from pole to pole

projection
a way of showing the round Earth on a flat map

physical map
a map that shows land and water features

political map
a map that shows the names and borders of countries

special-purpose map
a map that shows themes or patterns such as climate, natural resources, or population

scale
a measuring line that shows the distances on a map

cardinal directions
north, south, east, and west

choropleth
a special-purpose map that uses colored dots to show population density

migration
the movement of people from one place to settle in another place

culture
the set of beliefs, behaviors, and traits shared by a group of people

Essential Question
How does geography influence the way people live?

Guiding Questions
1. What methods do geographers use to show the Earth's surface?
2. How do geographers use the five themes and six essential elements of geography?
3. What are some of the key ways that maps are used?
4. What are the uses of charts, graphs, and diagrams?
5. How do geographers study population and culture?

Where in the World?

The World

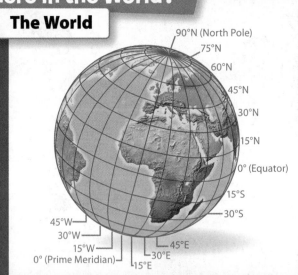

What Do You Know?

Directions: Label the globe above with the following:

North   South   East   West

Use a globe or map in your classroom and find the latitude and longitude of your town or city. _____

Displaying the Earth's Surface

Geographers use globes and maps to show where things are on the Earth. *Globes* are round models of the Earth. Maps are flat drawings of the Earth. On a globe, the land and water look the same as on the Earth. This is not true for a map. A flat map has to stretch the Earth out. This means the size and shape of the land and water are changed. Mapmakers choose different ways to do this. Each way of showing the Earth on a flat map is called a **projection.**

Globe

A round, 3-D model surface that shows the shape of the Earth as it is.

Map Projection

A flat drawing that stretches and twists the Earth's surface out of proper size and shape.

How do you know exactly where something is on Earth? Mapmakers use imaginary lines. One key line is the Equator. It circles the Earth from east to west. The Equator divides Earth into two hemispheres, north and south. A **hemisphere** is half of a globe. Another key line is the Prime Meridian. It circles the Earth from north to south. It divides Earth into the eastern and western hemispheres.

Lines of **latitude** circle the Earth from east to west. They run above and below the Equator. Lines of **longitude** circle the Earth from north to south. They run to the east and west of the Prime Meridian. Together, these lines form a grid. This means that the two sets of lines cross each other. Each point where they cross has a latitude measurement and a longitude measurement. These are shown in units called degrees. If you know the longitude and latitude of a spot, you know its exact location on the Earth.

Five Themes and Six Essential Elements of Geography

Geographers also want to know about other features of our world. They study the people who live on Earth.

1. Identify the Main Idea
Why do maps and globes show the Earth in different ways?

_____

_____

_____

_____

_____

_____

Think Critically

2. Infer Why do mapmakers use imaginary lines on maps and globes?

_____

_____

_____

_____

3. Analyze How are the Equator and Prime Meridian related to latitude and longitude?

_____

_____

_____

_____

_____

Show Your Skill

5. **Compare and Contrast** How are physical maps different from political maps?

_____

_____

_____

_____

_____

_____

Take the Challenge

6. In a small group, draw an example of a physical map, political map, and special-purpose map. Choose a theme so that your maps are related. Put your maps on a poster to show to the class.

For many years, geographers have used the Five Themes of Geography to study the world. The Five Themes of Geography are (1) location, (2) place, (3) human-environment interaction, (4) movement, and (5) regions.

Geographers now divide their field into Six Essential Elements. Each element looks at a different set of facts about our world and the people on it.

Geographers who study *The World in Spatial Terms* want to know where things are. People interested in *Places and Regions* want to know what places are like. They study the land, the weather, and the plants and animals of an area. Geographers studying *Physical Systems* look at how natural events such as earthquakes and volcanoes shape the Earth's surface. They also learn how living things depend on each other and their surroundings. *Human Systems* deals with how people shape the world. Why do people settle in one place and not another? How do they choose the borders of countries? How do people, ideas, and goods move from place to place? Human Systems tries to answer these questions. Those who study *Environment and Society* want to know how people act toward the natural world around them. They ask how people change their environment and are changed by it. *The Uses of Geography* deals with how geography helps us understand the world we live in. It looks at the tools geographers use to study and describe the world.

Types of Maps

Geographers use different types of maps to show the Earth. **Physical maps** show land and water on the surface of Earth. **Political maps** show the names of countries. They also show borders between countries. **Special-purpose maps** show specific kinds of information. They might show weather patterns. They could show the number of people who live in a place. Such maps can even show you where events took place throughout history.

To understand a map, you must be able to read it. Most maps have a map key. It tells you what the lines and colors used on a map represent, as well as the meaning of any symbols, or pictures, shown on a map. A map **scale** is a line that helps you measure distances on a map. Many maps also show you the **cardinal directions**—north, south, east, and west. A compass rose directs you to due north. Some maps also have a locator map. This small map shows you where the area on the main map is found.

Using Charts, Graphs, and Diagrams

Charts, graphs, and diagrams are all tools for showing information. Reading the title tells you the subject. Charts display data such as facts and numbers. They place numbers and other data in rows and columns. To read a chart, look at the labels at the top of each column and on the left side of the chart. They explain what the numbers or other data on the chart are measuring.

There are different types of graphs. Bar graphs use wide lines to show data. They are useful for comparing amounts. Line graphs work well for showing changes over time. To read line and bar graphs, first look at the labels along the side and bottom of the graph. The left side has a line that runs up-and-down. This line is called the y-axis. The line that runs left-to-right along the bottom is the x-axis. Each axis is labeled. One label tells what is measured. The other label tells how much is measured. Pie, or circle, graphs are circular graphs that show how the whole of something is divided into parts. Each divided "slice" section of the circle is labeled and shows a part or percentage of the whole "pie," circle. The entire pie circle should add up to 100 percent.

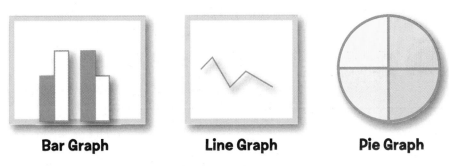

Bar Graph   **Line Graph**   **Pie Graph**

Diagrams are special drawings. They show steps in a process, point out the parts of an object, or explain how something works.

Sample Diagram

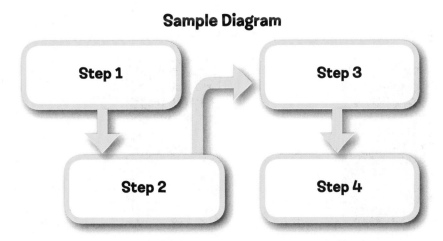

7. Explain How do charts and graphs help show data?

_____

_____

_____

_____

_____

_____

Take the Challenge

8. Create a bar graph, line graph, or pie graph based on a study you do of students in your classroom or school. Select a topic and collect the data. Display your findings in one of the tools shown on this page.

_____

_____

_____

_____

10. Analyze Why are meetings between cultures important in world history?

_____

_____

_____

_____

Population and Culture

Population is the number of people who live in a specific place. Geographers study this in great detail. They record how fast the number of people increases or decreases over time. They also measure population density. This is the average number of people living in a square mile or square kilometer. A **choropleth** map uses colors to show population density. Geographers also study **migration,** or the movement of people from one place to another.

Geographers are also interested in how people think and act. They study this by looking at culture. **Culture** is the set of beliefs and behaviors shared by the members of a group. Scholars study cultures by learning about the key ideas that groups share. For example, they study language, religion, and government. They also look at what people eat, what they wear, and their activities.

Throughout history, different peoples have met through exploration, migration, and trade. Change often happens as a result of such meetings. Strong groups may conquer weaker ones. Different groups may share part of their culture with others. In this way, ideas are spread from one group to another. Sometimes the mixing of two or more groups forms a new culture. Such meetings between different peoples are a key part of world history.

NGSSS Check Why do geographers use different types of maps and map projections? SS.6.G.1.2

_____

_____

_____

_____

In your own words, describe the Six Essential Elements of Geography. SS.6.G.6.1

The World in Spatial Terms		Human Systems	
Places and Regions		Environment	
Physical Systems		The Uses of Geography	

2 EXPLORING ECONOMICS

NGSSS

SS.6.E.1.2 Describe and identify traditional and command economies as they appear in different civilizations.

SS.6.E.1.3 Describe the following economic concepts as they relate to early civilization: scarcity, opportunity cost, supply and demand, barter, trade, productive resources (land, labor, capital, entrepreneurship).

SS.6.E.3.2 Categorize products that were traded among civilizations, and give examples of barriers to trade of those products.

SS.6.E.3.4 Describe the relationship among civilizations that engage in trade, including the benefits and drawbacks of voluntary trade.

Essential Question
Why do people trade?

Guiding Questions
1. What are the basic ideas of economics?
2. What are the different types of economic systems?
3. What are the benefits and disadvantages of trade?

Terms to Know

capital
money and goods used to help people make or do things

entrepreneurship
the act of running a business and taking on the risks of that business

supply
the amount of something that is available

demand
the desire that a person has to buy something

scarcity
a lack of a resource

opportunity cost
what a person gives up when they choose to buy or make something

traditional economy
an economic system based on custom

command economy
an economic system in which a central government makes economic decisions

recession
a period of slow economic growth

inflation
a rise in prices and a drop in the value of money

exports
goods sent from one country to another in trade

imports
goods brought into one country from another in trade

barter
to trade by exchanging one good for another

globalization
the growth in free trade between countries

It Matters Because

Products are made all over the world. Through trade, different countries are able to import goods or raw materials that they do not produce.

- Look at the labels of your clothing or other items around the classroom.
- Check out where those things have been made by looking for a "Made in _____" label.
- Make a list of the countries that made your clothing or items in your classroom.
- Mark the countries from your list on the world map.

What patterns do you see?

_____

_____

_____

_____

What Do You Know?

Directions: Select three or four vocabulary terms from the list at left, write an example of what that term means in everyday life, and then come back later to add more detail.

Now	Later

Show Your Skill

1. Identify Main Ideas and Details What are the three main questions that economists ask?

_____

_____

_____

_____

_____

_____

Mark the Text

2. Circle the word *resources* and each of the four key resources.

Take the Challenge

3. Take on the role of an entrepreneur! Think of a product or service. Answer the questions that entrepreneurs must ask themselves when developing a product or service. Consider supply and demand for the product or service. Make an advertisement for your product or service, including details about it, where to buy it, and how much it costs.

What Is Economics?

Economics is the study of how and why people make, buy, and sell things. Economists ask three questions. *What* goods and services should people offer? *How* should they make and sell them? *Who* will use them?

Resources

Land — The surface of the Earth and the resources found in and on it	**Labor** — The ability of people to do work
Capital — The money and goods used to help people make or do things	**Entrepreneurship** — The act of running a business and taking risks to succeed

Resources are the things that people need to make goods and offer services. In economics, there are four key resources. *Land* is the surface of the Earth. It also includes things found in the Earth, such as oil or water. *Labor* is the ability of people to do work. Without workers, goods cannot be made. **Capital** is the money and goods used to help people make or do things. For example, if a company wants to make shoes, it needs a factory. It also needs money to pay workers to make the first set of shoes. The factory and the money are each kinds of capital. **Entrepreneurship** is the act of running a business. It also means taking on risks. If a company is poorly run, it is more likely to fail. If no one is willing, however, to take risks, it would be harder to start new companies.

Having the right resources is just the first step in making something. How much should you make? What price should you charge for it? These choices are shaped by the law of supply and demand.

Supply is how much of something people want to sell. It is also how much of a good or service is available. **Demand** is how much of something people want to buy. It can also show how strongly someone wants to buy something. In general, people want to sell goods at high prices and buy goods at low prices. How do they agree on a price? In a *free market*, where people can choose what to buy or sell, supply and demand balance out. If a seller charges too high a price, no one will buy those high-priced goods. If a buyer demands too low a price, no one will be willing to sell goods at that price. Over time, each side finds a price they can agree on.

Prices also depend on how uncommon something is, or its **scarcity.** If something is very rare, it is usually worth more than something that is easy to find. This means that buyers have to choose between paying a high price or not buying the good.

Such choices happen all the time when people buy and sell. One name for these kinds of choices is opportunity cost. The **opportunity cost** of something is based on what you gave up to make or buy it. For example, you are a farmer. You must choose what to grow. Whatever you choose will use up resources. These include land, water, money, and time. If you grow wheat, you cannot grow something else. You gave up that chance, or opportunity, when you chose to grow wheat.

Managing and Measuring Economies

There are four major kinds of economic systems. These systems are ways of deciding who should make goods and who should use them.

The oldest system is a **traditional economy.** In a traditional economy, people live in small groups. They make what their family or others in their group need. Children often do the same kind of work as their parents. Choices about what to make are based on custom. Customs are ways of doing things that have been followed for a long time.

The first civilizations, such as those in Egypt, China, and Mesopotamia, often had command economies. In a **command economy,** a central government decides what goods will be made and who will get them. The government often

Show Your Skill

4. Make a Connection Think of something you chose to buy or do recently. Write down its opportunity cost, or what you gave up when you made your choice.

_____

_____

_____

_____

_____

_____

5. Compare and Contrast How are traditional and command economies different from each other?

_____

_____

_____

_____

_____

_____

_____

_____

_____

Traditional Economy

People make goods or offer services for their local group according to custom.

Command Economy

The central government decides what people make and who should get it.

Market Economy

Each person chooses for himself or herself what goods or services to make, buy, or sell.

Mixed Economy

The government makes some choices about what to make and how much to make, while individuals make the rest of the economic choices.

collects taxes from people. It may also make them work on large projects. A command economy can bring together many resources. This may make the government powerful. People, however, have limited choices.

In a *market economy*, each person makes their own choices about what to make, sell, or buy. The United States has a market economy. In a *mixed economy*, the government has some control over what is made and how much is made, while individuals make the rest of the economic choices.

When an economy grows, more goods are made. When an economy shrinks, fewer goods are made. Economies tend to grow for a while, then shrink, then grow again, shrink again, and so on. This up-and-down pattern is called the business cycle. When an economy grows very slowly or shrinks, it is called a **recession.** Companies may close and people may lose their jobs. One sign of economic trouble is inflation. **Inflation** means that money is worth less. Prices go up as a result. This makes it more expensive to buy the things needed to live. Governments want to avoid recessions and limit inflation. But no one is sure just how this should be done.

Reading Check

7. Why is inflation a problem?

_____

_____

_____

_____

_____

Trade in World History

People have been trading with each other for thousands of years. Trade takes place when each side has something to gain. This means that each side has something that the other side wants. Trade between countries is based on exports and imports. When a country **exports** a good, it ships that good from the country to another place. When a country **imports** a good, it brings it into the country from another place.

Mark the Text

8. Underline what a country does when it exports a good and circle what it does when it imports a good.

How does a country decide what to export? An export can be a good that is common at home but uncommon in other places. This means that it can be sold for a higher price than it cost to make. Or it can be something rare that brings a high price. The same ideas apply to imports. Countries want to import goods that they do not have. Countries also import goods when they can buy those goods more cheaply than they can make them at home.

Imports   goods brought into a country   **Country**   **Exports   goods sent out to another country**

People first traded with each other using a system called **bartering.** When bartering, goods are traded directly for each other. People might trade fish for furs. But bartering only works if you have what the other person wants. If all you have is fish and the other person wants wood, you have no deal. Once money was invented, trade became simpler. Money has an agreed-upon value. This means it can be traded for almost anything.

Trade is not always possible. If people cannot travel, trade cannot happen. Sometimes geography makes it hard to travel between places. A wide desert, a tall mountain, or a large sea can limit trade. Fighting or other kinds of conflict can also make travel too dangerous.

Sometimes one group does not want to trade with other groups. This might happen because the two groups disagree with each other about politics or other issues. Or, a country may want to limit trade if it hurts some of its own people. Farmers in a country may not be able to grow rice as cheaply as it can be bought from another country. Those farmers may be driven out of business if everyone buys cheap imported rice from another country. Their government may tax that imported rice to make it more expensive. This action protects its farmers.

Today many countries trade with each other. This growth in world trade is called **globalization.** It is the result of efforts to increase free trade. The goal of free trade is a world market where people are free to choose what to buy and sell. People who are in favor of free trade say that it boosts trade. It also reduces the prices of goods. These changes help economies grow. Those against free trade say that it makes imports and foreign labor costs too cheap. They fear that this can cause a country to lose its companies and jobs to other countries.

Globalization has increased the ties between the world's economies. When a large economy like that of the United States struggles, it affects the economy of the whole world.

NGSSS Check List two reasons why countries trade. Then list two reasons why countries may refuse to trade with one another. SS.6.E.1.3

_____

_____

_____

_____

_____

Show Your Skill

9. Draw Conclusions What might happen to trade today if there was no money?

_____

_____

_____

_____

_____

10. Draw Conclusions Why are there barriers to trade?

_____

_____

_____

_____

_____

_____

_____

_____

Think Critically

11. Infer Why do you think that free trade has grown over time, leading to globalization?

_____

_____

_____

_____

_____

_____

_____

_____

LESSON 3 — PRACTICING CITIZENSHIP

NGSSS

SS.6.C.1.1 Identify democratic concepts developed in Ancient Greece that served as a foundation for American constitutional democracy.

SS.6.C.1.2 Identify how the government of the Roman Republic contributed to the development of democratic principles (separation of powers, rule of law, representative government, civic duty).

SS.6.C.2.1 Identify principles (civic participation, role of government) from Ancient Greek and Roman civilizations which are reflected in the American political process today, and discuss their effect on the American political process.

Essential Question

Why do people form governments?

Guiding Questions

1. What are the key principles of the U.S. government?
2. What are the civic rights, duties, and responsibilities of U.S. citizens?
3. What does it mean to be a global citizen?

Terms to Know

representative government
a form of government in which people vote for officials who represent their interests

federal system
a type of government in which power is divided between a central government and state governments

separation of powers
the idea that power should be divided between specific branches of government

legislative branch
the branch of government that passes laws

executive branch
the branch of government that enforces laws

judicial branch
the branch of government that interprets laws

checks and balances
a system in which each branch of government can limit the power of another branch

It Matters Because

Our system of government needs active citizens who understand their rights and responsibilities.

Think about what it means to be a U.S. citizen. What are your responsibilities?

Now think about what it means to be a global citizen. How are the responsibilities alike or different from those of a U.S. citizen?

What Do You Know?

Directions: Draw a diagram to show what you think the three branches of the U.S. government are, and how checks and balances work with the branches. Use arrows to show how each branch checks on the other branches. When you have completed your diagram, look at the diagram in the lesson and make any necessary changes.

Principles of Government

The government of the United States is based on the rules written down in the U.S. Constitution. The United States has a **representative government.** This means that citizens vote to elect, or choose, people who will serve in government. These people are supposed to act in the interests of the citizens who voted for them.

The Constitution also limits the powers of the government. The United States has a **federal system.** The federal, or central, government has the most power. But it shares power with the state governments. The Constitution also divides the federal government into three branches, or parts. Each branch has its own set of powers. This idea is called **separation of powers.**

What powers does each branch have? The **legislative branch** makes laws. The U.S. Congress is the legislative branch. It is made up of the House of Representatives and the Senate. The **executive branch** carries out the laws. The president is the leader of the executive branch. The **judicial branch** reviews and interprets the laws. The Supreme Court is the leading court of the judicial branch.

The Constitution also creates a system of **checks and balances.** This means that each branch can check, or limit, the power of another branch. For example, the president can veto, or block, a law proposed by Congress. However, Congress can overturn a veto with enough votes. The system of checks and balances keeps any one part of government from becoming too powerful.

Show Your Skill

1. Explain What is a *federal system?*

_____

_____

_____

_____

Mark the Text

2. Circle each of the branches of government.

Show Your Skill

3. Draw Conclusions How do separation of powers and checks and balances limit the power of government?

_____

_____

_____

_____

_____

Legislative Branch

Checks on other branches

Checks on other branches

Executive Branch

Judicial Branch

Checks on other branches

Mark the Text

4. Highlight or underline the rights and freedoms of U.S. citizens.

Show Your Skill

5. **Identify Main Ideas and Details** List the duties of citizenship.

_____

_____

_____

_____

_____

_____

_____

What Is Citizenship?

American citizens have rights, duties, and responsibilities. Rights are freedoms protected by law. All Americans have the right to seek, or look for, life, liberty, and happiness. All Americans may speak their minds freely. They can also write what they think. Together these rights are called freedom of expression. Americans have the right to go to meetings and other gatherings that are peaceful. If they have a problem, they can write to government officials and ask them to help. This is called the right to petition. The Constitution also protects freedom of religion. This means that people can worship as they choose. If someone is accused of a serious crime, they have a right to a trial by jury.

A jury is a group of people who listen to both sides in a court case. Jury members are guided by a judge. They decide if the accused person is guilty or innocent of the crime.

Citizens also have the right to vote. This allows them to choose their leaders. Citizens are free to serve in public office. These and other rights are discussed in the Bill of Rights and other amendments to the Constitution.

The Constitution also says that citizens have some duties. These are things that all citizens must do. All citizens must obey the law and pay taxes. This applies to federal, state, and local laws and taxes. Citizens must serve on a jury if asked. They must also be ready to defend the United States and the Constitution.

Responsibilities are actions that are not required by law. They are still very important. Carrying out these acts helps protect the freedoms that Americans enjoy. Being responsible also helps local communities. Citizens should stay informed about important issues. Issues are topics that affect many people, such as crime or education. Learning about issues helps citizens make wise choices when they vote. In addition to being a right, voting is a key responsibility of citizenship. Citizens should vote and vote with care. If they do not, they have less chance of being represented in government.

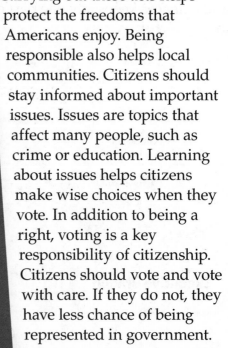

Citizens are called to serve on a jury. As a jurist, you will listen to a case and deliberate.

Citizens should also respect the rights and views of other people. The United States welcomes people of many different backgrounds. All these people share the same freedoms. Before you deny a right to someone else, think about how you would feel if someone tried to take away your rights.

Finally, citizens should take part in their local community. By working with each other, we help make our neighborhoods and towns better places to live. There are different ways to keep our communities strong. We can volunteer our time. We can join neighborhood groups, and we can serve in public office.

Being a Global Citizen

Today the world faces many problems. Often these problems are too big for any one country to handle alone. Pollution is one example. It can spread from one country to another. Trade is a world issue. Most countries trade with at least one other country. Some rely on trade to help their economies, so the laws about trade are important to many countries.

Another global issue is human rights. Around the world, many people do not have the same rights as Americans. Improving this situation is a goal of the United States and the United Nations. The United Nations is an international organization that promotes peace, human rights, and cooperation between the countries of the world.

Being a global citizen means learning about these and other issues that affect the world as a whole. It also means understanding better how people live in other countries. A key goal of global citizenship is working together with others. One way to do that is to respect the views of others.

Being a global citizen does not mean giving up your duties and responsibilities as a U.S. citizen. It means thinking about how you can make the world a better place by your actions.

NGSSS Check How is being a global citizen like being a U.S. citizen? SS.6.C.2.1

_____

_____

_____

_____

_____

_____

6. Make Generalizations
Why is being a responsible citizen important?

_____

_____

_____

_____

_____

_____

Mark the Text

7. Circle three world issues given as examples in the text.

Take the Challenge

8. Think about how you can be a responsible citizen. Make a mini-citizenship booklet just for kids. Illustrate your examples. Show your booklet to a partner.

MY REFLECTIONS

Reflect on What It Means...

Where people live affects what activities they do, clothes they wear, and food they eat. How does geography influence how you live? Your community? Your world?

Draw a picture to show how geography influences you, your community, and a place in the world. Draw a picture in each box below or on another piece of paper. Write a brief description to go with your picture.

Me

My Community

My World

TAKE THE CHALLENGE

With the help of an adult, go online and connect with other students your age around the world. Ask them how geography influences the way they live.

EARLY HUMANS
AND THE AGRICULTURAL REVOLUTION

NGSSS

LA 6.1.6.2 The student will listen to, read, and discuss familiar and conceptually challenging text.

ESSENTIAL QUESTION *How do people adapt to their environment?*

These archaeologists study remains from the past. Richard Leakey is an important anthropologist. He has spent his life studying how human life developed and adapted during pre-historic times. He made this statement in a book he wrote in 1977.

" For three million years we were hunter-gatherers, and it was through the evolutionary pressures of that way of life that a brain so adaptable and so creative eventually emerged. "

RICHARD LEAKEY

hunter-gatherers

What do you think a hunter-gatherer might be?

_____

_____

way of life

What pressures might hunter-gatherers face as a way of life?

_____

_____

DBQ BREAKING IT DOWN

Why do you think it might be important for individual people or entire communities to adapt to new situations?

_____

_____

_____

McGraw-Hill
netw⊙rks™
There's More Online!

LESSON

1 HUNTER-GATHERERS

NGSSS

SS.6.G.4.3 Locate sites in Africa and Asia where archaeologists have found evidence of early human societies, and trace their migration patterns to other parts of the world.

SS.6.W.2.1 Compare the lifestyles of hunter-gatherers with those of settlers of early agricultural communities.

SS.6.W.2.2 Describe how the developments of agriculture and metallurgy related to settlement, population growth, and the emergence of civilization.

Essential Question
How do people adapt to their environment?

Guiding Questions
1. What was life like during the Paleolithic Age?
2. How did people adapt to survive during the ice ages?

Terms to Know

Paleolithic
the early part of human history, also known as the Old Stone Age

nomads
people who move from place to place to survive

technology
the use of new ideas and tools to do work

ice ages
long periods of extreme cold on Earth

Where in the World?

Paleolithic Europe and the Near East

Historians have found evidence of human activity dating from Paleolithic times at each of these sites.

When Did It Happen?

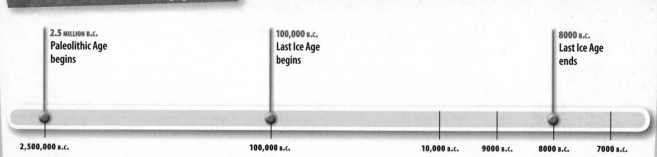

2.5 MILLION B.C. Paleolithic Age begins

100,000 B.C. Last Ice Age begins

8000 B.C. Last Ice Age ends

2,500,000 B.C.   100,000 B.C.   10,000 B.C.   9000 B.C.   8000 B.C.   7000 B.C.

The Paleolithic Age

The early period of human history is called the Stone Age. That's when people made tools and weapons from stone. The early part of the Stone Age is the **Paleolithic** Age. The Paleolithic Age began about 2.5 million years ago. It lasted until about 8000 B.C.

The first humans spent most of their time looking for food. They hunted animals and gathered, or collected, plants, nuts, and berries. For this reason, early people are known as "hunter-gatherers." Early people moved from place to place looking for food. People who move from place to place in order to survive are called **nomads.**

In the Paleolithic Age, men hunted large animals. They learned how animals behaved. They learned the best way to hunt them. At first, men used clubs to kill the animals. They also drove animals over the edge of cliffs. Over time, Paleolithic people created better tools and weapons. These new traps and spears made hunting easier.

Paleolithic women spent most of their time looking for food. They gathered berries, nuts, and grains from woods and meadows. They also took care of the children.

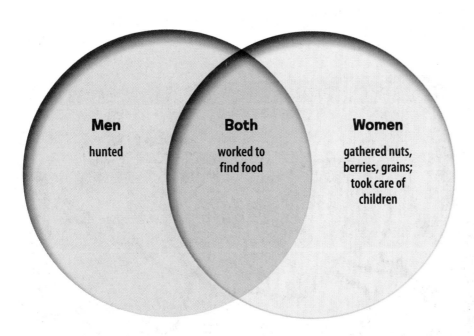

Men
hunted

Both
worked to find food

Women
gathered nuts, berries, grains; took care of children

Technology is the use of new ideas and tools to do work. Technology was first used by Paleolithic people. They made tools and weapons from flint. Flint is a hard stone with sharp edges. Paleolithic people made sharp knives and ax heads from flint.

Think Critically

1. Predict The Stone Age gets its name from the type of tools people used. What do you think people in the future will call our time period? Why?

_____

_____

_____

_____

_____

_____

_____

Mark the Text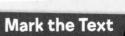

2. Circle the foods that early people ate.

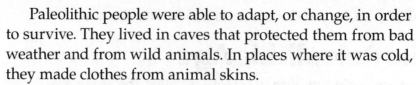

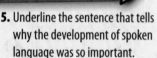
Paleolithic people were able to adapt, or change, in order to survive. They lived in caves that protected them from bad weather and from wild animals. In places where it was cold, they made clothes from animal skins.

During the Paleolithic Age, people learned how to make fire. Can you imagine how hard life was before that? Once people had fire, they could eat cooked food. They had light at night. Fire also provided warmth and scared away wild animals.

Early people probably produced fire by friction. They rubbed two pieces of wood together until the wood became so hot it caught on fire. They also started fires by hitting one stone against another. This would create a spark that could set dry grass or leaves on fire.

Other advancements took place during the Paleolithic Age. During this time, people developed spoken language. Before this, humans communicated through sounds and gestures. Spoken language made it easier for people to work together. Just like language today, the language of early people was constantly growing and changing. Just like today, new ideas and new technology gave rise to new words.

Early people expressed their ideas through language. They also expressed themselves through art. Early artists painted the walls of their caves with paints made from crushed rock mixed with animal fat. Early cave paintings show animals in bright colors.

This Paleolithic cave painting of a horse, and many others, were discovered in Lascaux, France. These cave paintings could be as many as 17,000 years old.

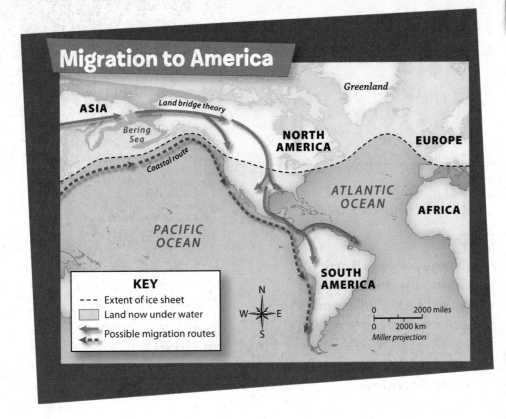

Migration to America

ASIA

Greenland

Land bridge theory

Bering
Sea

NORTH
AMERICA

EUROPE

Coastal route

ATLANTIC
OCEAN

AFRICA

PACIFIC
OCEAN

SOUTH
AMERICA

KEY
- - - Extent of ice sheet
☐ Land now under water
← Possible migration routes
◄--

N
W E
S

0   2000 miles
0   2000 km
Miller projection

Show Your Skill

7. Make a Connection The ice ages are an example of climate change. Where else have you heard about climate change?

The Ice Ages

About 100,000 B.C. Earth began to get very cold. Thick sheets of ice moved across much of the land. Early people had to adapt, or change, if they were to survive. This was the beginning of Earth's most recent Ice Age. **Ice ages** are long periods of extreme cold on Earth.

During the ice ages, more and more ice formed on the Earth. The levels of the oceans dropped because so much water was taken from the oceans to form the ice. Land that was once covered by water was now visible above it. One place this happened was between Asia and North America. During the ice ages, a land bridge connected the two land masses. A land bridge is a strip of dry land that was once covered by water. People could now walk from Asia into the Americas.

Think Critically

8. Analyze Why were the first people nomads?

Take the Challenge

9. Draw an illustration or illustrations on a separate piece of paper to show how land bridges were created during the ice ages.

NGSSS Check List two advancements of the Paleolithic Age, and tell how each one made life easier for early humans. SS.6.W.2.2

2 THE AGRICULTURAL REVOLUTION

NGSSS

SS.6.G.3.1 Explain how the physical landscape has affected the development of agriculture and industry in the ancient world.

SS.6.G.4.1 Explain how family and ethnic relationships influenced ancient cultures.

SS.6.W.2.1 Compare the lifestyles of hunter-gatherers with those of settlers of early agricultural communities.

SS.6.W.2.2 Describe how the developments of agriculture and metallurgy related to settlement, population growth, and the emergence of civilization.

Essential Question
How do people adapt to their environment?

Guiding Questions
1. How did farming change people's lives?
2. What was life like during the Neolithic Age?
3. What characteristics did early civilizations share?

Terms to Know

domesticate
tame

systematic agriculture
the growing of food on a regular basis

Neolithic Age
the period of time from 8000 to 4000 B.C.

shrine
a place where people worship

Bronze Age
the period of time from 3000 to 1200 B.C.

monarchy
a government led by a king or a queen

specialization
performing jobs people are good at

Where in the World?

Early Farming

NORTH AMERICA
SOUTH AMERICA
EUROPE
ASIA
AFRICA
AUSTRALIA

PACIFIC OCEAN
ATLANTIC OCEAN
PACIFIC OCEAN
INDIAN OCEAN

N W E S

0   2,000 miles
0   2,000 km
Mercator projection

KEY

Barley
Corn/maize
Millet
Oats
Potatoes
Rice
Rye
Squash
Wheat
Yams

When Did It Happen?

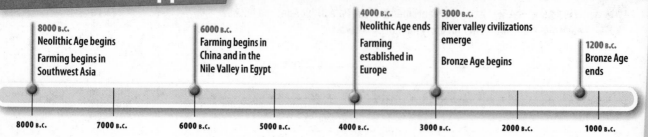

8000 B.C.
Neolithic Age begins
Farming begins in Southwest Asia

6000 B.C.
Farming begins in China and in the Nile Valley in Egypt

4000 B.C.
Neolithic Age ends
Farming established in Europe

3000 B.C.
River valley civilizations emerge
Bronze Age begins

1200 B.C.
Bronze Age ends

8000 B.C.   7000 B.C.   6000 B.C.   5000 B.C.   4000 B.C.   3000 B.C.   2000 B.C.   1000 B.C.

Neolithic Times

The last Ice Age ended about 10,000 years ago. The climate on Earth became warmer and the ice melted. People began to stay in one place. They started to grow grains and vegetables. This was **systematic agriculture,** or the growing of food on a regular basis. Farming slowly replaced hunting and gathering as the main source of food for people. People also began to **domesticate,** or tame, animals.

This change in the way people lived marked the start of the **Neolithic Age.** The Neolithic Age began about 8000 B.C. and ended about 4,000 years later. Agriculture was the biggest change that took place during the Neolithic Age. This change happened very slowly.

The Neolithic Age

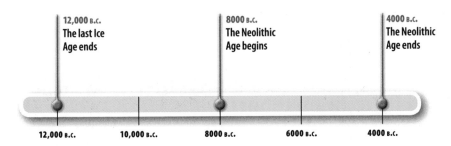

12,000 B.C.
The last Ice Age ends

8000 B.C.
The Neolithic Age begins

4000 B.C.
The Neolithic Age ends

12,000 B.C.   10,000 B.C.   8000 B.C.   6000 B.C.   4000 B.C.

The switch from hunting and gathering to farming is called the Agricultural Revolution. Once humans learned how to grow crops and tame animals, their lives became very different. There was a better supply of food. People stopped moving around to look for food. They began to live in settled communities. People built houses in which to live. They also built **shrines,** or holy places, where they worshiped their gods and goddesses. These changes took place around the world.

Life in the Neolithic Age

Neolithic farmers grew fruits, nuts, and different grains. Some farmers also raised sheep, goats, and cattle. People ate fish and eggs. Some men continued to hunt. People in early communities often had more and better food than nomads.

Better food led to healthier people. Healthier people lived longer and had more children. The population grew. Eventually, farmers grew more food than they could eat. They began to trade food for things they could not produce themselves.

Mark the Text

1. Circle the word that means the same as *tame*. Circle the term that means *farming on a regular basis*.

Show Your Skill

2. Define What was the Agricultural Revolution?

_____

_____

_____

_____

_____

Think Critically

3. Explain How did the spread of farming change the life of nomads?

_____

_____

_____

_____

Show Your Skill

4. Identify Cause and Effect What effect did healthier food have on people?

_____

_____

_____

Mark the Text 🖊️

5. Underline the work done by men. Circle the work done by women.

6. Circle the areas on the map where civilizations emerged.

People began to do work other than farming. **Specialization** occurred. People took up jobs that they were good at. Some people made jewelry or weapons. Others made pottery or wove cloth. These people also traded their products for goods they did not have.

In Neolithic communities, most men were farmers. They grew the crops and protected the village. Women took care of the children and wove cloth for clothing.

People continued to make advancements. In western Asia, people discovered that mixing tin and copper created bronze. Bronze was stronger than copper. Bronze tools and weapons were better than those made of stone. Bronze became widely used between 3000 and 1200 B.C. This period is known as the **Bronze Age.**

Civilizations Emerge

By the beginning of the Bronze Age, four great civilizations had appeared in river valleys. These civilizations were Mesopotamia, Egypt, India, and China.

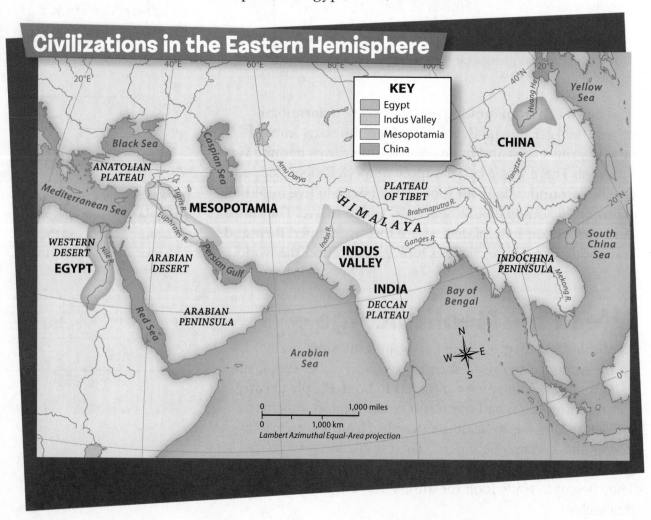

Civilizations in the Eastern Hemisphere

KEY
- Egypt
- Indus Valley
- Mesopotamia
- China

These civilizations were far apart. But they had things in common.

- They developed in river valleys. The rich soil in river valleys made it easier to grow crops. Rivers provided fish. Rivers also encouraged trade.
- Increased trade led to the development of cities. Cities became the centers of civilization.
- People formed governments. Governments protected their people and food supplies. The first governments were monarchies. A **monarchy** is a government led by a king or a queen.
- Religion became more complex. Priests performed ceremonies to win the approval of the gods and goddesses.
- People were organized into social classes. The classes were based on the type of work people did and the amount of wealth they had. Rulers and priests belonged to the highest class. Farmers and craftspeople were another class. Enslaved people formed the lowest class.

During this time, written language developed. Early writing was different from writing today. It used shapes and symbols. People in early civilizations also produced art. They created paintings and sculptures. They built huge buildings, such as the pyramids.

 NGSSS Check Put these events in order. Write the letters in the order that the events happened. SS.6.W.2.2

A River valley civilizations emerge
B Farming begins in Southwest Asia
C Bronze Age begins
D Neolithic Age ends

Think Critically

7. Analyze Why did early people form governments?

_____

_____

_____

Take the Challenge

8. Create your own written language using art, shapes, or symbols that shows characteristics shared by early river valley civilizations. Be creative!

Using the chart, underline one advance that is similar in both Ages and circle one improvement from the Paleolithic to the Neolithic Age. SS.6.W.2.1

Comparing the Neolithic and Paleolithic Ages		
	Paleolithic Age	**Neolithic Age**
How humans obtained food	People hunted animals, gathered nuts, berries, and grains	People began to farm in permanent villages. They continued to raise and herd animals.
How humans adapted	People learned to make fire, created a language, and made simple tools and shelter.	People built mud-brick houses and places of worship. They specialized in certain jobs and used copper and bronze to create more useful tools.
Work of men and women	Women gathered food and cared for children. Men hunted.	Women cared for children and performed household tasks. Men herded, farmed, and protected the village.

ESSENTIAL QUESTION *How do people adapt to their environment?*

Reflect on What It Means . . .

Adaptation is a part of life for all of us today. It sure looks different for us than it did for people living in pre-historic times. One example of a change that requires adaptation is transportation. In the distant past, people walked everywhere. Later, people used animals to help them get around. Today people use a variety of methods to get from one place to another. These changes have affected where people live and how cities are built.

Use the space below to illustrate a page from your own short graphic novel called "How Cars and Planes Changed Everything!" Be sure to show how your community, people around the world, and even you are adapting to changes in transportation.

TAKE THE CHALLENGE

Make a prediction about the future: How do you think transportation may be different for kids in the future? Draw an illustration on another piece of paper to show your ideas.

CHAPTER 4

MESOPOTAMIA

NGSSS

SS.6.W.2.7 Summarize the important achievements of Mesopotamian civilization.

ESSENTIAL QUESTIONS *How does geography influence the way people live? Why does conflict develop?*

In the Code of Hammurabi, the Babylonian king set forth laws that people in his kingdom should obey. His intentions were to make clear the rights of all men. The Code served as a model for future codes of law, like those in ancient Greece and Rome.

> "[T]o bring about the rule of righteousness in the land, to destroy the wicked and the evil-doers; so that the strong should not harm the weak; so that I should rule over . . . people like Shamash, and enlighten the land, to further the well-being of mankind."
>
> CODE OF HAMMURABI

righteousness

Write an antonym for the word *righteousness* below.

_____

_____

enlighten the land

Why does Hammurabi want to "enlighten the land" if *enlighten* means "to see clearly."

_____

_____

_____

DBQ BREAKING IT DOWN

Hammurabi was known for being a fair ruler. What does his code reveal about how he will rule the people in his kingdom?

_____

_____

Why does Hammurabi refer to "wicked and the evil-doers"? Who are they?

_____

_____

McGraw-Hill
networks™
There's More Online!

PHOTO: INTERFOTO / Alamy

LESSON **1**

THE SUMERIANS

NGSSS

SS.6.G.4.3. Locate sites in Africa and Asia where archaeologists have found evidence of early human societies, and trace their migration patterns to other parts of the world.

Essential Question

How does geography influence the way people live?

Guiding Questions

1. Why did people settle in Mesopotamia?
2. What was life like in Sumer?
3. What ideas and inventions did Sumerians pass on to other civilizations?

Terms to Know

silt
rich soil

irrigation
a system that supplies dry land with water through ditches, pipes, or streams

surplus
an amount that is left over after a need has been met

city-state
an independent nation made up of a city and the land around it

polytheism
a belief in many gods

ziggurat
a square, pyramid-shaped tower with each story smaller than the one below and a temple at the top

cuneiform
a system of writing developed by the Sumerians

scribe
a person who copies or writes out documents; often a record keeper

epic
a long poem that tells the story of a hero

Where in the World?

Mesopotamia

EUROPE

ASIA

ATLANTIC OCEAN

AFRICA

PACIFIC OCEAN

PACIFIC OCEAN

INDIAN OCEAN

0   2,000 miles
0   2,000 km
Mercator projection

When Did It Happen?

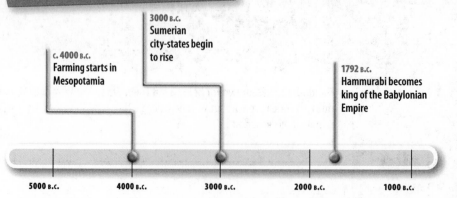

c. 4000 B.C.
Farming starts in Mesopotamia

3000 B.C.
Sumerian city-states begin to rise

1792 B.C.
Hammurabi becomes king of the Babylonian Empire

5000 B.C.   4000 B.C.   3000 B.C.   2000 B.C.   1000 B.C.

The First Civilizations in Mesopotamia

About 3000 B.C., the first civilizations began. A civilization is a group of people who have a high level of culture and order. For example, a civilization is divided into social classes. These classes often include upper, middle, and lower. People in the upper class often have power and a large amount of money. People in the middle class usually have some money. People in the lower class have little or no money. They also have no power. People in a civilization do different types of jobs.

A civilization has science and the arts. It also has a government, values, and beliefs. Civilizations began in river valleys. These valleys were located in Egypt, India, China, and Mesopotamia.

Mesopotamia is the land between the Tigris and Euphrates Rivers. It is located in Southwest Asia. The first known civilization started here. People first lived in Mesopotamia around 7000 B.C. These people hunted. They also raised animals for food. People started to farm around 4000 B.C. in the valley between the two rivers.

To grow crops, farmers need water for the soil. Farmers in Mesopotamia got water from the Tigris and Euphrates Rivers. Sometimes, though, little rain fell. As a result, these rivers did not have enough water. At other times, it rained too much. This caused the rivers to flood. A flood is when water overflows from a river onto land. Floods could destroy crops. However, they also left the land covered with **silt.** Silt is a rich soil. It is good for farming.

To control the floods, the people of Mesopotamia built dams. A dam is a wall that stops the flow of water. They also

Think Critically

1. Contrast How was the upper class different from the lower class?

_____

_____

_____

_____

_____

_____

_____

2. Describe How did the Mesopotamians solve the problem of flooding?

_____

_____

_____

_____

The Mesopotamia region, shown here in a satellite image, was also known as the Fertile Crescent. It has supported civilizations for thousands of years.

3. Make Inferences In Sumer, people began to live together in places that helped trade. What type of locations do you think would help trade?

_____

_____

_____

_____

_____

_____

4. Make a Connection Would you consider cities in Florida to be city-states? Why or why not?

_____

_____

_____

_____

_____

_____

_____

_____

_____

dug canals. A canal is a ditch that lets water flow to the fields. Watering crops using canals is called **irrigation.**

By using irrigation, farmers could grow large amounts of food. In fact, the people of Mesopotamia had extra food, or a **surplus.** As a result, not everyone had to farm. Some people could become artisans. An artisan is a person who makes a good. These goods can be cloth, tools, and weapons. Soon people began to trade goods. People began to live together in places that helped trade. Before long, small villages grew into cities. By 3000 B.C., many cities had grown up in Sumer. Sumer is the region in southern Mesopotamia.

Sumer's Civilization

The people of Sumer were called Sumerians. They built many cities. These cities became centers of their civilizations. The cities of Sumer had deserts around them. Deserts were hard to travel across. Deserts cut off each city from other cities. As a result, each city stood alone.

The people of each city grew their own crops. They also made their own goods. As cities grew, they gained control of the land around them. In this way, they formed **city-states.** Each city-state had its own government. Also, it did not belong to any larger nation.

Sometimes Sumerian city-states fought each other. During times of peace, they traded with each other. City-states also formed alliances. An alliance is an agreement between groups or states to help each other. By doing this, they can reach a common goal.

The Sumerian people worshiped many gods. This type of belief is called **polytheism.** Each city-state, though, claimed one god as its own. To honor this god, the city-state built a large temple called a **ziggurat.** A temple is a building used to worship a god or many gods.

The Sumerian Ziggurat of Ur, built about 2113 B.C., stands in present-day southern Iraq. The Sumerians built it as a shrine to one of their gods.

At first, priests of the ziggurat ruled the city-states. Later, these priests were replaced by kings. Over time, their rule became hereditary. This meant that after a king died, his son took over.

People in Sumer were divided into social classes. The upper class included kings, priests, and warriors. People who worked in the government also belonged to this class. People in this class had a large amount of power and money. The middle class had farmers, fishers, and artisans. Merchants were also members of this class. A merchant is a person who buys and sells goods. The lowest class had slaves and prisoners. They had no money and no power.

Mark the Text

5. Using different colored markers for each social class, highlight the people who belong to the upper class, the middle class, and the lowest class.

_____

_____

_____

_____

_____

_____

_____

Show Your Skill

6. **Identify Cause and Effect** Why did the Sumerians need to trade?

_____

_____

_____

_____

The basic unit of Sumerian life was the family. Men were the head of the home. Women ran the home and cared for the children. Most people in Sumer were farmers. Each farmer had a plot of land.

Trade was important in Sumer. Sumerians did not have some goods that they needed. Because of this, they traded their extra goods for goods that they needed. For example, Sumerians had more than enough wheat. However, they needed metals. As a result, they might trade wheat for metal.

PHOTO: Mesopotamian/The Bridgeman Art Library/Getty Images

7. Draw Conclusions Do you think people had to go to school to become scribes? Explain.

_____

_____

_____

_____

_____

Think Critically

8. Explain How did Sumerians learn what were the best times to plant crops?

_____

_____

_____

Take the Challenge

9. Create a clay tablet that describes an event in your own life. You can use pictures and words.

Sumerian Contributions

Sumerians began a way of writing called cuneiform. **Cuneiform** was written by using wedge-shaped marks. Sumerians used sharp reeds to cut these marks into damp clay. Only a few people learned to read and write cuneiform. Some of these people became **scribes.** A scribe is a person who records business dealings. Scribes also record important events.

The oldest known story in the world comes from Sumer. This story is called the *Epic of Gilgamesh.* An **epic** is a long poem that tells the story of a hero.

The Sumerians made many inventions. An invention is something new that is made. The Sumerians were the first people to use the wheel. They were also the first to use sailboats and wooden plows. In addition, they were the first to make bronze out of copper and tin.

The Sumerians studied mathematics. They also studied astronomy. Astronomy is the study of planets, stars, and other objects in outer space. In fact, Sumerians watched the position of the stars. By doing this, they learned the best times to plant crops. Also, they created a system of numbers based on 60. The 60-minute hour we use today is an idea that came from the Sumerians.

This cuneiform tablet includes mathematical text and geometric shapes.

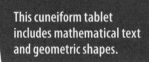

NGSSS Check Why did Sumerians need to trade, and how do we know what they traded? SS.6.G.4.3

_____

_____

_____

_____

_____

_____

LESSON 2 — MESOPOTAMIAN EMPIRES

NGSSS

SS.6.G.2.3 Analyze the relationship of physical geography to the development of ancient river valley civilizations.

Essential Question
Why does conflict develop?

Guiding Questions
1. How did Mesopotamia's first empires develop?
2. How did the Assyrians influence Southwest Asia?
3. Why was Babylon an important city in the ancient world?

Terms to Know

empire
a group of many different lands under one ruler

tribute
a payment made to a ruler or state as a sign of surrender

province
a district within a larger country or empire

caravan
a group of merchants traveling together for safety, usually with a train of camels

astronomer
a person who studies stars, planets, and the moon

Where in the World?

Mesopotamian Empires

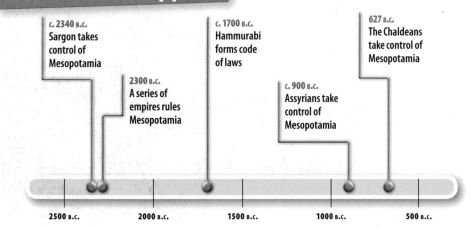

EUROPE

ASIA

ATLANTIC OCEAN

AFRICA

PACIFIC OCEAN

PACIFIC OCEAN

INDIAN OCEAN

0   2,000 miles
0   2,000 km
Mercator projection

When Did It Happen?

c. 2340 B.C. Sargon takes control of Mesopotamia

2300 B.C. A series of empires rules Mesopotamia

c. 1700 B.C. Hammurabi forms code of laws

c. 900 B.C. Assyrians take control of Mesopotamia

627 B.C. The Chaldeans take control of Mesopotamia

2500 B.C.   2000 B.C.   1500 B.C.   1000 B.C.   500 B.C.

Think Critically

1. Summarize How did the first empire form?

_____

_____

_____

_____

_____

_____

Mark the Text

2. Underline the name of the person who took over the Amorite cities.

Show Your Skill

3. Make Inferences Why do you think Hammurabi made a code of laws?

_____

_____

_____

_____

_____

_____

_____

The First Empires

The city-states of Sumer often fought each other. By 2400 B.C., the fighting weakened these city-states. Then, Sargon and his armies started to fight the city-states of Sumer. Sargon was the leader of the kingdom of Akkad. This region was in northern Mesopotamia. Soon Sargon defeated all the city-states of Sumer. He then united Akkad and Sumer to form an **empire.** An empire is a group of different lands under one ruler. The empire of Sargon was the first known empire ever formed. His empire lasted for more than 200 years.

The Amorites lived in a region west of Mesopotamia. They took over Mesopotamia in the 1800s B.C. These people built their own cities. The biggest of these cities was Babylon. Hammurabi was a king of Babylon. He began to take over many of the Amorite cities. By doing this, he formed the Babylonian Empire.

Hammurabi was a fair ruler. He made a law code, or a set of laws, for his empire. The Code of Hammurabi had laws for many different things. For example, it had laws for crimes, farming, and marriage. The code had a punishment for each crime.

The code called for "an eye for an eye, and a tooth for a tooth." What does this mean? If a man knocked out the teeth of someone, then the man would have his own teeth knocked out as punishment. The Code of Hammurabi shaped later law codes, such as those of Greece and Rome.

The Assyrian Empire

The Assyrians lived in northern Mesopotamia. Around 900 B.C., they built a strong army. Soon this army started to take over Mesopotamia. The Assyrians destroyed towns. They robbed

This stone engraving appears on the stone slab, or stele, of Hammurabi's Code.

This illustration shows a reconstruction of the capital of the Assyrian Empire, Nineveh.

the people they defeated. Also, they set crops on fire. The Assyrians forced the people they defeated to pay them money. This forced payment is called a **tribute.**

Why was the Assyrian army so strong? One reason was their weapons. They made their weapons out of iron. Before this, people made weapons out of tin or copper. Iron is much stronger than tin or copper.

Nineveh was the major city of the Assyrian Empire. This city was located on the Tigris River. The empire was ruled by a king and divided into regions called **provinces.** Roads connected the provinces. The king chose a person to rule each province. These people were under the control of the king.

The Assyrians used a law code that had harsh punishments. The Assyrians worshiped the same gods as the Babylonians. The Assyrians built large temples and palaces. They also wrote stories, which they put in a large library. This library was the first library ever built.

The Assyrians did a large amount of trading. They brought in wood and metal from far away and used these materials to make buildings, tools, and weapons.

The Chaldean Empire

The Assyrian Empire lasted for about 300 years. Around 650 B.C., the Assyrians began to argue about who would be the next ruler. As a result, they fought each other. This fighting weakened the empire. While the Assyrians were divided, a group of people called the Chaldeans fought the Assyrians and defeated them.

Take the Challenge

4. Using the image above and what you read about Nineveh, write a short journal entry from the perspective of a person who is visiting the city for the first time.

Think Critically

5. Explain How did iron help the Assyrians?

_____

_____

_____

_____

_____

_____

Show Your Skill

6. Compare How were the Assyrians similar to the Babylonians?

_____

_____

_____

Think Critically

8. Summarize What were some of the major contributions made during the New Babylonian Empire?

_____

_____

_____

_____

_____

Show Your Skill

9. Identify Cause and Effect What effect did caravans have on Babylon? Explain.

_____

_____

_____

_____

_____

The Chaldeans took over the lands held by the Assyrians. They moved the capital to Babylon. The empire of the Chaldeans came to be called the New Babylonian Empire. King Nabopolassar was the first ruler. After he died, his son, Nebuchadnezzar, took control.

King Nebuchadnezzar rebuilt Babylon, making it the largest and richest city in the world. A large wall surrounded the city, which had many temples and palaces. The king also built the Hanging Gardens of Babylon. These gardens had many levels. An irrigation system brought in water for the gardens.

A major trade route went through Babylon. As a result, many **caravans** passed through the city. A caravan is a group of traveling merchants. The merchants bought goods such as cloth, baskets, and jewelry in Babylon. Babylon grew rich from this trade.

The people of Babylon made advances in science. Chaldean **astronomers** studied the stars, planets, and the moon. The Chaldeans made the first sundial to measure time. They also were the first to use a seven-day week.

NGSSS Check How did the Mesopotamians obtain the resources they did not have? **SS.6.G.2.3**

_____

_____

_____

_____

The Chaldeans' contribution of the sundial influenced other civilizations to create sundials, like this one from South Korea.

ESSENTIAL QUESTION *Why does conflict develop?*

Reflect on What It Means . . .

Search online and in print resources for news about conflicts, what caused them, and how they are being resolved.

To My Community

Research a conflict in your community. Make a poster or ad that offers solutions to the conflict. With the supervision of an adult, post it on a community Web site or locally.

Keep Going!

To the World

Find a headline in a newspaper or online about a world conflict and any possible solutions that have been offered. Paste or tape it below. Then put labels on a blank outline map of the world, and write down how different countries have responded to the conflict and/or offered solutions.

To Me

Think about a conflict that you have had with a friend or family member. Write down ways to resolve the conflict. Meet with the person with whom you have had the conflict and try out your solutions. Did they work?

TAKE THE CHALLENGE

As a class, brainstorm a list of possible solutions to conflicts in the United States, the world, or your community. Choose one idea, and with the help of your teacher, work to pursue a solution. Advertise your solution by videotaping a commercial to show what you are doing to help solve the conflict, or draw a storyboard to show the steps that your class is taking to help resolve the conflict.

ANCIENT EGYPT AND KUSH

NGSSS

SS.6.W.2.6 Determine the contributions of key figures from ancient Egypt.

ESSENTIAL QUESTIONS *How does geography influence the way people live? What makes a culture unique? Why do civilizations rise and fall?*

Queen Hatshepsut was a powerful Egyptian female pharaoh.

> " Hatshepsut ... ordered herself crowned pharaoh.... She adopted the false beard signifying wisdom worn only by pharaohs, and occasionally she was depicted wearing masculine garb as well. An extraordinary and able monarch, she foreswore the military conquests of her forebears and concentrated instead on commercial enterprises. "
>
> —FROM *WOMEN WHO RULED*

garb

Knowing that Hatshepsut wore a false beard, what do you think *garb* means?

_____

_____

foreswore

Foreswear means "to reject."
Did Hatshepsut work more on military or economic issues?

_____

DBQ BREAKING IT DOWN

What did Queen Hatshepsut wear that was unusual for a woman?

_____

_____

_____

Why do you think Queen Hatshepsut dressed like a man?

_____

_____

_____

McGraw-Hill
networks™
There's More Online!

PHOTO: Chris Hill/National Geographic/Getty Images

THE NILE RIVER

NGSSS

SS.6.G.2.1 Explain how major physical characteristics, natural resources, climate, and absolute and relative locations have influenced settlement, interactions, and the economies of ancient civilizations of the world.

Essential Question
How does geography influence the way people live?

Guiding Questions
1. Why was the Nile River important to the ancient Egyptians?
2. How did the ancient Egyptians depend on the Nile River to grow their crops?
3. How did Egypt become united?

Terms to Know

cataracts
dangerous, fast-moving waters

delta
a fan-shaped area of marshy land at a river's mouth

shadoof
a bucket attached to a long pole, used to move water for irrigation

papyrus
a reed plant that grows along the Nile River

hieroglyphics
ancient Egyptian writing system using picture symbols

dynasty
a line of rulers from one family

Where in the World?

Location of the Nile River Valley

NORTH AMERICA

ATLANTIC OCEAN

EUROPE

ASIA

PACIFIC OCEAN

AFRICA

PACIFIC OCEAN

SOUTH AMERICA

INDIAN OCEAN

N
W—E
S

0   2,000 miles
0   2,000 km
Mercator projection

When Did It Happen?

5000 B.C.
Settlement begins in Nile River Valley

4000 B.C.
Egypt is divided into Upper Egypt and Lower Egypt

3100 B.C.
King Narmer rules in Upper Egypt

| 5000 B.C. | 4000 B.C. | 3000 B.C. | 2000 B.C. | 1000 B.C. | 750 B.C. |

The Nile River Valley

By 5000 B.C., hunters and gatherers moved into the Nile River Valley. They settled there, farmed the land, and built villages. These people became the earliest Egyptians. Because Egypt gets little rainfall, Egyptians relied on the Nile River for water. They fished and bathed in the Nile and used the water for farming, cooking, and cleaning. The Nile River flows north from the heart of Africa to the Mediterranean Sea, about 4,000 miles. Two rivers meet to form the Nile. They are the Blue Nile in eastern Africa and the White Nile in central Africa. The water forms rapids where the rivers meet. These are called **cataracts.** Large ships cannot sail through the cataracts.

In Egypt, the Nile runs through a narrow valley. Just before it reaches the Mediterranean Sea, it divides into many branches. These branches spread out over an area of rich soil. This area is called a **delta.** Deserts lie on both sides of the Nile River Valley. To the east is the Eastern Desert. It stretches to the Red Sea. Because the deserts were so hot, the ancient Egyptians called them "the Red Land." These areas could not support human life. However, they kept outside armies away from Egypt. Geography helped protect Egypt in other ways. To the south, dangerous cataracts blocked enemy boats. In the north, the delta marshes kept enemies from sailing into Egypt.

Mark the Text

1. Underline the reason why the Egyptians had to rely on the Nile River for water.

Show Your Skill

2. **Identify the Main Idea**
   Why did early settlers decide to live near the Nile River?

   _____

   _____

   _____

   _____

   _____

The Nile River is still important to Egypt today. Just as in the past, the river provides water for people as well as for farming. It is also used for transportation.

_____

_____

_____

_____

4. Draw Conclusions Why was the Nile River Valley good for farming?

_____

_____

_____

_____

_____

The geography of Mesopotamia did not protect people in the same way. The deserts and the rivers did not keep out invaders. Mesopotamians constantly fought off attackers. Egypt rarely faced such threats. As a result, Egyptian civilization grew and prospered. The deserts and Nile rapids did not completely close Egypt to the outside world. The Mediterranean Sea was to the north. Beyond the desert to the east was the Red Sea. These allowed Egyptians to trade outside its borders. Within Egypt, people used the Nile for trade and transportation. Winds from the north pushed sailboats south. The flow of the Nile carried them north. This made Egypt different from Mesopotamia. There, city-states constantly fought against each other. Egyptian villages, however, had friendly contact with one another.

People of the River

Farmers in Mesopotamia never knew when the nearby rivers would get flooded or if the floods would be bad. So, it was difficult to farm there. In Egypt, the Nile River also flooded, but its floods were regular. Farmers did not have to worry that floods would destroy crops or farms. Water came to the Nile from rain and melted snow. Then, during the summer, the Nile spilled over its banks. When the waters lowered, they left behind a layer of dark, rich mud.

The Egyptians became successful farmers. They planted wheat, barley, and flax seeds. They grew enough food to feed themselves and their animals. They used irrigation when the weather was dry. To trap floodwaters, Egyptian farmers first dug basins, or bowl-shaped holes in the earth. Then they dug canals to carry water from the basins to the fields. They used a **shadoof,** a bucket on a long pole. It would lift water from the river to the basins. Egyptians also developed geometry to measure land.

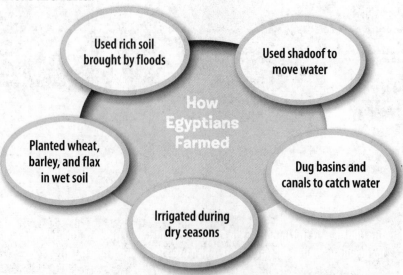

Used rich soil brought by floods

Used shadoof to move water

How Egyptians Farmed

Planted wheat, barley, and flax in wet soil

Dug basins and canals to catch water

Irrigated during dry seasons

Papyrus reeds, shown here, were a valuable resource to the ancient Egyptians. Papyrus was used to create many things.

Mark the Text

5. Underline the definition of *papyrus*. Circle the things it was used to make.

Think Critically

6. Analyze Why do you think it was important for Egyptians to develop a system of writing?

_____

_____

_____

_____

_____

_____

Take the Challenge

7. Make a diorama of Egyptian civilization with a small group. Show the resources that they used to live and to trade and how they benefited from their geographic location.

Egyptians developed ways to use **papyrus.** This was a reed plant that grew along the shores of the Nile. They harvested papyrus to make baskets, sandals, and river rafts. The Egyptians also used papyrus to make writing paper. Like the Mesopotamians, Egyptians developed their own system of writing called **hieroglyphics.** It was made up of thousands of picture symbols. Some symbols stood for objects and ideas. For example, to communicate the idea of a boat, a scribe would draw a tiny boat. Other symbols stood for sounds, like the letters of our own alphabet.

In ancient Egypt, few people could read and write. However, some Egyptian men went to special schools in temples. They studied reading and writing. They learned to become scribes, or record keepers for the rulers, priests, and traders. Some hieroglyphics showed public messages. Scribes carved these into stone walls and monuments. For everyday use, scribes invented a simpler script and wrote on papyrus.

Uniting Egypt

Skillful farming led to more food than was needed, or a surplus. This freed some people to work as artisans instead of farmers. Artisans wove cloth, made pottery, and carved statues. They also shaped copper into weapons and tools. Egyptians traded with each other, and then they traveled to Mesopotamia to trade. There they may have learned new ideas about writing and government.

PHOTO: Reza/Webistan/Corbis

Copyright © by The McGraw-Hill Companies, Inc.

8. Read a Map Scale About how many miles would a trader travel from the Mediterranean Sea to Thebes if they used the Nile River the whole way?

_____

Upper Egypt and Lower Egypt

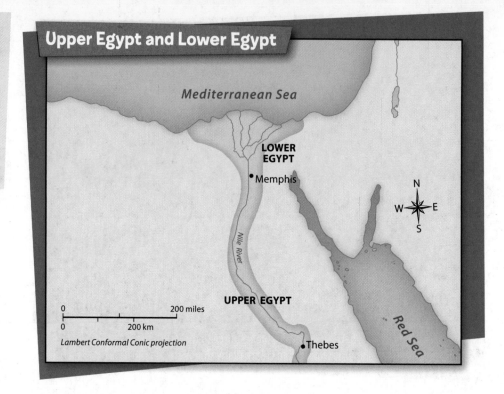

Lambert Conformal Conic projection

Irrigation systems needed to be built and maintained. Grain had to be stored. Disputes over land needed to be settled. Over time, a government formed. The earliest rulers were village chiefs. A few strong chiefs united villages into small kingdoms. By 4000 B.C., Egypt was made up of two large kingdoms. Lower Egypt was in the north in the Nile delta. Upper Egypt was in the south along the Nile River.

About 3100 B.C., Narmer was king of Upper Egypt. He led his armies north and took control of Lower Egypt. Narmer's kingdom held together long after his death. His family passed power from father to son to grandson. This is called a **dynasty.** Over time, ancient Egypt would be ruled by 30 dynasties for about 2,800 years. Historians group Egypt's dynasties into three main time periods—the Old Kingdom, the Middle Kingdom, and the New Kingdom. Each kingdom had a long period of strong leadership and safety.

NGSSS Check How did the Nile River valley provide the resources the Egyptians needed to thrive as a civilization? SS.6.G.2.1

_____

_____

_____

_____

_____

2 LIFE IN ANCIENT EGYPT

 NGSSS

SS.6.W.2.4 Compare the economic, political, social, and religious institutions of ancient river civilizations.

Essential Question
What makes a culture unique?

Guiding Questions
1. How was ancient Egypt governed?
2. What kind of religion did the ancient Egyptians practice?
3. Why and how were pyramids built?
4. How was Egyptian society organized?

Terms to Know

pharaoh
ancient Egyptian leader

theocracy
a government in which the same person is the political and religious leader

bureaucrat
government official

embalming
the process of preserving dead bodies

pyramid
a huge triangular tomb built of stone

What Do You Know?

Directions: In the "K" column, list what you already know about life in ancient Egypt. In the "W" column, list what you want to know. After reading the lesson, fill in the "L" column with the information that you learned.

K	W	L

When Did It Happen?

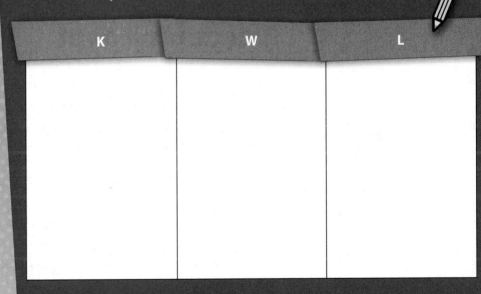

5000 B.C.
Settlement begins in Nile River Valley

4000 B.C.
Egypt is divided into Upper Egypt and Lower Egypt

3100 B.C.
King Narmer rules in Upper Egypt

2600 B.C.
Old Kingdom begins

2450 B.C.
Great Pyramid is built

5000 B.C.   4000 B.C.   3000 B.C.   2000 B.C.   1000 B.C.

Think Critically

3. **Summarize** List three ways that religion affected life in ancient Egypt.

_____

_____

_____

_____

_____

_____

_____

_____

_____

_____

_____

netw**rks** Read Chapter 5 Lesson 2 in your textbook or online.

Egypt's Early Rulers

The Old Kingdom began in Egypt around 2600 B.C. It lasted about 400 years. During this time, the Egyptians built cities and expanded trade. Their kings, or **pharaohs,** set up a government. Egypt was a **theocracy.** That means that the pharaoh was both the political and religious leader of the people.

The pharaoh had total power. He could use all the land in Egypt any way he wanted. His orders were obeyed without question. Pharaohs appointed officials called **bureaucrats.** Bureaucrats were in charge of irrigation canals and crop planting. They made sure grain was saved to help people get through hard times. Bureaucrats also controlled trade and collected tax payments from farmers.

As religious leader, a pharaoh participated in ceremonies that helped the kingdom. For example, he was the first to cut the grain at harvest time. Egyptians believed their pharaoh was the son of Re, the Egyptian sun god. He would protect the people during hard times.

Religion in Egypt

Religion affected every part of Egyptian life. Egyptians worshiped many gods and goddesses. They believed that the gods controlled nature. The sun god, Re, was important because the sun was necessary for good harvests.

Egyptians believed that life after death would be better than this life. They thought that the dead made a long journey through the afterlife. At the end, they came to a place of peace and plenty.

The *Book of the Dead* was a collection of spells and prayers. Egyptians studied this writing to reach life after death. They learned the spells and tried to lead good lives. They believed that the god Osiris would then grant them life after death.

For centuries, Egyptians believed that only the pharaohs and a few others could enjoy the afterlife. To live in the afterlife, the pharaoh's spirit needed a body. If his body decayed, his spirit would wander forever. If the pharaoh's spirit reached the next world, he would continue to care for Egypt. The Egyptians developed a process called **embalming** to protect the pharaoh's body. It involved removing organs from the dead body and then drying and wrapping the body in cloth. Then the pharaoh

This papyrus from the *Book of the Dead* shows oxen, which were offered as gifts to Osiris.

was ready for burial. The Egyptians learned about the human body by embalming the dead. They learned how to treat illnesses. They wrote down what they discovered in the world's first medical books.

Pyramid Tombs

Egyptians built **pyramids,** or large triangle-shaped tombs, to hold the bodies of the pharaohs. Pyramids protected the bodies from floods, heat and dust, wild animals, and grave robbers. They also held the things the pharaoh might need in the afterlife, such as clothing, furniture, jewelry, and food.

Thousands of people worked for many years to build a pyramid. Farmers, surveyors, engineers, carpenters, stonecutters, and enslaved people all worked on pyramids. Each pyramid sat on a square base with a north entrance. To find true north, the Egyptians studied the sky and developed principles of astronomy. They also invented a 365-day calendar.

Egyptians had to figure out the amount of stone and the angles for the walls. They developed and used mathematics and geometry to do this. They also invented a system of written numbers based on 10 and created fractions.

Workers found the stone. Artisans cut the stone into blocks. Others tied the blocks to wooden sleds and pulled them to barges, or boats. The barges floated to the building site. There workers unloaded the blocks, pushed them up ramps, and set them in place.

About 2540 B.C., the Egyptians built the Great Pyramid for King Khufu. It is one of three pyramids still standing in Giza. The Great Pyramid is 500 feet tall and has more than 2 million stone blocks.

Mark the Text

4. Underline what Egyptians learned from embalming their dead pharaohs.

Think Critically

5. **Make Inferences** Why do you think the Egyptians worked so hard to build the pyramids?

_____

_____

_____

_____

_____

_____

_____

_____

_____

_____

_____

_____

Daily Life

Every member of Egyptian society had a place in the social structure. A person's social status, or position in society, was decided by the job he or she did.

Egypt's Class Structure

Ruler

Pharaoh

Upper Class

Nobles
Generals
Priests

Middle Class

Merchants
Artisans
Shopkeepers

Lower Class

Farmers
Unskilled workers
Enslaved people

These Nubians, probably captured during a battle, were enslaved and formed part of the lower class in ancient Egypt.

The pharaoh and his family were at the very top of the social structure. Egypt's upper class included nobles, army commanders, priests, and government officials. They lived in cities and on large estates along the Nile. They dressed in linen and wore makeup and jewelry. Servants waited on them.

Egypt's middle class included merchants, artisans, and shopkeepers. They ran businesses or produced goods. They lived in smaller homes and dressed more simply. Artisans produced cloth, jewelry, pottery, and metal goods.

Farmers, unskilled workers, and enslaved people formed the largest class. Farmers lived in villages along the Nile. They had one-room huts and ate bread, beer, vegetables, and fruit. Unskilled workers did physical jobs. They unloaded cargo from boats or made and stacked bricks. They lived in small mud-brick homes with dirt floors.

PHOTO: David W. Hamilton/Riser/Getty Images

In ancient Egypt, the father headed the family. However, Egyptian women could own property, buy and sell goods, make wills, and get divorced. Upper-class women were in charge of temples and could perform religious ceremonies.

Few Egyptians sent their children to school. Mothers taught their daughters to sew, cook, and run a household. Boys learned farming or skilled trades from their fathers. Young children played games.

Mark the Text ✎

7. Underline the rights of ancient Egyptian women.

Take the Challenge

8. Write a short skit with a small group and role-play the different classes in ancient Egypt.

 NGSSS Check Complete the chart by giving three examples of how each topic was part of Egyptian life. SS.6.W.2.4

The Pharaoh	Religion	Pyramids	Social Status
•	•	•	•
•	•	•	•
•	•	•	•

NGSSS

SS.6.W.2.5 Summarize important achievements of Egyptian civilization.

SS.6.W.2.6 Determine the contributions of key figures from ancient Egypt.

3 EGYPT'S EMPIRE

Essential Question
Why do civilizations rise and fall?

Guiding Questions
1. Why was the Middle Kingdom a "golden age" for Egypt?
2. Why was the New Kingdom a unique period in ancient Egypt's history?
3. How did two unusual pharaohs change ancient Egypt?
4. Why did the Egyptian empire decline in the late 1200s B.C.?

Terms to Know

envoy
a person who represents his country in a foreign place

incense
a material burned for its pleasant smell

What Do You Know?

Directions: Read the list of pharaohs. Circle the names that you know or have heard before. For each circled name, write one fact that you know about the pharaoh.

Hatshepsut

_____

Akhenaton

_____

Thutmose III

_____

King Tut

_____

Ramses II

_____

When Did It Happen?

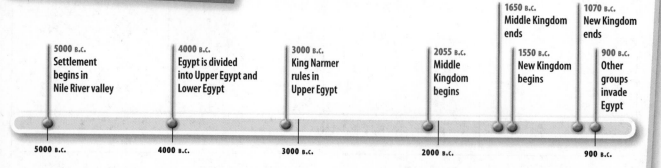

| 5000 B.C. Settlement begins in Nile River valley | 4000 B.C. Egypt is divided into Upper Egypt and Lower Egypt | 3000 B.C. King Narmer rules in Upper Egypt | 2055 B.C. Middle Kingdom begins | 1650 B.C. Middle Kingdom ends / 1550 B.C. New Kingdom begins | 1070 B.C. New Kingdom ends / 900 B.C. Other groups invade Egypt |

5000 B.C.   4000 B.C.   3000 B.C.   2000 B.C.   900 B.C.

networks Read Chapter 5 Lesson 3 in your textbook or online.

A Golden Age

The Middle Kingdom lasted from about 2055 B.C. to 1650 B.C. It was a time of power, wealth, and achievement for the Egyptians. During the Middle Kingdom, Egypt took control of new lands. Egyptian soldiers captured Nubia and attacked what is now Syria. The conquered peoples sent tributes, or payments, to the pharaoh. The pharaoh used this wealth to build dams and improve farmlands. The pharaoh also built a canal between the Nile River and the Red Sea.

During the Middle Kingdom, arts and architecture grew more popular. Painters covered tombs and temples with colorful scenes. Sculptors created large carvings of the pharaohs. These statues showed the pharaohs as ordinary people, not as gods. Instead of building pyramids, pharaohs had their tombs cut into cliffs. This area became known as the Valley of Kings.

The Middle Kingdom ended when nobles tried to take power from the pharaohs. This fight weakened Egypt, making it easy to conquer. The Hyksos invaded from western Asia. The Hyksos army rode chariots and used weapons made of bronze and iron. The Egyptians had copper and stone weapons that could not stop the invaders. The Hyksos ruled Egypt for about 100 years. During that time, the Egyptians learned how to make and use Hyksos weapons. Around 1550 B.C., an Egyptian prince named Ahmose drove the Hyksos out of Egypt.

Think Critically

1. Explain Why was the Middle Kingdom a golden age for Egypt?

_____

_____

_____

Mark the Text

2. Underline the details about how art and architecture experienced a golden age.

Show Your Skill

3. Draw Conclusions Why were the Hyksos able to defeat the Egyptians?

_____

_____

_____

_____

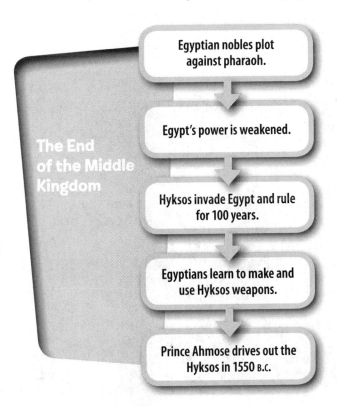

The End of the Middle Kingdom

Egyptian nobles plot against pharaoh.

↓

Egypt's power is weakened.

↓

Hyksos invade Egypt and rule for 100 years.

↓

Egyptians learn to make and use Hyksos weapons.

↓

Prince Ahmose drives out the Hyksos in 1550 B.C.

4. Explain Why was Phoenicia an important trading partner for the Egyptians?

_____

_____

_____

_____

_____

_____

5. Contrast What made Hatshepsut's rule different from that of Thutmose III?

_____

_____

_____

_____

_____

_____

Building an Empire

Ahmose's rule began an era known as the New Kingdom. From 1550 B.C. to 1070 B.C., Egypt grew richer and more powerful. Most pharaohs focused on bringing other lands under their control. They sent **envoys,** or representatives, to make political ties.

About 1480 B.C., a queen named Hatshepsut came to power. First she ruled with her husband. After he died, she ruled for her young nephew. Finally, she made herself pharaoh. Hatshepsut became the first woman to rule Egypt by herself.

Hatshepsut used trade to expand the empire. During her rule, Egyptians traded beads, metal tools, and weapons for ivory, wood, and leopard skins. Traders also brought **incense,** a material burned for its pleasant smell. One important trading partner was Phoenicia. The Phoenicians lived on the Mediterranean and had contact with many cultures. They had their own alphabet and system of writing. They traded goods all over the ancient world. The Egyptians traded their own goods for Phoenician wood and furniture.

When Hatshepsut died, Thutmose III became pharaoh. Thutmose expanded the empire through war. His armies extended the northern border of Egypt. His troops also took back control of Nubia, which had broken free from Egypt. The empire grew rich. It took gold, copper, ivory, and other goods from conquered peoples. Egypt also enslaved prisoners of war. These slaves were put to work building palaces, temples, and monuments. In Egypt, slaves could own land, marry, and gain their freedom.

Thutmose III disliked Hatshepsut so much that he had her name removed from many statues and monuments that were dedicated to her.

Two Unusual Pharaohs

About 1370 B.C., Amenhotep IV came to the throne. He and his wife, Nefertiti, tried to lead Egypt in a new direction. The pharaohs were losing power to the priests. So Amenhotep IV started a new religion. People could worship only one god, called Aton. When the priests protested, Amenhotep IV removed many from their positions. He seized their lands and closed their temples. He changed his name to Akhenaton, or "Spirit of Aton." He began ruling Egypt from a new city.

Most Egyptians resisted Akhenaton's changes. They refused to accept Aton as the only god. Meanwhile, Akhenaton neglected his duties. He took no action when enemies attacked Egypt. These people were called the Hittites. Their invasion cost Egypt most of its lands in western Asia.

When Akhenaton died, his son-in-law took the throne. The new pharaoh, Tutankhamen, was only 10 years old. He relied on help from officials and priests. He restored the old religion. After nine years, Tutankhamen died. In 1922 Howard Carter, a British archaeologist, unearthed Tutankhamen's tomb and all its treasures. The boy king and his riches fascinated people living in the modern world. He became known around the world as "King Tut."

Think Critically

6. Summarize How did ancient Egypt change under Amenhotep IV?

_____

_____

_____

_____

_____

_____

_____

Show Your Skill

7. Identify Cause and Effect What happened to Egypt after Ramses II came to power in 1279 B.C.?

_____

_____

_____

_____

_____

_____

_____

_____

Amenhotep

He changed the religion.

People could only worship one god.

Priests lost power.

Egyptian Religion

Tutankhamen

He restored the old religion.

He relied on priests to run Egypt.

Recovery and Decline

The most successful leader during the New Kingdom was Ramses II. Ramses II, who came to power in 1279 B.C. took back much of the territory lost by earlier pharaohs. He fought the Hittites in what is now Turkey and signed peace treaties. The Hittites and the Egyptians agreed to keep a peace between them. They would also fight together if an enemy attacked one of them.

Think Critically

9. Draw Conclusions Why was Ramses II considered a successful leader?

_____

_____

_____

_____

_____

Take the Challenge

10. Choose an Egyptian pharaoh that ruled during the New Kingdom. Create a biography card that includes interesting facts about the pharaoh. Draw or glue a picture on the other side of the card. With a small group, test each other's knowledge of the Middle Kingdom pharaohs using the cards you made.

Under Ramses II and other New Kingdom leaders, many temples were built. The most magnificent temple was Karnak at Thebes. Karnak has a huge hall that still impresses visitors today.

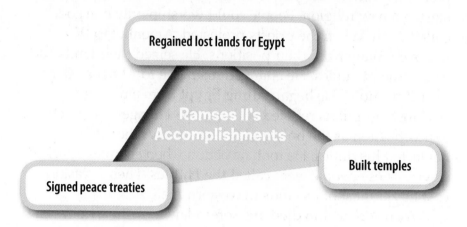

Regained lost lands for Egypt

Ramses II's Accomplishments

Signed peace treaties

Built temples

The Egyptians believed that their gods and goddesses lived in the temples. Priests and priestesses served the gods by leaving food for them and by washing their statues. Temples also served as banks. Egyptians stored valuables in them.

After Ramses II, Egypt's power faded. Egypt was attacked by groups with more and better weapons. By 1150 B.C., Egypt had lost its empire. Starting in 900 B.C., one outside group after another took over Egypt. These outside groups included the Libyans, the people of Kush, and the Assyrians.

 NGSSS Check List one accomplishment for each pharaoh. SS.6.W.2.6

Ahmose

_____

Hatshepsut

_____

Thutmose III

_____

Amenhotep IV

_____

Tutankhamen

_____

Ramses II

_____

NGSSS

SS.6.G.2.4 Explain how the geographical location of ancient civilizations contributed to the culture and politics of those societies.

SS.6.E.3.2 Categorize products that were traded among civilizations, and give examples of barriers to trade of those products.

LESSON 4 — THE KINGDOM OF KUSH

Essential Question

Why do civilizations rise and fall?

Guiding Questions

1. How did Nubia and Egypt influence each other?
2. Why did the kingdom of Kush prosper?

Terms to Know

savanna
a grassy plain with some scattered trees

textiles
woven cloth

What Do You Know?

Directions: Read each statement. Circle **T** if you think the statement is true. Circle **F** if you think the statement is false.

1. All civilizations that lived by the Nile River were the same.	T	F
2. The Egyptians were the only civilization to build pyramids.	T	F
3. The kingdom of Kush became famous for making iron.	T	F
4. Egypt and Kush received very little rainfall.	T	F

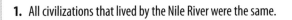

When Did It Happen?

1400s B.C. Thutmose III invades Nubia

850 B.C. The Kingdom of Kush rises

728 B.C. Kush rules over Egypt

540 B.C. Kush moves capital to Meroë

A.D. 350 Meroë is burned

2000 B.C. — 1000 B.C. — 100 B.C. — A.D. 100 — A.D. 350

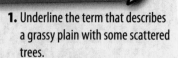
PHOTO: Gabriela Staebler/CORBIS

Mark the Text

1. Underline the term that describes a grassy plain with some scattered trees.

Think Critically

2. **Contrast** How was Nubia's land different from Egypt's?

_____

_____

_____

_____

_____

Mark the Text

3. Underline the items that Egypt received in trade from Kerma.

The Nubians

Egypt was not the only civilization along the Nile River. The Nubians lived on the Nile south of Egypt. Nubia later became known as Kush.

The first Nubians were cattle herders. Their cattle grazed in **savannas,** or grassy plains. Nubia also got plenty of rainfall. As a result, the Nubians did not need water from the Nile River. They settled in villages, grew crops, and hunted with bows and arrows.

	Nubia	Egypt
Land	savannas	desert lands river valley
Water Source	rainfall	Nile River
Crops	beans, yams, rice, grains	wheat, rice, other grains

In time, the Nubians formed the kingdom of Kerma. Farming and gold mining made Kerma wealthy. The kingdom also became an important trade center. The Egyptians traded with Kerma for cattle, gold, ivory, and enslaved people. Egyptians also hired Nubians to fight in their armies.

Kerma's craft-makers made fine pottery, jewelry, and metal goods. As in Egypt, Kerma kings were buried in tombs that held gold, jewelry, and pottery.

In the 1400s B.C., the Egyptian pharaoh Thutmose III invaded Nubia. After a 50-year war, Kerma collapsed and the Egyptians seized much of Nubia. They ruled it for the next 700 years. During this time, the people of Nubia adopted Egyptian ways. They worshiped Egyptian gods and goddesses. They worked with copper and bronze. They also adapted Egyptian hieroglyphics to their own language.

Today, Nubia is part of southern Egypt and northern Sudan. The land is mostly savanna, as shown here, unlike the desert land of northern Egypt.

The Kushite Kingdom

By 850 B.C., a Nubian group had formed the kingdom of Kush. Powerful Kushite kings ruled for the next few centuries. Their capital was the city of Napata. It was located south of Egypt, along the Nile River. Trade caravans carried gold, ivory, valuable woods, and other goods from Kush to Egypt.

In time, Kush became strong enough to take over Egypt. About 750 B.C., a Kushite king named Kashta headed north. He began the conquest of Egypt. His son Piye completed the conquest in 728 B.C. He ruled both Egypt and Kush from the city of Napata. The kings of Kush built temples and monuments similar to those built by the Egyptians. The Kushites also built small pyramids in which to bury their kings.

Kush's rule over Egypt was short. During the 600s B.C., the Assyrians invaded Egypt. They drove the Kushites back to their homeland. Kushites, however, gained something from the Assyrians—the secret to making iron. The Kushites became the first Africans to make iron. Soon, farmers in Kush could use iron to make stronger plows. Now they could grow more crops. Kush's warriors also began using iron spears and swords. Traders from Kush carried iron products and enslaved peoples to Arabia, India, and China. In return, they brought back cotton, textiles, and other goods.

4. Explain How did learning to make iron help the Kushites?

_____

_____

_____

_____

_____

_____

This gold bracelet was found in the pyramid tomb of Queen Amanishakheto near Meroë. Many jewels and other treasures were discovered in her tomb in 1837.

PHOTO: INTERFOTO/Alamy

Copyright © by The McGraw-Hill Companies, Inc.

PHOTO: DEA / A. DAGLI ORTI/De Agostini Picture Library/Getty Images

Mark the Text

5. Circle two items that helped Meroë become an iron-making center.

In about 540 B.C., Kush's rulers moved to the city of Meroë. It became the capital city. Like Napata, the new capital was near the Nile River. In addition, the land near Meroë had iron ore and trees for fuel. As a result, Meroë became an iron-making center. Kush's kings rebuilt Meroë to look like an Egyptian city. It included small pyramids, a grand avenue, and a huge temple.

Meroë became an important center of trade in the ancient world. Kush's traders received leopard skins and valuable woods from other places in Africa. They traded these, plus iron products and enslaved workers for cotton **textiles,** or woven cloth, and other goods. By the A.D. 200s, the kingdom began to weaken. As Kush declined, another kingdom called Axum took its place. Around A.D. 350, the armies of Axum burned Meroë to the ground.

This painted Nubian cup portrays a crocodile.

NGSSS Check Complete the Venn diagram about Egypt and Nubia. SS.6.G.2.4

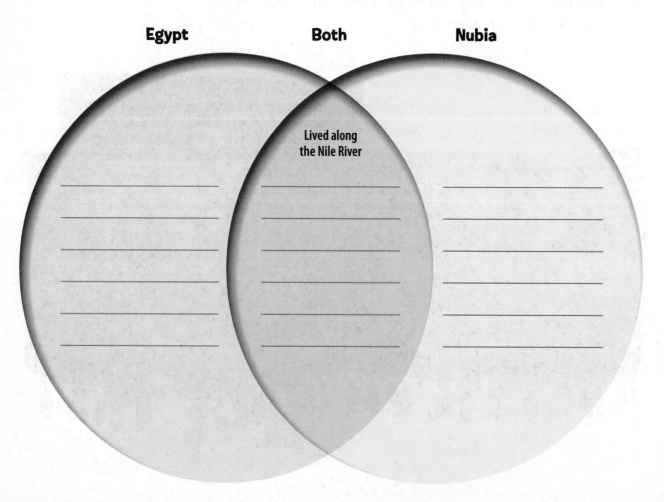

Egypt — Both — Nubia

Lived along the Nile River

MY REFLECTIONS

ESSENTIAL QUESTION *What makes a culture unique?*

Reflect on What It Means . . .

There are many factors that influence settlement, and whether civilizations rise or fall. Often, cultures develop within civilizations and are affected by similar influences. Today, there are many diverse cultures in our civilization. They may share some beliefs, traditions, and even their spoken or written language with other cultures. They may blend with other cultures to make a new culture.

Use the space within the culture wheel below to illustrate characteristics of Egypt's culture. You can use drawings or words.

art

ideas

language

music

custom

clothing

religion

tradition

TAKE THE CHALLENGE

Create your own model civilization. Choose a location. Think about what physical features will be important to your civilization's survival. Determine what natural resources will be used, what crops will be grown, and what cultural characteristics your civilization will have. Then make an advertisement to let other civilizations know about yours and to perhaps attract trade partners. Be creative!

Keep Going!

Use the circle below to illustrate characteristics of your culture. Draw a culture wheel with 6–8 spokes and include in it pictures and words that represent your culture. Be sure that your culture wheel shows how your community and your world are part of your culture.

CHAPTER
6
THE ISRAELITES

NGSSS

SS.6.W.2.9 Identify key figures and basic beliefs of the Israelites and determine how these beliefs compared with those of others in the geographic area.

ESSENTIAL QUESTIONS *How do religions develop? What are the characteristics of a leader? How does religion shape society? Why does conflict develop?*

Ruth was a poor woman who was a foreigner and a widow. She faced a difficult choice: whether to stay with her people or to join Naomi, her mother-in-law, who was an Israelite.

PHOTO: Peter Willi/SuperStock

Copyright © by The McGraw-Hill Companies, Inc.

"Where you go I will go, and where you stay I will stay. Your people will be my people and your God my God. Where you die I will die, and there I will be buried."

RUTH 1:16-17, THE HOLY BIBLE (NIV)

In Your Own Words

What is Ruth trying to say?

_____

_____

What does this image reveal about Ruth and Naomi?

_____

_____

DBQ BREAKING IT DOWN

Why do you think Ruth chose to join Naomi and follow the people of Israel?

_____

_____

_____

McGraw-Hill
networks™
There's More Online!

1 BEGINNINGS

NGSSS

SS.6.W.2.9 Identify key figures and basic beliefs of the Israelites and determine how these beliefs compared with those of others in the geographic area.

Essential Question
How do religions develop?

Guiding Questions
1. What did the ancient Israelites believe?
2. How did the Israelites settle Canaan?

Terms to Know

monotheism
the belief in only one god

prophet
a messenger sent by God

tribe
a group of people who share a family member in the past

Exodus
the journey of the Israelites from slavery in Egypt

covenant
an agreement with God; the Israelites agreed to follow God's laws if he would lead them safely to Canaan

Torah
the laws that Moses received from God on Mount Sinai; they are also a part of the Hebrew Bible

commandment
a rule that God wanted the Israelites to follow

alphabet
a group of letters that stand for the sounds made when talking

Where in the World?

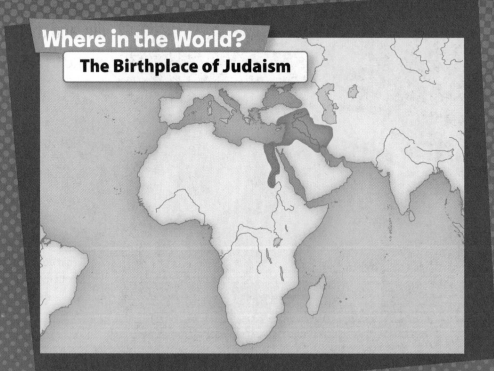

The Birthplace of Judaism

When Did It Happen?

3000 B.C.
Nomadic tribes probably settle in Canaan

1800 B.C.
Israelites emerged in the eastern Mediterranean region

1200 B.C.
Philistines invaded the Mediterranean area

4000 B.C.   3000 B.C.   2000 B.C.   1000 B.C.

networks Read Chapter 6 Lesson 1 in your textbook or online.

Beginnings

Around 1800 B.C., a group called the Israelites appeared in southwest Asia. The Israelites were different from many other groups at the time. They practiced **monotheism.** This means they believed in only one god. Other groups practiced polytheism. This is the worship of more than one god. The Israelites also believed that God sent **prophets.** These prophets were messengers who shared God's words with the people.

The Israelites wrote about their religious beliefs and history. Some of these writings became the Hebrew Bible. These religious beliefs eventually became a religion called Judaism. Today, the followers of this religion are called Jews.

Jewish belief states that the Israelites descended from a man named Abraham. The Hebrew Bible says that God told Abraham to settle in Canaan. God promised that Abraham and his descendants would always control Canaan.

Abraham's grandson Jacob was later named Israel. Jacob had 12 sons. Over time his family eventually divided into separate family groups. These groups are called **tribes.** Jacob's 12 sons became the leaders of the Twelve Tribes of Israel.

Famine eventually forced the Israelites to leave Canaan. Many of them moved to Egypt. However, Egypt's leader, the pharaoh, enslaved them. The Israelites had to work at hard labor. They prayed to their God for freedom.

The Hebrew Bible says that a prophet named Moses led the Israelites from Egypt. One day, Moses saw a burning bush. God spoke to him from this bush. God told Moses to tell the pharaoh to let the Israelites go. The pharaoh refused and God sent ten plagues to Egypt. Plagues are events that cause great problems for many people. The plagues eventually convinced the pharaoh to let the Israelites leave.

The Torah scrolls are part of the Hebrew Bible. The Torah is still read today.

Mark the Text

1. Underline what God promised Abraham in exchange for settling in Canaan.

Show Your Skill

2. **Identify Cause and Effect** What caused the Israelites to leave Canaan, and what did they face in the place where they fled?

_____

_____

_____

_____

_____

PHOTO: Steve McAlister/Photographer's Choice/Getty Images

Copyright © by The McGraw-Hill Companies, Inc.

_____

_____

_____

_____

Think Critically

4. **Contrast** How were the Israelites different from other groups at the time?

_____

_____

_____

5. **Explain** What challenge did the Israelites face when they returned to Canaan?

_____

_____

_____

Show Your Skill

6. **Draw Conclusions** How could an alphabet have helped the Phoenicians trade?

_____

_____

_____

After the Israelites left, the pharaoh changed his mind. He sent his army to catch the Israelites. The Hebrew Bible says that God parted the Red Sea so the Israelites could cross. When the Egyptians followed, they were drowned. The journey of the Israelites from slavery in Egypt is called the **Exodus.** The Jewish holy day of Passover celebrates their freedom from slavery.

During their journey, the Israelites received a **covenant** with God. A covenant is an agreement. According to the Hebrew Bible, God promised to guide the Israelites safely back to Canaan. In exchange, they had to follow his laws. Moses received these laws on top of Mount Sinai. The laws are known as the **Torah.** These laws include the Ten Commandments. The Torah later became part of the Hebrew Bible. The Ten Commandments are also a part of the Torah. A **commandment** was a rule that God wanted the Israelites to follow. The main idea of the Ten Commandments is loyalty to God. The belief in only one God became the basis for other religions. The laws of many nations are also based on principles in the Ten Commandments.

The Land of Canaan

The Hebrew Bible says that Moses died before reaching Canaan. A new leader named Joshua led the Israelites to Canaan. They found other groups already living there. Two of these groups were the Phoenicians and the Philistines. These groups had different beliefs and ways of life than the Israelites.

The Phoenicians lived in cities by the Mediterranean coast. They used their location to become skilled sailors and traders. Over time, the Phoenicians gained control of Mediterranean shipping and trade. They traded goods and founded settlements around the Mediterranean world. These settlements helped spread Phoenician ideas. They developed an **alphabet** to help them trade. An alphabet is a group of letters that stands for sounds made when talking. Their alphabet influenced the Greek and Roman alphabets. We still use the Roman alphabet today.

The other group was the Philistines. They had come from near present-day Greece. They built walled towns by the Mediterranean coast in southern Canaan. The Philistines made tools and weapons, and they built a strong army.

The Israelites wanted to establish Canaan as their new homeland. However, these two groups made that difficult. The Israelites believed that God wanted them to claim this land. According to the Hebrew Bible, Joshua led them into battle to achieve this goal. At the city of Jericho, the Israelites marched around the city walls for six days. On the seventh day, the walls fell. The Israelites took control of Jericho.

Groups Living in Canaan

Phoenicians
- sailors and traders
- settlements throughout Mediterranean world
- created an alphabet

Philistines
- settled in southern Canaan
- built walled cities along Mediterranean coast
- made tools and weapons; built a strong army

Joshua continued to lead the Israelites into other battles. Then, they divided the lands they captured between the 12 tribes. When Joshua died, leaders called judges ruled the tribes. The judges settled disputes and led troops into battle. A woman judge named Deborah became known for her bravery. She helped advise troops in battle. These troops defeated another army seeking control of Canaan.

After many battles, the Israelites won control of central Canaan. The Hebrew Bible states that they worshiped God in a tabernacle. This is a large tent-like building that could be taken along as they moved from place to place. The tabernacle housed the Ark of the Covenant. The Ark was a wooden chest. The Israelites believed the Ten Commandments were written on tablets kept in the Ark. They carried the Ark into battle with them. They believed it would ensure a victory, or make certain they won.

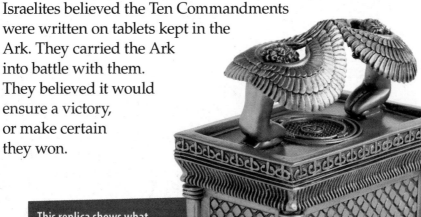

This replica shows what the Ark of the Covenant may have looked like.

NGSSS Check Explain why Canaan was important to the Israelites. SS.6.W.2.9

_____

_____

Mark the Text

7. Underline in the text what part of Canaan the Israelites reclaimed.

Think Critically

8. Explain Who was Deborah?

_____

_____

Take the Challenge

9. Make a storyboard to show the sequence of events of the Israelites taking control of Canaan.

LESSON

2 THE ISRAELITE KINGDOM

NGSSS

SS.6.W.2.9 Identify key figures and basic beliefs of the Israelites and determine how these beliefs compared with those of others in the geographic area.

Essential Question
What are the characteristics of a leader?

Guiding Questions
1. What was the role of kings in Israelite history?
2. How did neighboring empires respond to the Israelites?

Terms to Know

psalm
sacred song or poem

proverb
a familiar saying that shares lessons for living

exile
forced absence from one's home or country

Where in the World?

The Israelite Kingdom and Assyrian Empire

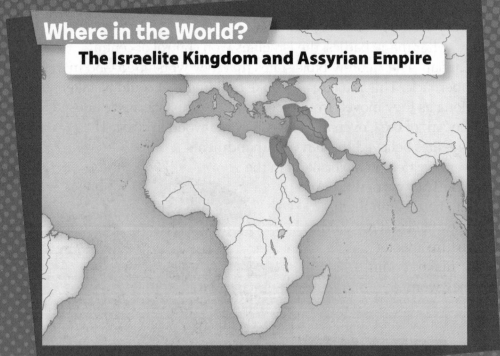

When Did It Happen?

1200 B.C.
Philistines invaded the Mediterranean area

1100 B.C.
Israelites settle much of Canaan

970 B.C.
Solomon becomes Israelite king

922 B.C.
Solomon dies

722 B.C.
Assyrians invade Israel

1200 B.C.   1000 B.C.   800 B.C.   600 B.C.

Early Kings

The Israelites had settled much of Canaan by 1100 B.C. However, they feared the powerful Philistines. The Israelites called for a king to unite them against this enemy. They asked the judge Samuel to choose a king. He warned that a king might tax or enslave them. Still, the Israelites demanded a king. Samuel chose Saul to become the first Israelite king.

Saul helped the Israelites win many battles against the Philistines. However, according to the Hebrew Bible, he disobeyed some of God's commands. God told Samuel to choose a new king. Samuel then chose a young shepherd named David to be king.

David was already known for his bravery. The Hebrew Bible tells the story of his victory over the giant Philistine warrior, Goliath. Goliath dared any Israelite to battle one-on-one. David accepted the challenge. He used a shepherd's staff, a slingshot, and five stones to kill Goliath. Saul put David in charge of his army. David won victories, and he became even more well-known. Saul then became jealous and tried to kill David, but David escaped. Saul later died in battle and David became king.

As king, David united the Twelve Tribes. The Israelite army finally defeated the Philistines, and David set up a capital city at Jerusalem. It is believed that David wrote many of the sacred songs, or **psalms,** in the Hebrew and Christian Bibles. Today, David is considered the greatest Israelite king.

David is shown here using his slingshot to defeat Goliath. When David was older, he became king of Israel and established a capital at Jerusalem.

Mark the Text

1. Underline the names of the three Israelite kings described in this section.

Show Your Skill

2. Make a Connection What characteristics do leaders in your school or community in Florida share with David?

_____

_____

_____

_____

_____

_____

Think Critically

3. Analyze Why is David considered a great Israelite king?

_____

_____

_____

_____

_____

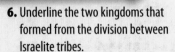

Think Critically

4. Evaluate How did Solomon eventually lose the support of the Israelites?

_____

_____

_____

5. Infer Why was the time period following Solomon's death difficult for the Israelites?

_____

_____

_____

Mark the Text

6. Underline the two kingdoms that formed from the division between Israelite tribes.

Take the Challenge

7. The Assyrians have hired you to make an advertisement for them. They want the ad to remind the people they have conquered to pay tribute.

After David died, his son Solomon became king. Solomon made peace with many nearby groups. He also built cities and Jerusalem's first temple. Solomon was known as a wise leader. His **proverbs** are found in the Hebrew Bible. Proverbs are familiar sayings that share lessons for living. Solomon did many good things as king. However, the Israelites eventually turned against him. They did not like working on his many building projects or paying his high taxes. Solomon died about 922 B.C. After that time, the Israelites entered a difficult period. Their kingdom became divided and powerful neighbors threatened them.

Two Kingdoms

The ten northern tribes rebelled against Jerusalem after Solomon died. These tribes started a new kingdom called Israel. Samaria was its capital. The two southern tribes formed Judah. The capital of this smaller kingdom was Jerusalem.

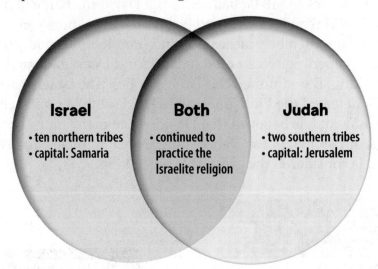

Israel
• ten northern tribes
• capital: Samaria

Both
• continued to practice the Israelite religion

Judah
• two southern tribes
• capital: Jerusalem

During this time, large empires grew around Israel and Judah. The Assyrians and Chaldeans became powerful. They wanted to control the trade routes that ran through the Israelite kingdoms.

The Assyrians spread fear across the region. They forced the people they conquered to pay tribute. This meant that people had to give the Assyrians money or enslaved people. If they did not receive a tribute, the Assyrians would destroy buildings or entire towns. The kingdom of Israel refused to pay tribute to the Assyrians. As a result, the Assyrians invaded Israel in 722 B.C. They captured Samaria and other major cities. They brought people into Israel from other parts of the Assyrian Empire. These new settlers mixed with the Israelites. This produced a new culture, whose people were called Samaritans.

The Israelite prophets' teachings were very important to the Jewish faith. This painting shows a prophet under the hand of God.

The Samaritans accepted many Israelite religious beliefs. They also adopted religious practices that the Israelites did not accept. Eventually, the two groups had little in common. Present-day Judaism grew from the religious practices of the tribes of Judah.

Later, the Chaldeans conquered Jerusalem and began making major changes. At first, the Chaldeans chose a Judaean king to rule Judah. This king planned to set Judah free. He did not listen to those people who warned against a revolt. After a long conflict, the Chaldeans retook the city. They then destroyed much of it, including the temple. The Chaldeans took the king and thousands of other people to live in Babylon. This time became known as the Babylonian Exile.

During this difficult time, prophets played an important role in Jewish life. They provided encouragement and guidance for the Israelites. Their goal of making the world a better place influenced many people who came after them.

 NGSSS Check Were David and Solomon successful kings? Explain. SS.6.W.2.9

_____

_____

_____

_____

Show Your Skill

8. Draw Conclusions Why might the Chaldeans have decided to send so many Israelites to live in Babylon?

_____

_____

_____

_____

Think Critically

9. Summarize Why did the Assyrians and Chaldeans want to take over the Israelite kingdoms?

_____

_____

_____

_____

THE DEVELOPMENT OF JUDAISM

NGSSS

SS.6.W.2.9 Identify key figures and basic beliefs of the Israelites and determine how these beliefs compared with those of others in the geographic area.

Essential Question

How does religion shape society?

Guiding Questions

1. How did the people of Judah practice their religion while in exile and in their homeland?
2. How did religion shape the Jewish way of life?

Terms to Know

synagogue
a Jewish house of worship

Sabbath
in Judaism, a day of rest and worship that lasts from sundown on Friday to sundown on Saturday each week

scroll
a long document made up of pieces of rough paper called parchment; the pieces are sewn together to make scrolls

kosher
describes food that has been made while following Jewish dietary laws

Where in the World?

Babylon, Judah, and Israel

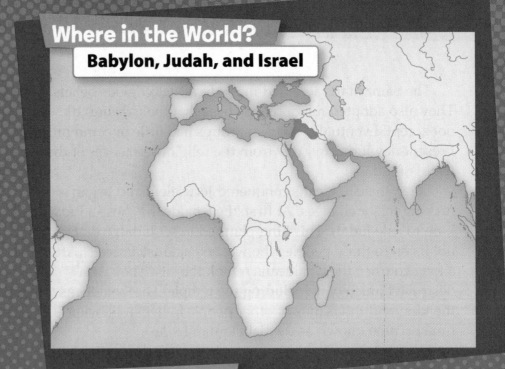

When Did It Happen?

722 B.C.
Assyrians invade Israel

c. 586 B.C.
Chaldeans retake Jerusalem; many Jews are sent to live in exile in Babylon

538 B.C.
Persian king Cyrus II lets Jews return to Judah

750 B.C.   700 B.C.   650 B.C.   600 B.C.   550 B.C.   500 B.C.

Return to Judah

The Judaeans' time in Babylon was called an exile. This is a period of time when people are forced to live away from their homes. During this time, they became known as the Jews. Their religion also became known as Judaism.

The Jews did not have a large temple in Babylon. Instead, they gathered in smaller houses of worship. These were called **synagogues.** The Jews came together on the **Sabbath.** This is a weekly day of rest and worship. According to tradition, it lasts from sundown Friday to sundown Saturday. A tradition is a custom or way of life that has been handed down from generation to generation. Jews still observe the Sabbath today.

Many Jews in Babylon hoped to go back to Judah. Eventually, a group called the Persians defeated the Chaldeans. In 538 B.C., the Persian king Cyrus II allowed Jews to return to Judah. Many Jews returned to Judah. They began to rebuild Jerusalem. They built the Second Temple. This replaced the temple that was destroyed by the Chaldeans.

The Jews could not have their own government or king under Persian rule. They looked to religious leaders to guide their society. These leaders included priests and scribes. Scribes were religious scholars that taught the Jewish faith. The scribes wrote down the books of the Torah on rough pieces of paper called parchment. They sewed these pieces together to make **scrolls.** These writings make up the Hebrew Bible.

The Hebrew Bible has three main parts. These parts are the Torah, the Prophets, and the Writings. The Hebrew Bible contains 24 books. It presents the laws and rules of the Israelites. It also tells about Jewish history, art, literature, poetry, and proverbs. The first book of the Hebrew Bible is Genesis. It gives the Israelite view of how humans began. Genesis also explains how God punished the world for wicked behavior. This is told through the story of Noah's ark. This book also describes why the world has many languages.

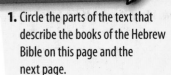

Mark the Text

1. Circle the parts of the text that describe the books of the Hebrew Bible on this page and the next page.

Show Your Skill

2. Identify Cause and Effect How did exile affect the way the Jews practiced their religion?

_____

_____

_____

_____

Think Critically

3. Explain Why did priests and scribes become leaders when the Jews returned from exile?

_____

_____

_____

_____

When a Jewish boy reaches the age of 13, it is Jewish tradition for him to read the Torah at his Bar Mitzvah.

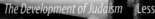

4. Identify the Main Idea What traits did the Torah encourage the Jews to show in their daily lives?

_____

_____

_____

_____

5. Draw Conclusions Why do you think Ruth became a model for Jewish girls?

_____

_____

_____

_____

_____

Take the Challenge

6. Create a menu for a kosher restaurant. Include choices for breakfast, lunch, and dinner. Do additional research if needed.

The book of Isaiah details God's plan for a peaceful world. The book of Daniel says that the Jews believed that goodness would eventually replace evil and suffering. Daniel was a king's advisor who refused to worship Babylonian gods. The Chaldeans threw him in a lion's den. However, God protected Daniel. This story reminds Jews that God will also rescue them from evil. Christians and Muslims also share this hope for a better world.

Jewish Daily Life

The laws of the Torah shaped daily life for the early Jews. These laws affected family life, food, and clothing. The Torah required Jews to help others and treat them fairly. It also encouraged self-control and loyalty to God.

The Torah described roles for Jewish fathers and mothers. Jewish families valued education. Sons learned a trade and how to read the Torah. Daughters learned to be wives, mothers, and housekeepers. They studied Jewish laws about food and clothing. They also learned about women of ancient Israel, such as Ruth and Naomi.

- Ruth was Naomi's daughter-in-law.
- Naomi's husband and two sons died.
- One of the sons was married to Ruth, who was not a Jew.
- Ruth made a difficult decision.
- To help Naomi, she left her homeland to go to Bethlehem.
- Ruth's courage and devotion became a model for Jewish girls.

Jewish dietary laws tell what Jews can eat. Ancient Jews could only eat animals that were considered clean. These included cattle and sheep, but not swine (pigs). Food prepared according to Jewish dietary laws is called **kosher.** Animals used in kosher meat must be killed in a certain way. This meat is inspected, salted, and soaked in water. Jews cannot eat meat and dairy products together. They also cannot eat crab, shrimp, or other shellfish.

NGSSS Check List five features of Judaism. SS.6.W.2.9

_____

_____

_____

_____

NGSSS

SS.6.W.2.9 Identify key figures and basic beliefs of the Israelites and determine how these beliefs compared with those of others in the geographic area.

Essential Question
Why does conflict develop?

Guiding Questions
1. What was life like for the Jews in Greek-ruled lands?
2. How did the Jews react to Roman rule of their homeland?

Terms to Know

Diaspora
the groups of Jewish people living outside of the Jewish homeland

rabbi
Jewish religious leaders who explained the Torah and offered moral guidance

Where in the World?

Judaea and the Roman Empire

When Did It Happen?

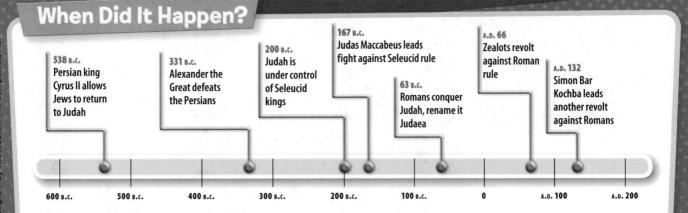

538 B.C.
Persian king Cyrus II allows Jews to return to Judah

331 B.C.
Alexander the Great defeats the Persians

200 B.C.
Judah is under control of Seleucid kings

167 B.C.
Judas Maccabeus leads fight against Seleucid rule

63 B.C.
Romans conquer Judah, rename it Judaea

A.D. 66
Zealots revolt against Roman rule

A.D. 132
Simon Bar Kochba leads another revolt against Romans

600 B.C. 500 B.C. 400 B.C. 300 B.C. 200 B.C. 100 B.C. 0 A.D. 100 A.D. 200

Mark the Text

1. Underline the result of the Maccabees' revolt.

Think Critically

2. **Summarize** How did Jewish ideas spread throughout the Mediterranean world?

_____

_____

_____

3. **Explain** What does the annual festival of Hanukkah celebrate?

_____

_____

_____

_____

_____

_____

_____

The Arrival of Greek Rule

In 331 B.C., Alexander the Great defeated the Persians. Alexander brought Greek language and culture to Judah. He also allowed Jews to stay in Judah.

Judah remained the center of Judaism. Many Jews, however, moved to other parts of Alexander's empire. Some lived in Babylon, Egypt , and other Mediterranean lands. Jews living outside of Judah became known as the **Diaspora.** *Diaspora* is a Greek word that means "scattered." The members of the Diaspora remained loyal to Judaism. They also spoke Greek and adopted parts of Greek culture.

Some Jewish scholars in Egypt copied the Hebrew Bible into Greek. This Greek version of the Hebrew Bible is called the Septuagint. A version is a different form or type of something. This Greek version brought the Hebrew Bible to people who were not Jews. It helped spread Jewish ideas throughout the Mediterranean world.

When Alexander died, four of his generals divided his empire. One kingdom covered most of Southwest Asia. A family called the Seleucids gained control of Judah by 200 B.C. The Seleucid king Antiochus IV required Jews to worship Greek gods and goddesses. Many Jews refused to give up their religion.

A priest named Judas Maccabeus fought against the Seleucids. His army was called the Maccabees. They drove the Seleucids out of Judah. They removed all statues of Greek gods and goddesses from the temple. The annual festival of Hanukkah celebrates this event.

These boys celebrate the annual Jewish tradition of Hanukkah by lighting menorahs.

Roman Rule in Judaea

In 63 B.C., Roman forces conquered Judah and named it Judaea. The name *Roman* came from their capital, Rome. This city was located far away from Judaea in what is now Italy. At first, the Romans chose a follower of Judaism as king of Judaea. This ruler, Herod, built forts and cities. The Second Temple in Jerusalem was also rebuilt during his reign. This temple was the center of Jewish worship.

When Herod died, Roman officials ruled Judaea. Jews began to disagree about how to practice Judaism. They also disagreed about how to interact with the Romans.

One group was called the Pharisees. They had the support of the common people. The Pharisees taught in synagogues. They also applied the Torah's teachings to daily life. The Pharisees worked to make Judaism a religion of the home and family. They focused on both written and oral law.

The Sadducees included wealthy noble families. Many served as priests and scribes in the Temple. They focused on applying the Torah's laws to temple ceremonies. They opposed many of the Pharisees' teachings. For example, they rejected the Pharisees' focus on oral law.

A third group was called Essenes. These priests had broken away from the Temple in Jerusalem. They lived in the desert by the Dead Sea. They prayed and waited for God to deliver them from Roman rule. They also followed only the written law of the Torah. The Essenes may have written the Dead Sea Scrolls.

The Zealots lived in Judaea. They believed that the Jews should fight the Romans for their freedom. In the A.D. 60s, many Jews were waiting for a deliverer. A deliverer is a person sent by God to rescue people from trouble. Anger at Roman rule reached its peak during this time. The Zealots got ready for battle.

| Jewish Groups Respond to Roman Rule ||
Group	Response
Pharisees	• wanted Judaea free from Roman rule • urged resistance through greater devotion to the Torah
Sadducees	• favored cooperation with Romans • wanted to keep peace and order in Judaea
Essenes	• prayed for God to deliver them from Roman rule
Zealots	• prepared to fight the Romans for their freedom

Mark the Text

4. Underline the accomplishments of the first king of Judaea.

Show Your Skill

5. **Make Inferences** Why is the Talmud a valuable record of Jewish law?

_____

_____

_____

_____

_____

_____

Take the Challenge

6. Write a newspaper article from the point of view of someone living in Judaea under Roman rule.

The Western Wall is an extremely sacred place for Jews, and as these Jews illustrate, serves as a common place of prayer.

PHOTO: Panoramic Images/Getty Images

Show Your Skill

7. Identify Cause and Effect
What was the outcome of the second Jewish revolt against Roman rule in A.D. 132?

_____

_____

_____

_____

_____

Think Critically

8. Infer How did rabbis help to unify the Jews?

_____

_____

_____

_____

_____

In A.D. 66, the Zealots revolted. They drove the Romans from Jerusalem. However, the Romans reclaimed Jerusalem four years later. They killed many Jews and forced many others to leave. The Romans also destroyed the Second Temple. Today, the temple's Western Wall is all that remains.

In A.D. 132, the Jews again revolted. The Romans also defeated this rebellion. The Jews were no longer allowed to live in or visit Jerusalem. The Romans renamed Judaea and called it Palestine.

The Jews regrouped with help from religious leaders called **rabbis.** The rabbis became important because the Jews no longer had temples or priests. One famous rabbi was named Yohanan ben Zaccai. When the Romans captured Jerusalem in A.D. 70, he persuaded them to spare the city of Yavneh. There, he set up a school to keep teaching the Torah. His efforts helped the Jewish religion survive the destruction of the temple and loss of Jerusalem. The rabbis eventually put their teachings about Jewish laws in writing. These writings are called the Talmud. The Talmud discusses issues faced in daily life. It remains an important record of Jewish law.

 NGSSS Check For each cause, identify one effect. SS.6.W.2.9

Cause	Effect
Alexander the Great conquered Judah.	1. _____
The Seleucids took control of Judah.	2. _____
The Zealots rebelled against Roman rule.	3. _____

Reflect on What It Means . . .

Throughout history, religious beliefs have shaped societies. Using what you learned in this chapter, reflect on the ways that the religious beliefs of the Ancient Israelites shaped their society.

With a small group, work to create a mini-television program or podcast on the history of the Ancient Israelites discussed in this chapter.

Then prepare a special segment on the relationship between the religion of the Israelites and their society. Use the space below and on the next page to jot down your ideas.

Our Ideas

Keep Going! ➤➤

Artifacts We Could Show

Scenes to Re-enact

TAKE THE CHALLENGE

Write a short story about the history of Judaism. Use illustrations in your short story. When you have completed it, exchange short stories with a partner. Have the class vote on the short story that does the best job of portraying the story of Judaism.

THE ANCIENT GREEKS

NGSSS

SS.6.W.3.5 Summarize the important achievements and contributions of ancient Greek civilization.

ESSENTIAL QUESTIONS *How does geography influence the way people live? Why do people form governments? Why does conflict develop? How do governments change?*

The Peloponnesian War pitted two Greek city-states against each other. The city-state that was defeated championed democratic ideas that would influence future civilizations.

" Our constitution is called a democracy because power is in the hands not of a minority but of the whole people. When it is a question of settling private disputes, everyone is equal before the law. . . . in positions of public responsibility, what counts is the actual ability which the man possesses. . . . "

— *PARAPHRASED FROM* THE HISTORY OF THE PELOPONNESIAN WAR

minority

What does the term *minority* mean here?

_____

_____

ability

Write another word (synonym) for *ability* below.

_____

DBQ BREAKING IT DOWN

In a democracy, what are some examples of "public responsibility"?

_____

_____

According to this excerpt, what is the connection between a person's social class and their skill or knowledge?

_____

_____

McGraw-Hill
networks™
There's More Online!

PHOTO: Rainey, William (1852-1936) / Private Collection / The Stapleton Collection / The Bridgeman Art Library International

1 RISE OF GREEK CIVILIZATION

SS.6.G.2.2 Differentiate between continents, regions, countries, and cities in order to understand the complexities of regions created by civilizations.

SS.6.G.2.5 Interpret how geographic boundaries invite or limit interaction with other regions and cultures.

Essential Question
How does geography influence the way people live?

Guiding Questions
1. How did physical geography influence the lives of the early Greeks?
2. How did the civilization of the Minoans develop?
3. How did the Mycenaeans gain power in the Mediterranean?
4. How did early Greeks spread their culture?
5. How did Greek city-states create the idea of citizenship?

Terms to Know

peninsula
a body of land with water on three sides

bard
someone who writes or performs epic poems about historical events and heroes and their deeds

colony
a group of people living in a new territory with close ties to their homeland; the territory itself

polis
Greek city-state

agora
a gathering place or marketplace in ancient Greece

phalanx
a formation of armed foot soldiers in ancient Greece

Where in the World?

Ancient Greece

When Did It Happen?

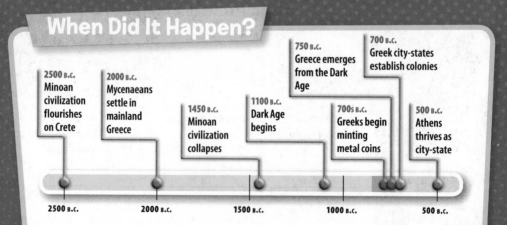

Copyright © by The McGraw-Hill Companies, Inc.

92 Chapter 7 *The Ancient Greeks*

Mountains and Seas

Greece is a **peninsula,** which is land that is surrounded by water on three sides. The land on the Greek peninsula has many mountains. Water and mountains have always influenced the Greek way of life. The sea and mountains greatly influenced how ancient Greek culture developed.

The water around Greece has many islands. Ancient Greeks traded goods and ideas with the people on those islands. Ancient Greeks also fished and farmed. The farmers settled in villages along the coast and between the mountains. The land there was fertile, and the climate was mild. The farmers grew wheat, barley, olives, and grapes. They also raised sheep and goats.

An Island Civilization

Another civilization developed on one of the islands off the coast of southern Greece. That island is Crete. Greek myths or stories tell about this civilization. However, it was not until the 1900s that a British archaeologist named Arthur Evans found items from this civilization.

The place he discovered on Crete is called Knossos. Evans dug up remains of an amazing palace. The palace had many rooms that were workshops. People made jewelry, vases, and statues in those rooms. There were also rooms used for storing food. The ancient people called Minoans built the palace. The Minoan civilization lasted over a thousand years, from 2500 B.C. to 1450 B.C.

Trade was an important economic activity for Minoans. Their wooden ships sailed to Egypt and Syria to trade goods. The Minoans made pottery and stone vases. They traded these

Show Your Skill

1. Identify Cause and Effect
How did the fact that Greece is a **peninsula** influence the way of life in Greece?

_____

_____

_____

_____

Mark the Text

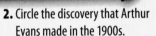

2. Circle the discovery that Arthur Evans made in the 1900s.

3. Circle the word that means "the system in a country that includes making, buying and selling goods."

Take the Challenge

4. Create a travel brochure to attract people to settle in the Mediterranean. Include the area's resources and beauty in your brochure.

Even though the land was mountainous, the ancient Greeks found flat areas to start villages and had access to water.

_____

_____

_____

_____

_____

6. Evaluate Why were the Mycenaean palaces important?

_____

_____

_____

_____

_____

Show Your Skill

7. Interpret Diagrams Name two things the Mycenaeans learned from the Minoans.

_____

_____

_____

_____

_____

_____

goods for ivory and metals. Their ships even patrolled the Mediterranean Sea to protect Minoan trade from pirates.

Sometime around 1450 B.C. the Minoan civilization ended. Historians do not know why. Some historians have decided that earthquakes destroyed the Minoan civilization. Other historians think that another civilization, the Mycenaeans, invaded Crete.

The Minoan island civilization was the first to develop in the area of Greece, but the Minoan people were not Greeks.

A Mainland Civilization

Another early civilization in the area was the Mycenaean civilization. These people moved to mainland Greece from central Asia. They lived in Greece from about 2000 B.C. to 1100 B.C.

Little was known about the Mycenaean until the late 1800s. That is when a German archaeologist named Heinrich Schliemann found the remains of palaces. The palaces were on the Greek mainland in a place called Mycenae.

In the Mycenaean civilization, each king lived in a palace built on a hill. Each palace had thick stone walls to protect against attackers. Nobles lived outside the walls on large farms called estates. Enslaved people and other workers lived in villages on the estates. The palaces were centers of government and workshops. People made clothes and jars for wine and olive oil there. Other workers made metal swords and leather shields.

Mycenaeans learned many things from Minoan traders. By the mid-1400s B.C., the Mycenaeans had conquered the Minoans. Their wealth grew. They built a strong military and fought in the Trojan War. Later the Mycenaean civilization grew weak. The many Mycenaean kings fought one another. Earthquakes destroyed their palaces. By 1100 B.C. the civilization had crumbled.

What Mycenaeans Adopted from Minoans

Minoans

Built ships for trade;
Navigated ships
using sun and stars;
Worked in bronze;
Worshiped Earth
Mother as chief god.

Mycenaeans Adopted

Built ships for trade;
Navigated ships
using sun and stars;
Worked in bronze;
Worshiped Earth
Mother as chief god.

About the time the Mycenaean civilization ended, groups of people moved around the eastern Mediterranean area. These groups fought wars with each other. Historians call the following period the Dark Age. Trade slowed down, and people made fewer things to sell. Farmers grew enough food only for their families. People were very poor.

Finally, around the 750s B.C., the difficult time started to end. Trade began to increase. People started making many items to trade. Many descendants of the people who had fled returned to the Greek mainland. They brought with them new ideas, crafts, and skills. Small communities formed. They were independent and ruled by kings. The people of these communities called themselves Greeks.

The Greek farmers grew more food than they could use. They traded this food with each other. They also built ships. The ships enabled them to trade the extra food with Egyptians and Phoenicians.

When trade increased, the Greeks needed a system of writing to record their trade. They adopted or used an alphabet from the Phoenicians.

The development of the Greek alphabet brought some important changes. It had 24 letters representing different sounds. It made reading and writing easier for the Greeks. Soon **bards,** or storytellers, were writing down the old stories. Until then, the old stories had always been spoken.

Colonies and Trade

The population increased in Greece when the Dark Age ended. By 700 B.C. farmers could not grow enough food for all of the people. Greek communities started to send people outside the

Think Critically

8. **Contrast** How were the beginning and end of the Dark Age different?

_____

_____

_____

_____

_____

Show Your Skill

9. **Identify the Main Idea** Why was the development of the Greek alphabet important?

_____

_____

_____

_____

_____

_____

_____

_____

Phoenician writing (shown here) served as a model for the development of the Greek alphabet.

Mark the Text

10. Underline the goods sent from the colonies to the mainland. Circle the goods sent from the mainland to the colonies.

area of Greece to form **colonies.** A colony is a settlement in a new territory. Greek people started colonies along the coasts of the Mediterranean Sea. That included coastal areas in Sicily, France, Spain, North Africa, and western Asia.

The colonies traded with their "parent" cities on the Greek mainland. They shipped grains, metals, timber, and enslaved people to Greece. In return, the cities in Greece shipped wine, olive oil, and pottery to the colonies.

To make trading easier, in the 700s B.C., the Greeks started to make coins from metals. Making coins is called minting. A coin is small and can be traded for many different types of goods. This makes it convenient to carry and use. Trade increased and made the Greek colonies wealthier.

The demand for food grew. People in the colonies started to specialize in what they grew or made. In some colonies the farmers raised sheep and made cloth from the sheep's wool.

This Greek jug from the 7th century B.C. might have been traded in the Mediterranean.

The Greek City-State

Mountains and seas separated the Greek city-states or communities. People in each community were very loyal to their city-state. At the end of the Dark Age, nobles who overthrew the kings were ruling the city-states. The nobles owned a lot of property around the city-states. Each city-state was very independent.

The **polis,** or city-state, was the basic political unit in Greece. At the center of each polis was a fort built on a hilltop. This fort was called an acropolis. When invaders attacked, people could be safe in the acropolis. The Greeks built temples on the acropolis. These temples honored local gods.

There was an open area outside the acropolis. This open area was called the **agora.** This space was used as a marketplace. Also the people gathered in the agora and debated issues, passed laws, and chose officials for the polis. City neighborhoods were located around the agora.

The villages and farmlands sat just outside the built-up city, yet were considered part of the polis. Most city-states were small. They were surrounded by mountains and seas.

The city-states were separated from each other, so each polis was governed by its own citizens. The Greeks developed the modern idea of citizenship. The citizens of each polis were members of a political community. They treated each other equally. Each citizen had rights and responsibilities.

In early Greece, only males who owned land were citizens. They had the right to vote, hold public office, own property, and defend themselves in court. They also had responsibilities. Their responsibilities included serving in government and fighting to defend their polis.

Citizenship in Greek city-states was different from citizenship in ancient Mesopotamia or Egyptian city-states. In Mesopotamia and Egypt, most people had no rights or say in their government. They had to obey their rulers. Besides being male and owning property, citizens in the Greek polis had to have been born in the polis. No foreigners were allowed to be citizens.

Citizens fought to defend their city-state. These citizen soldiers were called hoplites. They fought on foot. Each was armed with a round shield, a short sword, and a spear. When fighting, the hoplites would march shoulder to shoulder into battle. This formation was called a **phalanx.**

Later, many city-states ended the requirement for citizenship of owning property. Women and children, however, had no political rights.

The polis gave Greek citizens a sense of belonging. However, strong loyalty to their individual city-states divided Greece. This lack of unity weakened Greece and made it easier for outsiders to conquer Greece.

NGSSS Check How did physical geography affect trade in the ancient civilizations that developed in the Mediterranean region? SS.6.G.2.5

_____

_____

_____

_____

Mark the Text 🖉

14. Underline the definition of an *agora.*

Show Your Skill

15. Identify the Main Idea How did geography influence life and government on the Greek peninsula?

_____

_____

_____

_____

_____

_____

_____

_____

_____

_____

_____

_____

2 SPARTA AND ATHENS: CITY-STATE RIVALS

NGSSS

SS.6.W.3.2 Explain the democratic concepts (polis, civic participation and voting rights, legislative bodies, written constitutions, rule of law) developed in ancient Greece.

SS.6.W.3.3 Compare life in Athens and Sparta (government and the status of citizens, women and children, foreigners, helots).

SS.6.W.3.4 Explain the causes and effects of the Persian and Peloponnesian Wars.

Essential Question
Why do people form governments?

Guiding Questions
1. Which types of government did the Greek city-states have?
2. Why did the Spartans focus on military skills?
3. How did the culture in Athens differ from other Greek city-states?

Terms to Know

tyrant
a ruler who has total authority and is not bound by laws

oligarchy
a government in which a small group has control

democracy
a government by the people

helot
enslaved people in ancient Sparta

ephor
a high-ranking government official in Sparta

When Did It Happen?

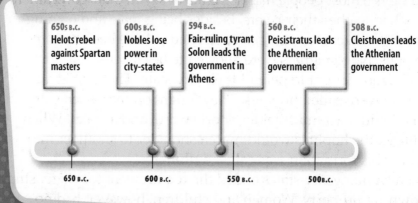

650s B.C. Helots rebel against Spartan masters	**600s B.C.** Nobles lose power in city-states	**594 B.C.** Fair-ruling tyrant Solon leads the government in Athens	**560 B.C.** Peisistratus leads the Athenian government	**508 B.C.** Cleisthenes leads the Athenian government

650 B.C.   600 B.C.   550 B.C.   500 B.C.

What Do You Know?

Directions: Read each statement. Circle the "T" if it is True or the "F" if it is False.

Before You Read True/False		Statement	After You Read True/False	
T	F	1. Tyrants were fair rulers who supported a democratic form of government.	T	F
T	F	2. Sparta and Athens became strong city-states.	T	F
T	F	3. Physical fitness was important in Sparta.	T	F
T	F	4. Sparta and Athens had the same ideas.	T	F

Political Changes

As the Greek city-states grew, there were political changes. The wealthy nobles seized power from the kings. The nobles did not rule long, however. Owners of small farms did not like the nobles ruling. Many of them had borrowed money from the nobles. When the farmers could not repay their loans, the nobles took their farms. Some of the farmers ended up working for the nobles or moving to the city to find jobs. Some farmers even had to sell themselves into slavery to repay the nobles.

By 650 B.C. small farmers wanted political change. They wanted a greater say in the government. Merchants and artisans also wanted change. They were not citizens because they did not own land. That meant they did not have a say in ruling the polis.

The growing political unrest led to the rise of **tyrants.** A tyrant is someone who seizes power and rules with total authority. Most of the tyrants who ruled city-states ruled fairly. It was the harsh rule of a few tyrants that gave the word tyranny its meaning as a cruel and unjust rule.

The common people supported the tyrants overthrowing the nobles. The hoplites, or citizen soldiers, also supported the tyrants. Tyrants increased their popularity by building new marketplaces, temples, and fortresses. Nevertheless, most people in the Greek city-states objected to rule by one person. They wanted a government in which all citizens had a say.

The tyrants ruled Greek city-states until about 500 B.C. Then, until about 336 B.C., most governments in Greek city-states changed. The form of government changed to either an **oligarchy** or a **democracy.** In an oligarchy, a few wealthy people run the government and hold power over the larger group of citizens. In a democracy, all citizens have a say in the government. Remember, each city-state was independent. Each polis chose its own type of government.

Sparta and Athens, two important Greek city-states, had different types of government. They also had very different societies.

Mark the Text

1. Circle the definition of a *tyrant*.

Think Critically

2. Categorize Which groups in Greek city-states did not want the nobles to rule?

_____

_____

3. Contrast How are an oligarchy and democracy different?

_____

_____

_____

_____

_____

_____

_____

_____

_____

| Nobles took control from kings, but farmers, merchants, and artisans all wanted more changes in government. | → | The people supported the rise of tyrants, most of whom ruled city-states fairly. | → | Greeks still wanted more say in government, so they replaced most of the tyrants with oligarchies or democracies to rule their city-states. |

Think Critically

5. **Summarize** What were Spartan men and women expected to do as adults?

_____

_____

_____

_____

_____

_____

_____

Show Your Skill

6. **Make Inferences** Life in Sparta was focused on what activity? Why?

_____

_____

_____

_____

_____

Warrior and Spartan king Leonidas clashed with King Xerxes of Persia in 480 B.C.

Sparta: A Military Society

Sparta was located on the Peloponnesus peninsula in southern Greece. The Spartans were descended from the Dorians. The Dorians had invaded Greece during the Dark Age.

Sparta's economy was based on farming. Unlike other city-states, Sparta did not set up overseas colonies. Sparta invaded nearby city-states. Then the Spartans enslaved the people of that conquered city-state. The Spartans called these enslaved people **helots.**

In about 650 B.C. the Spartan helots rebelled. The Spartans crushed the uprising. The Spartan leaders wanted to prevent further revolts. They decided to make Sparta a military society. A military society stresses discipline. The leaders thought this would make citizens more loyal.

All boys and men were prepared for a life of war. Boys left home at age seven and joined the military. They lived in military camps where they learned to read, write, and to use weapons. They were treated harshly. Spartan leaders believed harsh treatment would make boys into better adults. As adults the boys would survive the pain of battle.

At age 20, Spartan men joined the regular army. Men in their twenties stayed in military camps. They shared barracks and ate meals together. They could marry in their twenties, but had to remain living in the military camps. At age 30, the Spartan men could live at home, but they still had to train for war. They served in the military until they were age 60.

Spartan women enjoyed more freedom than women in other city-states. Because the men were often away serving in the military, Spartan women could own property and travel. Girls were trained in such sports as wrestling and racing. The main role of women was to raise sons for the military. The military dominated every aspect of life in Sparta.

Sparta's government was an oligarchy. Two kings ruled together, but they had little power. Their duties were to lead the army and perform religious ceremonies.

The council of elders held the power in Sparta. The council passed laws, however it was the king that made decisions about war and peace. Sparta's assembly was made up of all male citizens over the age of 30. The assembly elected five people each year called the **ephors.** These ephors enforced laws and collected taxes.

The Spartan government was strict. Leaders resisted change because they did not want free thinking and new ideas. Officials believed education could lead to unrest. For this reason, the government discouraged people from studying literature and the arts. Foreign visitors were not welcome, either. People could not leave Sparta except for military purposes.

Sparta continued to use heavy iron bars for money when other Greek city-states were minting coins. This policy hurt trade, and Sparta remained a poor farming society. Other city-states built up trade and businesses.

The only important goals to the Spartan army were military power and victory. Later, Sparta's army played an important role in defending Greece against invaders.

Athens: A Young Democracy

Athens was another important Greek city-state. It was located northeast of Sparta. It was about a two-day journey away from Sparta.

The people in Athens were descended from the Mycenaeans who settled in Greece in the 2000s B.C. The Athenian people had different ideas about government and society than the people of Sparta.

In Athens, boys studied a variety of subjects. They studied arithmetic, geometry, drawing, music, and public speaking. They also practiced sports. The people of Athens believed this type of education created adults with strong minds and bodies. Boys finished school at age 18. At that age, they were expected to be active in public affairs.

Girls in Athens were educated at home. They learned spinning, weaving, and other household duties. In some wealthy families they might learn to read, write, and play music. All

Think Critically

7. Evaluate Was Sparta's government at all democratic? Explain.

_____

_____

_____

_____

_____

8. Analyze Why did Sparta not focus on expanding trade?

_____

_____

_____

_____

_____

_____

Athenian boys were privileged to receive instruction at school, while girls received their education at home.

Think Critically

10. Analyze Why do you think the Athenians and Spartans had different ideas about government?

_____

_____

_____

_____

_____

_____

_____

_____

_____

_____

_____

_____

Show Your Skill

11. Draw Conclusions Why would Peisistratus have been popular with poor people?

_____

_____

_____

_____

women were expected to marry and care for children. Most women were not active in business or government in Athens.

The history of Athenian government was similar to that of many city-states. About 600 B.C. most farmers owed money to the nobles. Some had to sell themselves into slavery to pay their debt. People started to rebel. The farmers called for an end to all debt. To avoid an uprising, the nobles agreed to make changes. They turned to a respected merchant named Solon. He was a fair-ruling tyrant.

In 594 B.C. Solon ended the farmers' debts. He freed those farmers who had been enslaved. He opened the assembly and the courts to all male citizens. The assembly voted on laws written by a council of 400 wealthy citizens.

Education in Sparta and Athens

Sparta

Boys: Boys leave home at age seven and study only reading, writing, and use of weapons as they train to be soldiers.

Girls: Girls participate in sports and learn household duties.

Athens

Boys: Boys practice sports and study many subjects, such as arithmetic, geometry, drawing, music, and public speaking. They do not study the use of weapons.

Girls: Girls learn spinning, weaving, and household duties.

The common people considered the changes Solon made good changes. The wealthy people believed he had gone too far. By the time he left office, he had lost much support.

In 560 B.C. another tyrant took over the government. His name was Peisistratus. He made even more changes. He divided large estates among the farmers who had no land. He also gave citizenship to people who did not own land, like merchants and artisans. Peisistratus provided poor people with loans. He gave poor people jobs. He hired them to build temples and other public works.

When Peisistratus died, another tyrant led Athens. His name was Cleisthenes, and he took office in 508 B.C. He made the assembly the major governing body of the city-state. As before, all male citizens could participate in the assembly and vote on laws, but Cleisthenes gave them more powers. He let them discuss issues freely, hear legal cases, and appoint top army officers.

Cleisthenes also created a new council of 500 citizens. The job of the new council was to help the assembly manage daily government better. The new council introduced laws and controlled the treasury. The council also managed how Athens dealt with other city-states.

Each year a lottery was held to choose the council members. Terms on the council were one year. No one could serve more than two terms. Using a lottery to choose the council meant that every citizen had a chance to be a council member.

Cleisthenes made changes to make the Athenian government democratic. However, many people in Athens still did not have a say in the government. People who were not citizens could not participate in the government. That group included all women, foreign-born men, and enslaved people.

PEISISTRATOS

Peisistratus (Peisistratos) started a line of tyrannical rulers in Athens.

NGSSS Check How did Athens' democratic form of government include some citizens and not others? Explain. SS.6.W.3.2

_____

_____

_____

_____

Think Critically

12. Evaluate How was Athens' use of a lottery system democratic?

_____

_____

_____

_____

_____

_____

Mark the Text

13. Underline the actions that Cleisthenes took that led to a greater democratic government.

Take the Challenge

14. You are a member of the Athenian Council. Write a "to-do" list for the day of daily government tasks.

3 GREECE AND PERSIA

NGSSS

SS.6.G.2.2 Differentiate between continents, regions, countries, and cities in order to understand the complexities of regions created by civilizations.

SS.6.E.3.4 Describe the relationship among civilizations that engage in trade, including the benefits and drawbacks of voluntary trade.

SS.6.W.3.4 Explain the causes and effects of the Persian and Peloponnesian Wars.

Essential Question
Why does conflict develop?

Guiding Questions
1. How did the Persians rule a vast empire?
2. How did the Greeks defeat the Persians?

Terms to Know

satrapy
a province in ancient Persia

satrap
the governor of a satrapy in ancient Persia

Zoroastrianism
a Persian religion founded by the religious teacher Zoroaster

Where in the World?

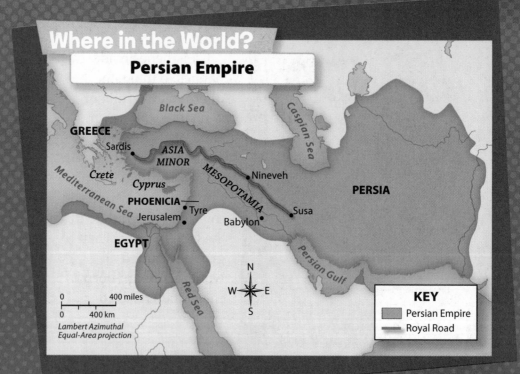

Persian Empire

KEY
▢ Persian Empire
— Royal Road

Lambert Azimuthal Equal-Area projection

When Did It Happen?

600s B.C. Zoroaster, a religious teacher in Persia preaches there is one god

540 B.C. Persian Cyrus the Great built a large empire

500s B.C. Government changing in Athens

522 B.C. Darius I rules Persia

490 B.C. Darius I sends fleet to conquer Athens

480 B.C. Persian King Xerxes invades Greece

479 B.C. United Greeks defeat Persians at Plataea

400s B.C. Persians begin to expand into Europe

600 B.C.   550 B.C.   500 B.C.   450 B.C.   400 B.C.

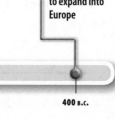

PHOTO: Gianni Dagli Orti/CORBIS

Copyright © by The McGraw-Hill Companies, Inc.

Persia's Empire

While Greek city-states were going through changes in their governments, the Persians were building a large empire in southwest Asia. The homeland of the Persians is Persia, which today is called Iran.

In the 500s B.C., a king named Cyrus the Great came to rule in Persia. He built a powerful army. He began conquering lands. Eventually Persia ruled the largest empire in the ancient world.

Around 540 B.C. Cyrus conquered Mesopotamia, Syria, and Canaan. He also conquered some Greek city-states that were in the area of Anatolia. Today Anatolia is called Turkey.

Cyrus ruled fairly. He allowed the people he conquered to keep their own languages, religions, and laws. For example, Cyrus allowed the Jews to return to their homeland. They had been exiled in Babylon.

After Cyrus, the empire continued to expand. Persia controlled Egypt, western India, and lands northeast of Greece. The Persian Empire stretched a distance of some 3,000 miles (4,800 km). This is about the size of the continental United States.

The Persians improved the network of roads that had been built by the Assyrians. They built an important road called the Royal Road. It ran from Persia to Anatolia. That was more than 1,500 miles (2400 km).

On this road, travelers could get food, water, and fresh horses at roadside stations. Before the road was built, travel between Persia and Anatolia was difficult. It would take a messenger about three months to travel from Persia to Anatolia. Using the road, the messenger could travel that distance in seven days.

The Persian Empire kept expanding. It became more difficult to manage it. Darius I ruled Persia from 522 B.C. to 486 B.C. He reorganized the government of the empire in order

Show Your Skill

2. **Draw Conclusions** Why it was important that Cyrus the Great let conquered people keep their own languages, religions, and laws?

_____

_____

_____

_____

_____

_____

_____

_____

_____

Darius I's division of the empire into satrapies consolidated his power.

3. Underline the meaning of the word *satrap*.

4. Circle the name of the male god of Zoroastrianism.

5. Graphic Organizer List facts about aspects of the Persian Empire.

Take the Challenge

6. Make a Help Wanted ad to attract soldiers to join the Persian army.

to manage it better. He divided the empire into provinces. He called the provinces **satrapies.** Each satrapy was ruled by a governor. The governor was called a **satrap.** The governor collected taxes and judged legal cases. He also managed the police and recruited soldiers for the Persian army.

It is important to remember that Persia had a full-time, paid professional army. The Greek city-states had armies of citizens that were called to serve only during times of war.

The best fighters in the Persian army were the soldiers trained to guard the king. There were 10,000 of them, and they were known as the Immortals. They got that name because when a soldier of the group died, another soldier immediately took his place.

At first the Persians worshiped many gods. Then in the 600s B.C., a man named Zoroaster started preaching. Zoroaster was a religious teacher who taught that there was one god. This new religion was called **Zoroastrianism.**

Zoroaster taught that the one god, named Ahura Mazda, was the creator of all things and the leader of the forces of good. Zoroaster believed there was evil in the world. People were free to choose between good and evil, but Zoroaster believed that at the end of time goodness would win. Zoroaster's teachings, prayers, and sacred songs were written down in a holy book.

Most Persians accepted Zoroastrianism. They also came to view the monarchy as sacred. Persian kings believed they ruled by the power of Ahura Mazda. The kings were responsible only to this male god.

King Darius I even made a statement about his relationship with Ahura Mazda. He had the statement carved on the side of a cliff for all the people to read. The Persians continued to practice Zoroastrianism for centuries.

Persian Empire	Facts
Cyrus the Great	
Zoroastrianism	
Royal Road	
satrapy	

The Persian Wars

In the 400s, the Persians wanted to expand their empire into Europe. They soon clashed with the Greeks. The Persians believed in an all-powerful king. Many of the Greeks believed that citizens should rule themselves.

The Persians already controlled Greek city-states in Anatolia. In 499 B.C. these city-states revolted. The people of Athens sent warships in support of the Greek rebels. The Persians crushed the revolt. However, the Persian king Darius I was angry at Athens for interfering. He decided to punish the mainland Greeks for meddling in his empire.

In 490 B.C. Darius I sent a fleet of 600 ships and an army to invade Greece. The Persians landed at Marathon. It was a plain about 25 miles (40.2 km) northeast of Athens. The Persians waited for the Greeks to fight them, but the Athenians did not attack the Persians. They had only 10,000 men. The Persians had 20,000. The Greeks knew they would lose if they attacked.

The Persians then decided to board their ships and sail directly to Athens. They planned to attack Athens by sea. The Persians started loading their ships with their strongest fighting units. It was only when those units were on the ships that the Athenians attacked. The Persians suffered a terrible defeat.

According to a Greek legend a young runner raced the 25 miles to Athens with the news. He reached Athens and cried out "Victory." Then he fell and died from exhaustion. Today, marathon races are named for that famous run. The marathon races are just over 26 miles (41.8 km) long, and are run all over the world.

PHOTO: Matt Stroshane/Disney/Getty Images

Think Critically

7. Explain Why did the Persians and Greeks start fighting?

_____

_____

_____

_____

_____

_____

8. Compare How did the Greek military compare to the Persian military?

_____

_____

_____

_____

Mark the Text

9. Circle the names of important battles where they appear in the text in this lesson.

The Greek tradition established at the Battle of Marathon is kept alive by Brazilian Fredison Costa, the winner of a 2011 marathon in Orlando.

10. Analyze Why was Thermopylae an important battle for the Greeks?

_____

_____

_____

_____

11. Identify Cause and Effect Were you surprised to read the outcome of the Persian Wars? Why or why not?

_____

_____

_____

_____

_____

_____

_____

The Persians vowed revenge against the Athenians after their defeat at Marathon. In 480 B.C., a new Persian king named Xerxes invaded Greece with a large army. His army consisted of 200,000 troops and thousands of warships. His force even had its own supply ships.

The Greek city-states joined together to fight the Persians. Sparta's King Leonidas supplied the most soldiers. Themistocles of Athens directed the Greek naval forces.

Themistocles wanted to attack the Persian supply ships to cut off the Persian army's supplies. To do that, the Greeks had to stop the Persians from reaching Athens.

For three days Spartan soldiers fought the Persians at Thermopylae. The Spartans fought bravely but could not stop the Persians. A traitor helped out the Persians. King Leonidas realized his army would be surrounded. He dismissed them. Only 300 Spartan soldiers remained to fight. They fought until the end.

The Spartans' heroic fight gave the Athenians time to carry out a plan to attack Persia's ships. The Battle of Salamis was a victory for the Greeks.

The Athenian fleet lured the Persian fleet into the strait of Salamis near Athens. A strait or **channel** is a narrow strip of water between two pieces of land. The large Persian ships crowded together in the channel. The Greeks had fewer ships than the Persians. Their ships were smaller and could maneuver more easily. The Greek navy destroyed most of the Persian fleet.

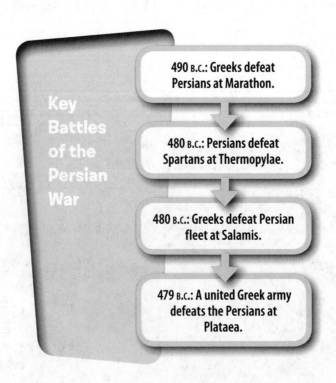

Key Battles of the Persian War

490 B.C.: Greeks defeat Persians at Marathon.

480 B.C.: Persians defeat Spartans at Thermopylae.

480 B.C.: Greeks defeat Persian fleet at Salamis.

479 B.C.: A united Greek army defeats the Persians at Plataea.

The Persian army continued to attack. It marched to Athens and burned Athens. Finally in 479 B.C. the last battle was fought. The Greek forces united. They had improved their forces with better armor and weapons. The Greeks defeated the Persians at Plataea, northwest of Athens.

After the battle at Plataea, the Persian Empire faced many challenges. Its army was no longer able to defend the whole Persian Empire. The people grew unhappy with their government. The kings taxed the people heavily. The royal family fought over who should rule.

Persia weakened and became open to outside attacks. In the 300s B.C. Persia was invaded by the powerful Greek ruler, Alexander the Great. As the Persian Empire ended, a new Greek empire grew. This empire eventually became even larger than the Persian Empire.

Alexander the Great, shown on his horse, brought greatness and unity to the Greeks.

 NGSSS Check How was the government of Persia different from that of the Greek city-states? SS.6.W.3.2

_____

_____

_____

 NGSSS Check What happened to the Persian Empire at the end of the war with Greece? SS.6.W.3.4

_____

_____

_____

Show Your Skill

12. Make Inferences Why did the Persian kings tax the people heavily?

_____

_____

_____

13. Predict What do you think Alexander the Great will do to the Persian Empire?

_____

_____

_____

LESSON

4

GLORY, WAR, AND DECLINE

NGSSS

SS.6.W.3.2 Explain the democratic concepts (polis, civic participation and voting rights, legislative bodies, written constitutions, rule of law) developed in ancient Greece.

SS.6.W.3.5 Summarize the important achievements and contributions of ancient Greek civilization.

Essential Question

How do governments change?

Guiding Questions

1. How did Pericles influence government and culture in Athens?
2. What was life like for Athenians under the rule of Pericles?
3. How did the Peloponnesian War affect the Greek city-states?

Terms to Know

direct democracy
a form of democracy in which all citizens can participate firsthand in the decision-making process

representative democracy
a form of democracy in which citizens elect officials to govern on their behalf

philosopher
a person who searches for wisdom or enlightenment

Where in the World?

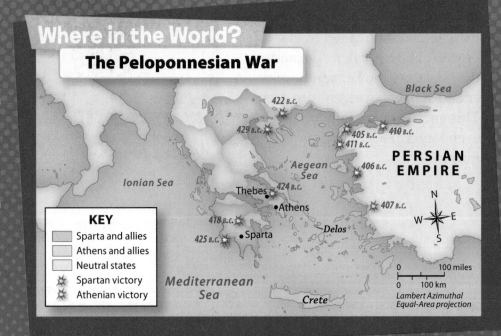

The Peloponnesian War

KEY
- Sparta and allies
- Athens and allies
- Neutral states
- Spartan victory
- Athenian victory

When Did It Happen?

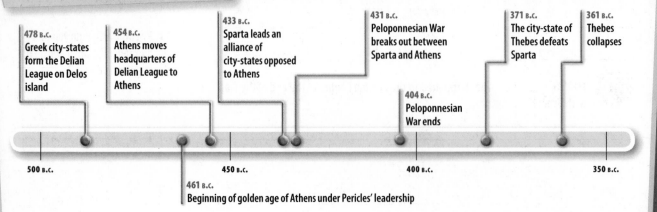

478 B.C. Greek city-states form the Delian League on Delos island

454 B.C. Athens moves headquarters of Delian League to Athens

461 B.C. Beginning of golden age of Athens under Pericles' leadership

433 B.C. Sparta leads an alliance of city-states opposed to Athens

431 B.C. Peloponnesian War breaks out between Sparta and Athens

404 B.C. Peloponnesian War ends

371 B.C. The city-state of Thebes defeats Sparta

361 B.C. Thebes collapses

500 B.C.   450 B.C.   400 B.C.   350 B.C.

110   Chapter 7   *The Ancient Greeks*

The Rule of Pericles

When the Persian wars ended, Athens became a powerful city-state. From 461 B.C. to 429 B.C. Athens enjoyed a golden age of prosperity and achievement. Athens became the economic and cultural center of Greece. Its leader was Pericles. The government was a democratic government.

The government of Athens was a **direct democracy.** That means that all citizens of Athens met to debate and vote on government matters. In the United States, we have a **representative democracy.** Citizens elect a smaller group of people. This group represents the citizens. It makes laws and governs on behalf of the citizens.

In ancient Athens direct democracy worked because of the small number of citizens. Often fewer than 6,000 citizens actually participated in the assembly meetings. The meetings were held every ten days. At those meetings citizens passed laws and elected officials. They made policy on war and foreign affairs. The ten officials elected every year were known as generals.

After the Persian Wars the most important general in Athens was Pericles. He led the city-state for more than 30 years. He gave people positions in government based on their abilities. He did not care which social class people belonged to. For the first time, Pericles brought ordinary Athenians into the government. Shopkeepers and laborers could share in the government with nobles and farmers. He emphasized equality.

Pericles rebuilt Athens after the Persians burned it. He built new temples, monuments, and statues. He supported artists, writers, and teachers. **Philosophers** also flourished during the rule of Pericles. A philosopher reflects or thinks about the meaning of life. Athens became a great center of knowledge. Pericles called it "the school of Greece."

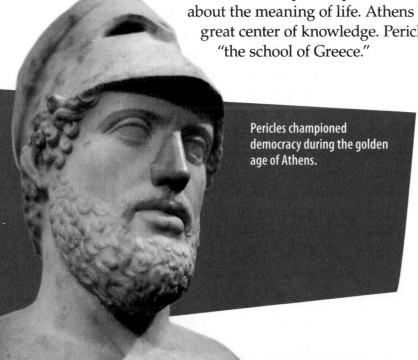

Pericles championed democracy during the golden age of Athens.

Show Your Skill

1. Compare and Contrast What kind of democracy do we have in the United States? How is it different from the democracy of Athens?

_____

_____

_____

_____

_____

_____

Mark the Text

2. Circle the words that mean "all citizens participate in government decision-making."

Think Critically

3. Summarize How did Pericles change the government of Athens?

_____

_____

_____

_____

_____

_____

4. Compare and Contrast How were women treated differently from men in Athens?

_____

_____

_____

_____

_____

_____

5. Analyze Why was slavery important in Athens?

_____

_____

_____

_____

_____

6. Explain Why was the Delian League created?

_____

_____

_____

_____

_____

7. Underline the city-state that came to control the Delian League.

Athenian Life

At its height, Athens was the largest Greek city-state. It had about 285,000 people in the city. Not all these people were citizens. Only about 43,000 males had political rights. The women, foreign-born men, and enslaved people could not be citizens. They had no political rights.

Citizens — Free native-born men

Athenian Citizenship

Non-Citizens — Women, foreign-born men, enslaved people

   Athenian men worked as farmers, artisans, and merchants. They often worked mornings and exercised in the afternoons. In the evenings upper-class men socialized at dinners. They discussed politics and philosophy at these dinners.

   The women of Athens had different lives. They focused on their homes and families. Girls married early, some when they were in their mid-teens. Their duties were to have children and take care of the households.

   Women in poor families helped with farm work or sold goods at the marketplace. Women in upper-class homes spun, dyed, or wove cloth. Most upper-class women rarely left their homes. Sometimes they attended a funeral or festival. When they did, they had to be with a male relative.

   Athenian women could not attend school. Many, however, learned to read and play music. Educated women in Athens were not considered equal to men. Women could not participate in political activities nor could they own property.

   Greek women were always under the care of males. Husbands were responsible for their wives and unmarried daughters. Sons took care of their widowed mothers.

   A few women had more freedom, however. Foreign-born women were not treated the same way as Athenian women. One such woman was Aspasia. She was known for her intelligence and charm. She taught public speaking. Her ideas were popular among Athenians. Pericles was influenced by her.

   Slavery was common in ancient civilizations. Even in a democracy like Athens, slavery existed. Most Athenian households had at least one enslaved person. The enslaved people were prisoners who had been captured in battle. These included both Greeks and non-Greeks.

Enslaved men worked on farms and in shops of artisans. Some worked at hard labor. Enslaved women were cooks and servants in wealthy homes. Sometimes they were teachers to upper-class children.

The treatment of enslaved people was different from place to place. Slavery was important in helping Athens develop a thriving economy.

Women in ancient Greece performed many household chores, such as sewing and spinning wool to make cloth.

War Between Athens and Sparta

The Greek city-states learned over time that their survival depended on cooperation. Even after the Persian Wars ended, Persia still remained a threat.

In 478 B.C. the Greek city-states joined together and formed a defensive league or protective group. The league's purpose was to defend its members against the Persians. Sparta did not join this league.

The league headquarters was the island of Delos. That is why the league was called the Delian League. Athens provided the league with most of its sailors and soldiers. The other city-states supplied money and ships. At first the league was a success. It drove the Persians out of Greek territories in Anatolia. As a result, trade increased and Greece became richer.

The Delian League had successes. In time, however, the league failed. Athens was the strongest city-state in the league. Over time, Athens began to control the other member city-states. The league was no longer an alliance of equal city-states but became a group of city-states controlled by Athens.

Show Your Skill

8. Identify Cause and Effect
What led to the outbreak of the Peloponnesian War?

_____

_____

_____

_____

_____

_____

_____

Take the Challenge

9. With a small group, write and deliver a news broadcast about the Delian League, discussing its successes and failures.

10. **Compare and Contrast** How did the Spartan and Athenian militaries compare to each other?

_____

_____

_____

_____

_____

Mark the Text

11. **Graphic Organizer** In the order that they took place, list in the graphic organizer the missing key events that happened in the Peloponnesian War. If you need more space to write, use the space to the left of the graphic organizer.

Pericles's leadership helped Athens dominate the other city-states. He demanded strict loyalty and required the city-states to make regular payments. He also insisted the other city-states use Athenian coins. In 454 B.C. the Athenians moved the Delian League's treasury to Athens.

Athens interfered in the governments of other city-states. Then the common people in some league city-states rebelled against the nobles in power. In response, the Athenians sent troops to support the common people.

Sparta, meanwhile, formed an alliance of Greek city-states opposed to Athens. Sparta and Athens were very different societies. They had a long history of being rivals. Both city-states wanted to be the major power in the Greek world.

In 433 B.C. Athens interfered with some of Sparta's alliances. These allies pressured Sparta to attack Athens. War broke out in 431 B.C. It lasted for 27 years. Historians call this conflict in Greece the Peloponnesian War. They named it that because Sparta was located in the Peloponnesus region of Greece.

Soon after the war started, Sparta surrounded Athens. Pericles understood that in an open battle Spartan soldiers would win. He kept his forces within Athens. While Athens was surrounded, the powerful Athenian navy brought supplies to the city. Sparta did not have a navy. It could not stop Athenian ships.

Key Events in the Peloponnesian War

1. Spartans surrounded Athens.

2. _____

3. A disease spread in Athens, killing many people.

4. _____

5. Spartans defeated the Athenian navy and conquered Athens.

For almost two years Athens remained surrounded. During that first winter Pericles made a speech at a funeral ceremony for soldiers and sailors killed in battle. This speech is still read today. It is called the *Funeral Oration*. In this speech Pericles gives reasons why democracy is worth fighting for.

After about two years, a deadly disease broke out in Athens. One-third of the people died, including Pericles. During the next 25 years each side won some victories. Neither side was able to defeat its opponent.

Then, Sparta made a deal with the Persians. The Spartans agreed to give Persia some territory in Anatolia. In return, Persia gave Sparta money to build a navy.

In 405 B.C. Sparta's new navy destroyed the Athenian fleet. Athens surrendered a year later. The Spartans and their allies knocked down the walls of Athens. The Athenian empire collapsed.

The Peloponnesian War brought disaster to Greek city-states. Most city-state governments were left weak and divided. Many people had died in battle and from disease. Fighting had destroyed many farms. People were left with no way to earn a living. Many young Greeks left Greece and joined the Persian army.

After the war ended, Sparta ruled its new empire. It ruled much like Athens had ruled. Sparta's allied city-states grew angry at how Sparta treated them, and many rebelled. In the next 30 years Sparta put down rebellions and fought Persia again.

In 371 B.C. the city-state of Thebes seized Sparta. That ended the Spartan empire. About ten years later, Thebes collapsed.

While the city-states fought each other, a kingdom grew to the north. The kingdom was Macedonia. Macedonia's strength and desire for expansion affected the Greek city-states. Eventually the strength of Macedonia cost the Greek city-states their independence.

 **NGSSS Check** Explain how the ancient Greeks used the democratic process. SS.6.W.3.2

Show Your Skill

12. Identify Cause and Effect What caused governments to change in Greece during the 400s B.C.?

_____

_____

_____

_____

_____

_____

_____

_____

_____

_____

This gold coin from about 330 B.C. shows the head of Athena, a Greek goddess, sporting a military helmet.

_____

_____

_____

_____

_____

CHAPTER 7 — MY REFLECTIONS

ESSENTIAL QUESTION *Why do people form governments?*

Reflect on What It Means . . .

Athens served as an early form of democracy that was a model for future democratic governments. The Athens model influenced concepts about voting rights, civic participation, legislative assemblies, and even constitutions. Research other early forms of democratic governments around the world.

With a partner or small group, make a mural to show how the use of democracy by different civilizations influenced individuals, the community, and the world. Do research to find specific examples from at least three different cultures. Use words and pictures in your mural.

TAKE THE CHALLENGE

Videotape or take pictures of the mural you created. Create a video blog or post the pictures on a blog, and write captions or descriptions to explain the mural. You may want to add dates or a time line, or even a world map to provide a big picture of the story of democracy.

CHAPTER 8

GREEK CIVILIZATION

NGSSS

SS.6.W.3.5 Summarize the important achievements and contributions of ancient Greek civilization.

SS.6.W.3.6 Determine the impact of key figures from ancient Greece.

ESSENTIAL QUESTIONS *What makes a culture unique? How do new ideas change the way people live? What are the characteristics of a leader?*

Hippocrates was a Greek physician in ancient Greece. This excerpt is from a Greek medical text called the *Hippocratic Oath*, which was most likely used to train early doctors:

> " I will follow that system of regimen which, according to my ability and judgment, I consider for the benefit of my patients, and abstain from [avoid] whatever is deleterious and mischievous. I will give no deadly medicine to any one if asked, nor suggest any such counsel. "
>
> HIPPOCRATIC OATH

regimen

What is a synonym for *regimen*?

_____

_____

deleterious

What words help you to understand the meaning of *deleterious*?

_____

_____

DBQ BREAKING IT DOWN

How would you summarize the goals of doctors who recited the *Hippocratic Oath*?

_____

_____

_____

Would Hippocrates have taken advice from a patient for his or her treatment? Explain.

_____

_____

_____

McGraw-Hill
networks™
There's More Online!

PHOTO: Stock Montage/Archive Photos/Getty Images

GREEK CULTURE

NGSSS

SS.6.W.3.5 Summarize the important achievements and contributions of ancient Greek civilization.

SS.6.W.3.6 Determine the impact of key figures from ancient Greece.

Essential Question
What makes a culture unique?

Guiding Questions
1. How did the ancient Greeks honor their gods?
2. Why were epics and fables important to the ancient Greeks?
3. How did Greek dramas develop?
4. What ideas did the Greeks express in their art and architecture?

Terms to Know

myth
a traditional story about gods and heroes that explains a culture's beliefs

ritual
words or actions that are part of a religious ceremony

oracle
a priestess who speaks for the gods and answers questions about what will happen in the future

fable
a story that teaches a lesson

oral tradition
the custom of passing stories from one generation to the next by telling the stories out loud

drama
a story that is told by the actions and spoken words of actors

tragedy
a drama in which characters struggle to overcome serious problems, but fail

comedy
a drama with a happy ending

Where in the World?

Ancient Greece

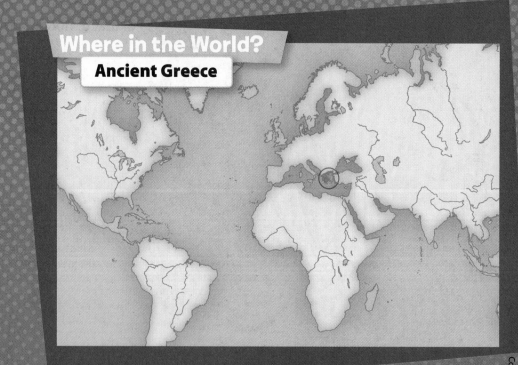

When Did It Happen?

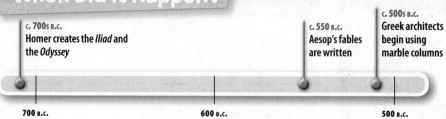

c. 700s B.C.	c. 550 B.C.	c. 500s B.C.
Homer creates the *Iliad* and the *Odyssey*	Aesop's fables are written	Greek architects begin using marble columns

| 700 B.C. | 600 B.C. | 500 B.C. |

Greek Beliefs

The Greeks believed in many gods and goddesses, and they told **myths** about them. Myths are traditional stories about gods and heroes. The Greeks believed these gods affected everyday life. Every city-state had a god or goddess who protected its people. The Greeks built beautiful temples in honor of their special gods.

The Greek gods and goddesses had great powers, but they looked and acted like human beings. They got married and had children. They sometimes acted like children. They played tricks on each other. The Greek people did not fear them, however, because the gods acted like humans. The 12 most important gods and goddesses lived on Mount Olympus and were protected by a gate of clouds. Zeus was the king of the gods.

To please their gods, the people performed **rituals,** or religious ceremonies in honor of the gods. They had festivals, or celebrations, and feasts for the gods. They prayed and offered gifts to the gods. They believed that the gods were pleased when they showed skill in the arts or athletics. Thus, they had athletic competitions, such as the Olympic Games They hoped that the gods would reward them.

The Greeks believed that everyone had a fate, or destiny. They also thought that the gods made prophecies, or predictions, to help people plan for the future. People who wanted to know the future or listen to other advice visited an **oracle.** The oracle chamber was a room deep inside a temple where a priestess talked to one of the gods. People asked the priestess questions. She told her answers to the priests. Then the priests translated the answers. The most famous oracle was at the Temple of Apollo in Delphi.

Many answers were riddles. One king named Croesus asked if he should go to war against the Persians. The oracle said that if Croesus attacked the Persians, he would destroy a mighty empire. Croesus attacked, and the Persian army crushed his army. It turned out that the mighty empire that was destroyed was Croesus's own.

Once believed to be a home to the Greek gods and goddesses, today Mount Olympus rises behind the village of Litohoro, Greece.

Mark the Text

1. Underline what the Greek gods and goddesses were like.

Think Critically

2. **Summarize** Why did the Greeks have festivals and rituals for their gods?

Show Your Skill

3. **Infer** Why would the ancient Greeks want advice from oracles about the future?

Show Your Skill

4. Make Inferences Why were the *Iliad* and the *Odyssey* written?

_____

_____

_____

Take the Challenge

6. Write an outline for an epic. Include heroes or heroines. Draw an illustration that describes a main theme in your epic. Share your epic with the class.

Epics and Fables

Greek poems and stories are the oldest in the Western world. Many writers have copied ideas from these old stories.

The earliest Greek stories were called epics. Epics are long poems about heroes and their brave deeds. Two great epics are the *Iliad* and the *Odyssey*. Homer wrote them both in the 700s B.C. The *Iliad* tells about a war between cities in Greece and the city of Troy. The *Odyssey* tells about the long journey home from that war for the hero Odysseus.

In the *Iliad*, a prince of Troy kidnaps Helen, the wife of a Greek king. The Greeks attack Troy. They trick the people of Troy, called Trojans, by building a big hollow wooden horse. They leave the horse outside the gates of Troy and all go away. The Trojans think they have won the war and the horse is a gift. They bring the horse inside their city. However, the horse is filled with Greek soldiers, and at night they come out. The Greeks capture the city of Troy and rescue Helen. A Trojan horse has come to mean something that seems like a gift, but is really a trick.

The *Odyssey* tells the story of Odysseus, a Greek hero at Troy. On his trip home from the Trojan War, he faces storms, giants, and witches. It takes him 10 years to get home. Today, people use the word *odyssey* to mean a long journey full of challenging adventures.

The Greeks believed that the *Iliad* and the *Odyssey* were true stories. These epics gave them a history filled with heroes and brave deeds. Homer's stories taught important lessons. They taught that friendship and marriage should be valued. Homer's heroes were role models for the Greeks.

Epics
- long poem
- has brave hero
- has adventures
- describes brave deeds
- is written down
- Greeks thought epics were true.

Both
- passed down from one generation to the next
- teaches a lesson

Fables
- about animals who talk
- told out loud
- ends with a moral
- often funny

Have you heard the story of "The Boy Who Cried Wolf?" This story and others like it were said to have been written by a man named Aesop. He is supposed to have lived around 550 B.C. Historians know now that there was probably never any one person named Aesop who wrote these stories. They were created by several different people. The stories are known as Aesop's **fables.**

Fables are short tales that teach a lesson. In most of Aesop's fables, animals talk and act like people. Fables always have a point, or moral. The moral is a truth that teaches a useful life lesson. Fables are often funny and show human weaknesses and strengths.

One of the best known of Aesop's fables is "The Tortoise and the Hare." In it, a tortoise, or turtle, challenges a hare, or rabbit, to a race. The hare is way ahead and is sure he will win, so he stops to take a nap. The tortoise keeps going at a slow but steady pace and wins the race. The moral of the fable is "Slow and steady wins the race."

Aesop's fables were part of Greece's **oral tradition** for about 200 years. This means that people told the stories out loud to their children and grandchildren. Later, people wrote down the fables. Aesop's fables are read and told today by people all around the world in many different languages.

One of Aesop's fables is called "The Crow and the Pitcher." Can you tell what the crow is doing?

ÆSOP'S FABLES
THE CROW AND THE PITCHER

The Impact of Greek Drama

A **drama** is a story told by people who act out the events. They play the parts of the characters in the story, saying their words and acting out their feelings and actions. Movies, plays, and television shows are often dramas.

The Greeks developed two types of drama—**tragedy** and **comedy.** A tragedy has an unhappy ending. The characters in a tragedy cannot solve their problems no matter how hard they try. The first Greek plays were tragedies. Later the Greeks

Think Critically

7. Explain How do fables end?

_____

_____

8. Infer Why do you think Aesop's fables are still told today?

_____

_____

_____

_____

_____

Mark the Text

9. The image shows the crow doing three things. Write next to each picture what the crow is doing to reveal the lesson of the fable.

Show Your Skill

10. Compare and Contrast
How is our idea of comedy today different from the ancient Greeks' idea of comedy?

_____

_____

_____

_____

_____

Mark the Text

11. Underline the names of three Greek writers of tragedies.

Show Your Skill

12. Identify Cause and Effect
How did Greek drama influence how people are entertained today?

_____

_____

_____

_____

Think Critically

13. Explain How were temples used?

_____

_____

_____

_____

wrote comedies. A comedy ends happily. Today, we use the word comedy to mean a funny story. For the Greeks, a comedy was any drama with a happy ending.

Aeschylus was the first writer of drama in Greece. He wrote a group of three plays called the Oresteia. They describe what happened after the Trojan War. They are about revenge and murder. They teach that evil acts can cause more evil acts. The plays are tragedies.

Sophocles also wrote tragedies. He accepted suffering as part of life. He wrote about courage and understanding. In his play *Antigone,* a character is ordered to do something she knows is wrong. She has to think about whether to obey the orders or do what is right.

Euripides also wrote tragedies. He wrote about everyday people. His plays often show the suffering caused by war, especially to women and children.

The comedies of Aristophanes poked fun at the leaders of his day. Aristophanes' plays included jokes. The plays encouraged the audience to think while they laughed.

In ancient Greece, only men could be actors. Women were not allowed to act, so men played all the parts, even the female characters. For the Greeks, drama was not just entertainment. Dramas were part of religious festivals. Greek dramas dealt with big ideas, such as the meaning of good and evil, the rights of people, and the role of gods in everyday life.

In the earliest dramas, the chorus—a group of singers—told the story by singing and dancing. A few times during the play, one actor would give a speech. Later, dramas used several actors on stage. Writers put more action and conflict in the plays.

Greek Art and Architecture

Greek artists created art that expressed the ideals of reason, moderation, balance, and harmony. The style of art that the Greeks developed is now known as the classical style.

Greek artists painted wall paintings. They also painted on pottery, using red and black paint. Large vases often have pictures from myths. Small pieces, like cups, have pictures from everyday life.

The Greeks built beautiful buildings. The most important buildings were the temples. Each temple was dedicated to a god or goddess. The Parthenon of Athens honored the goddess Athena. Temples contained a central room that housed statues of the gods.

Large columns supported the roofs of Greek buildings. The Greeks made columns from marble. Marble is a very hard stone. Stonecutters cut blocks of marble from places where there were deposits of the stone. Then they put the blocks on carts that were pulled by oxen. They hauled the blocks to the building site. Then they put the blocks on top of each other. They held them together with wooden pegs.

We still use marble columns in churches and government buildings today. For example, the White House and the Capitol building in Washington, D.C., both have columns.

Many Greek temples were decorated with sculpture. Sculpture, like all of Greek art, expressed ideas. Greek artists liked to copy the human body, but they did not copy it exactly. They did not include flaws. Instead, artists tried to show their ideas of perfection and beauty.

PHOTO: Adam Crowley/Getty Images

Show Your Skill

14. Make Inferences Why did the Greeks construct their buildings with marble columns?

_____

_____

_____

Mark the Text

15. Underline the buildings in the United States that have columns today.

The Parthenon was the temple of the Greek goddess Athena. The Greek use of columns has influenced the architecture of civilizations around the world.

NGSSS Check What contributions did the ancient Greeks make to literature? What impact have they had on our civilization today? SS.6.W.3.5

_____

_____

_____

_____

_____

2 THE GREEK MIND

NGSSS

SS.6.W.3.2 Explain the democratic concepts (polis, civic participation and voting rights, legislative bodies, written constitutions, rule of law) developed in ancient Greece.

SS.6.W.3.5 Summarize the important achievements and contributions of ancient Greek civilization.

SS.6.W.3.6 Determine the impact of key figures from ancient Greece.

SS.6.C.1.1 Identify democratic concepts developed in ancient Greece that served as a foundation for American constitutional democracy.

Essential Question

How do new ideas change the way people live?

Guiding Questions

1. What ideas did the Greeks develop to explain the world around them?
2. What did the Greeks believe about history and science?

Terms to Know

Sophists
Greek teachers of philosophy, reasoning, and public speaking

rhetoric
the art of public speaking and debate

Socratic method
philosophical method of questioning to gain truth; developed by Socrates

Hippocratic Oath
a set of promises that new doctors make to treat patients well; developed by Hippocrates

What Do You Know?

Directions: In the *K* column, list what you already know about ancient Greek philosophers, historians, and scientists. In the *W* column, list what you want to know. After reading the lesson, fill in the *L* column with the information that you learned.

K	W	L

When Did It Happen?

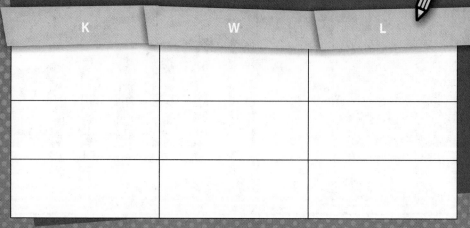

548 B.C.
Thales dies

435 B.C.
Herodotus writes history of Persian Wars

c. 424 B.C.
Thucydides writes history of Peloponnesian Wars

399 B.C.
Socrates sentenced to death

600 B.C.   500 B.C.   400 B.C.   300 B.C.

387 B.C.
Plato opens Academy in Athens

335 B.C.
Aristotle opens Lyceum in Athens

Greek Thinkers

The word *philosophy* comes from the Greek word for "love of wisdom." The first philosophers were Greek thinkers. They believed that people could understand everything. The **Sophists** were teachers in ancient Greece. They thought that students should improve themselves. Sophists taught **rhetoric,** the art of public speaking and debate, or formal argument.

Sophists did not believe that the gods influenced everyday life. They also did not believe in absolute, or definite, right and wrong. They thought that a thing could be wrong for one person and right for another.

Socrates was an artist in Athens. He loved philosophy but left no writings behind. We know about him from his students' writings. Socrates did not agree with the Sophists. He thought there was an absolute right and wrong. He thought that everybody could know everything. The knowledge was already buried deep inside each person.

Socrates believed that absolute truth existed. He tried to help people find the knowledge inside themselves through the **Socratic method** of teaching. This meant he did not lecture his students. Socrates asked them questions. He wanted them to use their own thinking to answer questions and learn to think for themselves.

Some leaders in Athens thought Socrates was dangerous. They said he encouraged people to question their leaders' decisions. In 399 B.C., Socrates was arrested and found guilty of teaching young people to rebel. He was sentenced to death.

Socrates could have left Athens, but he refused to do so. He said that he lived in Athens, so he had to obey the city's laws. He drank poison to carry out his death sentence.

Plato was one of Socrates' students. He wrote a book called *The Republic.* In it he described his plan for the ideal society. Plato did not like democracy. He did not believe that everyone in society could make good decisions. His ideal government divided people into three groups. The top group was philosopher kings. Philosopher kings ruled with wisdom and logic. They were well educated. Plato felt they were wise enough to think about what was best for everyone rather than just do what was best for themselves.

Think Critically

1. Explain Where does the word *philosophy* come from?

_____

_____

_____

Show Your Skill

2. Compare and Contrast How was Plato's plan for government different from Athenian democracy?

_____

_____

_____

_____

_____

_____

_____

_____

_____

Socrates was an influential Greek thinker and teacher. He taught by asking students questions instead of simply lecturing them.

Mark the Text

3. Underline one of the ideas of Plato that you think is the most important. Then write to explain your choice.

_____

_____

_____

_____

Think Critically

4. **Infer** Why do you think Aristotle's ideas influenced the Founders when they were creating a plan for the United States Government?

_____

_____

_____

_____

_____

_____

_____

_____

Mark the Text

5. Circle the name of the Greek writer who wrote a book about the Peloponnesian War.

Warriors were the second group in Plato's ideal society. Their job was to defend the society against attack.

The third group was everyone else. Plato thought the common people were not wise or brave, so they did all of the other jobs in the society that were necessary to provide food, clothing, and shelter. Plato believed that the common people could not think for themselves. He thought they were too easily influenced and would make foolish decisions.

Unlike most men at that time, Plato believed that women should be educated and be allowed to do the same jobs as men.

Plato started a school in Athens. It was called the Academy. His best student was Aristotle. Aristotle wrote more than 200 books on government, science, health, and the planets.

In 355 B.C., Aristotle opened his own school called the Lyceum. Aristotle taught his students the "golden mean." This idea says that people should live moderately. For example, a person should not eat too little or too much. His method of observation, or looking at the world around him, was an important step in the development of the scientific method.

Aristotle also wrote about government in his book *Politics*. He divided governments into three types. The first was monarchy, or government by one person, such as a king or queen, or a tyrant. The second was oligarchy, or government controlled by just a few people. The third was democracy, or government controlled by the majority of the people.

Aristotle thought that the best government was a combination of all three types. The Founders of the United States government were influenced by Aristotle's ideas.

New History and Science Ideas

For thousands of years, people did not write history. They used legends and myths to explain their past. Some civilizations kept lists of rulers, but no one wrote down events.

Then, in 435 B.C., Herodotus wrote a history book about the Persian Wars. He tried to separate fact from legend. He did careful research. He did believe, though, that the gods affected historical events. Today, he is called the "father of history."

Thucydides was another famous historian of the ancient world. Thucydides fought in the Peloponnesian War and later wrote *The History of the Peloponnesian War*. He did not believe that the gods affected human history. He believed that people made history. Thucydides tried to write everything as it actually happened. He wrote only about what he saw or what eyewitnesses saw.

In ancient times, most people thought that the gods controlled nature. For example, they thought that the gods threw bolts of lightning or clapped and made thunder. The early Greek scientists thought in new ways. They thought that people could discover the causes of natural events by observing, investigating, and thinking.

The first important Greek scientist was Thales of Miletus. He was born in the mid-600s B.C. He is thought to have used his studies to predict a solar eclipse. He believed that water was the basic substance of all matter. This idea was not correct, but it gave other scientists an idea to look into further.

Another Greek scientist, Pythagoras, believed that all relationships in the world could be expressed in numbers. He believed that the same laws governed music, numbers, and the whole universe. He came up with many new ideas in mathematics. He is famous for developing the Pythagorean theorem. It is still used in geometry to figure out the length of the sides of a triangle.

Most people in ancient Greece thought that disease was caused by evil spirits. One scientist who studied medicine, or the science of treating diseases, was Hippocrates. He believed that diseases came from natural causes. He traveled all over Greece to help sick people. He made important discoveries about different kinds of diseases. He also developed his own treatments to cure sick people.

Hippocrates wrote a list of rules about how doctors should treat their patients. The rules are listed in the **Hippocratic Oath.** The oath says doctors should do their best to help the patient get well. It says they should protect the patient's privacy. Today, some doctors around the world still promise to honor the Hippocratic Oath.

Greek Scientists

Hippocrates	numbers
Thales	water
Pythagoras	medicine

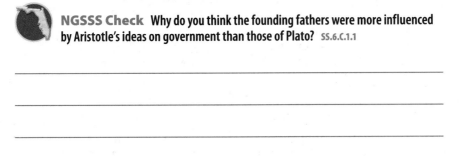 **NGSSS Check** Why do you think the founding fathers were more influenced by Aristotle's ideas on government than those of Plato? SS.6.C.1.1

_____

_____

_____

_____

Mark the Text

6. Chart Draw a line from the scientist's name to what he studied.

Show Your Skill

7. Make a Connection What Greek contribution is used in medicine today?

_____

_____

Take the Challenge

8. Write and deliver a persuasive speech about what you think the most important ancient Greek contribution was that is still used today.

3 ALEXANDER'S EMPIRE

NGSSS

SS.6.W.3.7 Summarize the key achievements, contributions, and figures associated with The Hellenistic Period.

Essential Question
What are the characteristics of a leader?

Guiding Questions
1. Why did Macedonia become powerful?
2. What were Alexander's goals as a ruler?
3. How successful was Alexander in achieving his goals?

Terms to Know

cavalry
soldiers who fight while riding horses

Hellenistic Era
period of time after Alexander died when Greek culture spread to all the lands that had been part of his empire

Where in the World?

Alexander the Great's Empire

When Did It Happen?

359 B.C.
Philip II becomes king of Macedonia

360 B.C.

334 B.C.
Alexander's cavalry defeats Persian army at Granicus

340 B.C.

338 B.C.
Philip conquers Greece

333 B.C.
Alexander defeats Persians at Issus

331 B.C.
Alexander conquers Egypt

Alexander builds city of Alexandria

Alexander defeats Persian army at Gaugamela and takes over Persian Empire

327 B.C.
Alexander leads armies into northwestern India

323 B.C.
Alexander leads armies to Babylon

Alexander dies in Babylon

320 B.C.

Philip II of Macedonia

Macedonia was a kingdom north of Greece. The people raised sheep and horses, and they farmed. Before the time of Philip II, Macedonia had never been a powerful country.

In 359 B.C., Philip II became king of Macedonia. He wanted to defeat the Persian Empire. First he had to unite the Greek city-states and put them under his rule. Philip built a strong army and trained them to fight like the Greeks.

The Greek city-states were weak. They had been divided by the Peloponnesian War. Philip took control of the city-states one by one. Some he defeated in battle. Some he bribed to join him. Others joined him by their own choice.

Demosthenes was a lawyer and one of Athens's great public speakers. He warned that Philip threatened the freedom of the Greeks. He urged Athens and other city-states to join together to fight the Macedonians. By the time the Athenians listened to Demosthenes, it was too late. In 338 B.C., the Macedonians crushed the Greeks at the Battle of Chaeronea near Thebes. Philip now controlled almost all of Greece.

Philip II was able to unite the Greek city-states. He defeated some in battles while others joined him voluntarily.

Alexander Takes Over

Before Philip could conquer the Persian Empire, he was killed. His son Alexander took over. Alexander was only 20, but he had already been in battle many times. His father had put him in the Macedonian army when he was young. By age 16, he was serving as a commander.

Alexander invaded Asia Minor in 334 B.C. He had about 40,000 soldiers. His **cavalry,** the soldiers who rode horses, crushed the Persian army at the battle of Granicus.

Alexander's armies continued across Asia Minor. They freed Greek city-states that had been under Persian rule. In 333 B.C., Alexander again defeated the Persian army at Issus in Syria. The Persian king, Darius III, had to run away.

Think Critically

1. Sequence How did Philip II gain control of most of Greece?

_____

_____

_____

_____

Mark the Text

2. Underline the sentences that explain how Alexander fulfilled his father's dream.

3. Graphic Organizer Underline
the event that you think was the
most important accomplishment
of Alexander. Then write to
explain your choice.

_____

_____

_____

_____

_____

Show Your Skill

4. Identify Cause and Effect
What impact did Alexander have
pouring the water on the ground
in the desert?

_____

_____

_____

_____

_____

_____

_____

_____

_____

Then Alexander went south. In 331 B.C., he conquered Egypt. There he built the city of Alexandria. It became one of the most important cities of the ancient world. Later that year Alexander went east. He defeated Darius's forces at Guagamela near the Tigris River. After that victory, Alexander's army took over the rest of the Persian Empire.

Defeating the Persian Empire

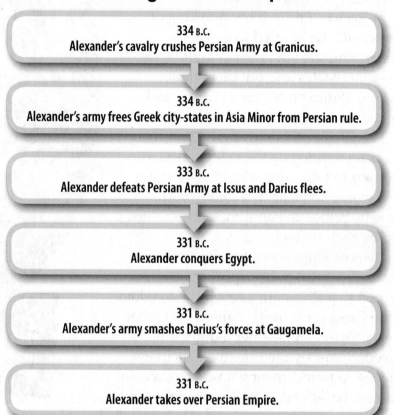

334 B.C.
Alexander's cavalry crushes Persian Army at Granicus.

334 B.C.
Alexander's army frees Greek city-states in Asia Minor from Persian rule.

333 B.C.
Alexander defeats Persian Army at Issus and Darius flees.

331 B.C.
Alexander conquers Egypt.

331 B.C.
Alexander's army smashes Darius's forces at Gaugamela.

331 B.C.
Alexander takes over Persian Empire.

Alexander did not stop. He marched east. In 327 B.C., Alexander and his army marched into northwestern India. They fought a number of bloody battles. His soldiers grew tired of war, so Alexander agreed to go home.

Going home, the army crossed a desert in what is modern Iran. There was very little water. Heat and thirst killed thousands of soldiers. When soldiers found some water, they gave it to Alexander in a helmet. Alexander poured the water on the ground. He showed his soldiers that he was willing to suffer the same thirst and pain that they did.

Alexander arrived back in Babylon in 323 B.C. The journey and all the battles had wrecked Alexander's health. He died in Babylon at the age of only 32 years old.

Alexander's Legacy

Alexander was a great and brave military leader. Sometimes he rode into battle before his army. Some might consider this foolish, but his bravery inspired his soldiers. Alexander is thought to have always tried to copy his hero Achilles. Achilles was one of the warriors in the *Iliad* by Homer.

When he died, Alexander was the most powerful ruler in the ancient world. That is one reason we call him Alexander the Great.

A legacy is what a person leaves to other people when he or she dies. Alexander's legacy was a world that knew about Greek culture. Wherever Alexander and his army went, they spread the Greek language, ideas, and art. This is another reason that Alexander is "the Great." Alexander also learned things in Asia and Africa. He brought those ideas back to Greece.

Alexander began the **Hellenistic Era.** Hellenistic means "like the Greeks." The Hellenistic Era is the time when Greek ideas spread to people in all the lands Alexander had conquered.

Alexander wanted the Macedonians, the Greeks, and the Persians to become one people. He had Persians serve in top government positions, and he encouraged his soldiers to marry women in the lands they conquered.

After Alexander died, his generals fought with each other. The empire fell apart. It became four Hellenistic kingdoms: Macedonia, Pergamum, Egypt, and the Seleucid Empire. Greek was the official language of these kingdoms. The kings often gave jobs to Greeks or Macedonians.

By 100 B.C., Alexandria was the largest city in the Mediterranean world. The Hellenistic kings built many other cities, too. These cities needed many workers. They needed architects, engineers, and artisans. They also needed philosophers and artists. The kings asked Greeks and Macedonians to move to these cities. These colonists helped spread the Greek culture into Egypt and as far east as India.

NGSSS Check How did Alexander try to unify the Greeks and Macedonians with the peoples he conquered? SS.6.W.3.7

_____

_____

_____

_____

5. Infer Why was Alexander called "Alexander the Great"?

_____

_____

_____

_____

_____

_____

_____

Mark the Text

6. Circle the names of the kingdoms that were created after Alexander's empire fell apart.

Think Critically

7. Describe What kinds of workers and thinkers did the Hellenistic kings need in their new cities?

_____

_____

_____

_____

_____

_____

_____

_____

HELLENISTIC CULTURE

NGSSS

SS.6.W.3.7 Summarize the key achievements, contributions, and figures associated with The Hellenistic Period.

Essential Question

How do new ideas change the way people live?

Guiding Questions

1. How did Greek culture spread during the Hellenistic Era?
2. What ideas and discoveries emerged during the Hellenistic Era?
3. How did Greece fall under Roman rule?

Terms to Know

Epicureanism
the philosophy of Epicurus, who believed that happiness was the goal of life and avoiding pain was the key to happiness; in modern times, associated with liking pleasure and comfort

Stoicism
the philosophy of the Stoics, a group founded by Zeno, believing that wise people should use reason over emotion; in modern times associated with not showing emotions

circumference
the outer boundary of a circle; the measurement of that boundary

plane geometry
branch of mathematics concerned with measurement and properties of points, lines, angles, and surfaces of figures that are flat or level

solid geometry
branch of mathematics concerned with measurement and properties of points, lines, angles, surfaces, and solids in three-dimensional space

What Do You Know?

Directions: In the first column, write your answers in the "Now" column based on what you know before you study. After this lesson, write your answers in the "Later" column.

	Now	Later
What do you know about Greek culture?		
Why did the Greeks fall to the Romans?		

When Did It Happen?

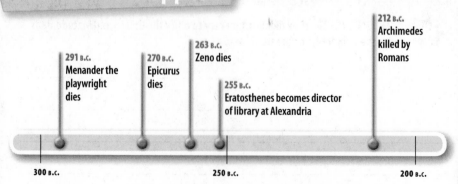

291 B.C. Menander the playwright dies

270 B.C. Epicurus dies

263 B.C. Zeno dies

255 B.C. Eratosthenes becomes director of library at Alexandria

212 B.C. Archimedes killed by Romans

300 B.C.   250 B.C.   200 B.C.

Hellenistic Arts

During the Hellenistic Era, scientists, writers, philosophers, and poets moved to the new Greek cities in Egypt and Southwest Asia. Many came to use Alexandria's library. It had more than 500,000 scrolls. Alexandria also had a museum that attracted people.

The Hellenistic kings built new cities and rebuilt old ones. They brought in Greek architects to design the new construction in the Greek style. The kings wanted Greek baths, temples, and theaters. The kings and other rich citizens hired Greek sculptors to make statues. Hellenistic sculptors developed new styles. They did not carve ideal versions of the perfect human body. They showed people more realistically.

Writers wrote drama, poetry, and histories at this time, but most of this writing has been lost or destroyed. Appolonius of Rhodes wrote an epic poem called *Argonautica*. It is about Jason, his crew, and their adventures. Another poet, Theocritus, wrote short poems about nature and its beauty.

Athens was still the center of Greek drama. Playwrights in Athens invented a new kind of comedy called Greek New Comedy. The plays were about love and relationships of ordinary people. Menander was the best-known of these new playwrights. He lived from 343 B.C. to around 291 B.C.

Thinkers and Scientists

During this time, the most famous philosophers still went to Athens. The two most important philosophers were Epicurus and Zeno.

Epicurus developed **Epicureanism.** This philosophy taught people that happiness is the goal of life. Today, *epicurean* means a love of good food and comfortable things. To Epicurus, happiness meant spending time with friends and not worrying.

Zeno developed **stoicism.** He taught at a building called the "painted porch." Since the Greek word for porch is *stoa*, his school was called the Stoics. Stoics thought that happiness came from following logic and reason. Emotions such as anger or sadness caused problems. Today we call people stoics if they keep going even if they are hurt or sad. Stoics also thought that people were happy when they did their duty to the community.

1. Identify the Main Idea How did the Hellenistic kings spread Greek culture?

_____

_____

_____

_____

Think Critically

2. Contrast How did Greek sculpture and drama change during the Hellenistic Era?

_____

_____

_____

_____

Sculpture from the Hellenistic Era was known for being realistic and highly detailed.

3. Compare and Contrast How were Epicureanism and Stoicism similar? How were they different?

_____

_____

_____

_____

_____

_____

4. Analyze If you wanted to figure out how much air is in a basketball, would you use plane geometry or solid geometry? Why?

_____

_____

_____

_____

_____

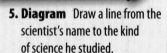

5. Diagram Draw a line from the scientist's name to the kind of science he studied.

6. Make a 2-column chart that lists items that could be measured using plane geometry or shape geometry. Use objects you see in your classroom to complete the chart.

Science also flourished during the Hellenistic Era. The scientists of that time had only simple instruments, but they performed experiments and made discoveries. Aristarchus was an astronomer who studied stars, planets, and other heavenly bodies. Aristarchus said that the sun was at the center of the universe. He said that Earth went around the sun, but no one believed him. At the time, people thought that the sun went around Earth.

Eratosthenes was an astronomer in charge of Alexandria's library. He figured out that Earth was round. He also measured the **circumference** of Earth, or how big around it was.

Here is how he did it. Eratosthenes put two sticks in the ground far apart from each other. He waited until the sun was directly over one stick. It had a shorter shadow than the other stick. After measuring the shadows, Eratosthenes used math to figure out the curve of Earth's surface.

Eratosthenes estimated that the distance around Earth was 24,675 miles (39,702 kilometers). He was only 185 miles (298 kilometers) off! He also measured the distance to the sun and the moon. But he did not come up with the correct measurements for these.

Euclid was a mathematician who wrote Elements. The book teaches **plane geometry**—a branch of mathematics concerned with how points, lines, angles, and surfaces work together.

Archimedes was the most famous scientist of the Hellenistic Era. He worked on **solid geometry**—the branch of mathematics concerned with the study of spheres [ball-like shapes] and cylinders [tubes]. He figured out the value of *pi*, which is used to measure the area of circles. Its symbol is π.

Hellenistic Scientists

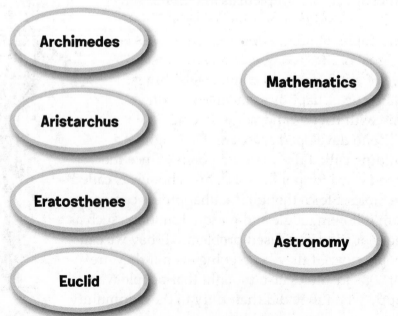

Archimedes measures the range of his invention, the catapult. The weapon could hurl rocks as heavy as 500 pounds.

Archimedes was also an inventor. He invented the catapult. Catapults are war machines that hurl rocks, arrows, and spears at the enemy. The catapults worked well. In 212 B.C., the Romans attacked Syracuse. The catapults kept the Romans from getting into the city. The catapults worked so well that it took the Romans three years to capture Syracuse. Finally the Romans got inside the city walls. They massacred most of the city, including Archimedes.

Hellenistic thinking and culture had long-lasting effects. Seven hundred years after the Hellenistic Era, the mathematician Hypatia lived in Alexandria. Like the earlier Greeks, she studied philosophy and mathematics. She believed in the use of reason rather than superstition.

Greece and Rome

The four kingdoms formed from Alexander's empire did not get along very well. They often fought wars against each other. Some Greek city-states became independent, but they did not have strong armies. They were not free for very long.

Rome was a city-state in central Italy. In the late 200s B.C., Rome conquered all of Italy. Greece had had some lands in southern Italy, but those lands were taken by the Romans.

The Greeks tried to stop Rome. They supported Rome's enemies in wars. The Romans won all those wars, though. Soon, Rome gained control of Greece.

NGSSS Check List three discoveries made in mathematics and astronomy during the Hellenistic Era that are still important to us today. SS.6.W.3.7

_____

_____

_____

Show Your Skill

7. Identify the Main Idea
What kind of technology did Archimedes introduce to Hellenistic culture?

_____

_____

_____

_____

Think Critically

8. Explain How did the Greek city-states react to Rome's growing power?

_____

_____

_____

ESSENTIAL QUESTION *How do new ideas change the way people live?*

Reflect on What It Means . . .

Alexander the Great blended Greek culture with the culture of the lands that he conquered. He did not want to impose Greek culture on these peoples, but the influence of Hellenistic culture spread and thrived. We can see many examples of it in our culture today.

Find examples of Hellenistic culture or the influence of it today. Make a model or a diorama to show the influences of Hellenistic culture in your community and in the world. From these examples that you found, write about how they influence you or your life.

TAKE THE CHALLENGE

With a small group, create a commercial about one of the major influences of Hellenistic culture. To prepare, create a storyboard to plan out your commercial. Rehearse it, and then record it. Show your finished product to the class.

ANCIENT INDIA

NGSSS

SS.6.W.4.4 Explain the teachings of Buddha, the importance of Asoka, and how Buddhism spread in India, Ceylon, and other parts of Asia.

SS.6.W.4.5 Summarize the important achievements and contributions of ancient Indian civilization.

ESSENTIAL QUESTIONS *How does geography influence the way people live? How do religions develop? What makes a culture unique?*

The Dhammapada is a collection of verses based on Buddha's teachings. This excerpt is from the "Twin Verses":

> " Our life is shaped by our mind; we become what we think. Suffering follows an evil thought as the wheels of a cart follow the oxen that draw it.
> Our life is shaped by our mind; we become what we think. Joy follows a pure thought like a shadow that never leaves. "
>
> —*translated from* THE DHAMMAPADA

How does the second verse describe *joy*?

_____

_____

What words do this first verse use to describe *suffering*?

_____

_____

DBQ BREAKING IT DOWN

What do you think "Our life is shaped by our mind" means?

_____

_____

_____

Why do you think the writer repeats the first two lines in both verses?

_____

_____

_____

McGraw-Hill
networks™
There's More Online!

PHOTO: Saam Diephuis/Corbis

EARLY CIVILIZATIONS

 NGSSS

SS.6.W.4.1 Discuss the significance of Aryan and other tribal migrations on Indian civilization.

SS.6.W.4.2 Explain the major beliefs and practices associated with Hinduism and the social structure of the caste system in ancient India.

SS.6.W.4.5 Summarize the important achievements and contributions of ancient Indian civilization.

Essential Question
How does geography influence the way people live?

Guiding Questions
1. How did physical geography and climate influence the development of civilization in India?
2. How did the people of the Indus River Valley build cities?
3. How did the Aryans influence early India?
4. How was society in ancient India organized?

Terms to Know

subcontinent
a large landmass that is smaller than a continent

monsoons
seasonal winds, especially in the Indian Ocean and southern Asia

language family
a group of similar languages

raja
an Indian prince

Sanskrit
the ancient written language of India

Vedas
sacred writings of India

caste
an Indian social class whose members are restricted in the jobs they may take and in their association with members of other castes

guru
a teacher

Where in the World?
The Indus River Valley

When Did It Happen?

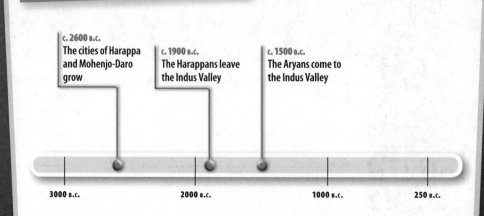

c. 2600 B.C.
The cities of Harappa and Mohenjo-Daro grow

c. 1900 B.C.
The Harappans leave the Indus Valley

c. 1500 B.C.
The Aryans come to the Indus Valley

3000 B.C.   2000 B.C.   1000 B.C.   250 B.C.

The Geography of India

India's border starts to the south of the continent of Asia. The Himalaya block off India from the rest of Asia. This makes India a **subcontinent.**

The Ganges and Indus rivers are in northern India. The Ganges runs southeast into the Indian Ocean. The Indus flows southwest into the Arabian Sea. Their water comes from melting snow in the Himalaya.

The Deccan Plateau is south of the Ganges and Indus river valleys. It is dry and hilly. The coastal areas have plains, or flat land, that is good for farming.

India's climate, or usual weather, has **monsoons,** or strong winds. The winter monsoon blows in cold, dry air from the mountains. The summer monsoon brings warm, wet air from the Arabian Sea. Summer monsoons bring the rainy season. If the rain comes in time, the crops will be good. If the rains are late, then there may be a drought, or a long time without rain for crops.

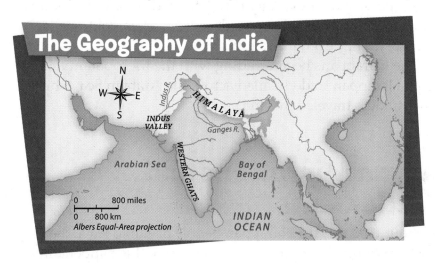

The Geography of India

The Indus Valley Civilization

India's first civilization began in the Indus River valley, where the floods wash up rich soil. The Harappa, or Indus, civilization lasted from about 2600 B.C. until 1500 B.C. Over 1,000 towns and cities stretched from the Himalaya to the Arabian Sea.

Harappa and Mohenjo-Daro were large cities with populations of about 35,000 people each. The cities had wide main streets and smaller side streets. Fortresses, or strong buildings made for defense, protected the people. Most houses were built with bricks made of dried mud. The houses had flat roofs, an open courtyard, wells, and indoor bathrooms. Brick pipes took wastewater to pits outside the city walls. Houses also had garbage chutes that led to bins in the streets.

Mark the Text

1. On the map, circle the landform that separates India from the rest of Asia.

Show Your Skill

2. **Identify Cause and Effect**
   How does monsoon season affect India's climate?

   _____

   _____

   _____

   _____

   _____

   _____

Think Critically

3. **Infer** How do you think we know about the early civilizations in the Indus River valley?

   _____

   _____

   _____

   _____

   _____

   _____

   _____

Once a thriving Indus Valley civilization, the ancient city of Harappa lies in ruins with just the layouts of buildings visible.

Think Critically

4. Describe What was the social class structure like in Harappa?

_____

_____

_____

_____

_____

_____

Show Your Skill

5. Compare and Contrast The Aryans were made up of different groups of people. However, in what way were they alike?

_____

_____

_____

Mark the Text

6. Underline the name of the area where the Aryans came from before entering India.

The Harappans left no written records. Experts have studied what is left of the cities to learn what life was like there. The royal palace and the temple may have been built together inside a fortress.

Most Harappans were farmers. They grew rice, wheat, barley, peas, and cotton. City dwellers made clay pots, cotton cloth, and metal tools. They made jewelry from gold, shells, and ivory. They even made toys.

The Harappans began trading with the Mesopotamians. Some Harappan traders sailed across the Arabian Sea, while other traders traveled by land.

Aryan Migrations and Settlements

In about 1900 B.C., the Harappan people began to leave their cities. Although historians don't know why this happened, there are two possible reasons. A very long drought dried up all the farms and there was no food, or an earthquake shook the river and caused a huge flood. Many years after most Harappans had left, the Aryans began settling the river valley.

The Aryans came from central Asia. They were nomads, so they traveled around to find food for their herds of cattle, sheep, and goats.

The Aryans were not a single race or a tribe. They were a group of people that spoke similar languages. This **language family** is called Indo-European. A language family is a set of similar languages. The Aryans were good warriors, expert horse riders, and expert hunters.

The Aryans left Asia about 2000 B.C. and crossed into India. They arrived in the Indus River valley around 1500 B.C.

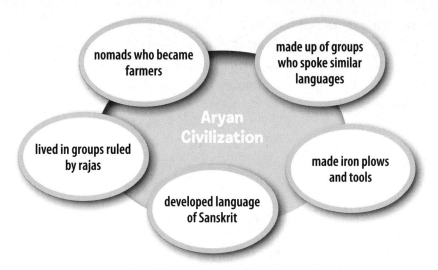

Aryan Civilization
- nomads who became farmers
- made up of groups who spoke similar languages
- lived in groups ruled by rajas
- made iron plows and tools
- developed language of Sanskrit

After awhile, the Aryans stopped living as nomads and became farmers. Over time, they decided that cattle were sacred, so people in India stopped eating meat from cattle. The Aryans found better ways to farm. They made iron plows and iron tools. With these, they cleared India's forests and dug canals to bring water from the river to the fields. This made the Ganges River valley good for growing crops. Farmers in north India grew wheat, barley, and other grains. In the river valleys, farmers grew rice. In the south, they grew spices like pepper, ginger, and cinnamon.

The Aryans did not write things down when they were nomads. When they became farmers, they developed a written language called **Sanskrit.** Using Sanskrit, they wrote down songs, stories, poems, and prayers in books called the **Vedas.**

The Aryans lived in groups, each ruled by a **raja,** or prince. Rajas often fought with each other over treasure and cattle.

Ancient Indian Society

In the Aryan society, social groups developed. They were based on a person's place in the Hindu religion and the work they did. These groups became the **caste** system. A caste system is a system of social position and rules. A person was born into one caste and could never change to any other. The caste system had rules for almost every part of a person's life, including marriage, work, and friendships.

The many different castes in Indian society were grouped into four classes called *varnas*. The top *varna* was the Brahmin. Brahmins were priests. The next *varna* was the Kshatriyas. These were warriors. They ran the government and the army. After the Kshatriyas came the Vaisyas, or "common people." They were farmers and merchants. Then came the Sudras. They were lower-class workers and servants. They had few rights. Most Indians were Sudras.

Think Critically

10. **Summarize** What was family life like In Indian society?

_____

_____

_____

_____

_____

_____

_____

Take the Challenge

11. Do research on education in India today. Design a Web page to display what you learned.

One group was not part of the caste system—the Untouchables. Untouchables did work considered too dirty for caste members. Most Indians thought Untouchables were unclean. As a result, Untouchables were made to live apart from everyone else.

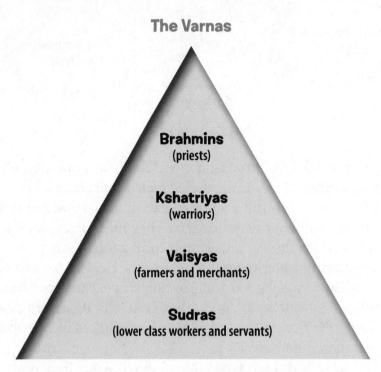

The Varnas

Brahmins
(priests)

Kshatriyas
(warriors)

Vaisyas
(farmers and merchants)

Sudras
(lower class workers and servants)

Grandparents, parents, and children all lived together with the oldest man in charge. This is called an extended, or enlarged, family. Men had many more rights than women. Only men went to school. Men had to have 12 years of schooling before they could marry. When they were young, boys studied with a **guru,** or teacher. When they were older, they went to schools in the cities. Only Brahmin men could become priests.

Parents chose marriage partners for their children. Divorce was not allowed. But if a couple could not have children, the husband could marry a second wife.

NGSSS Check Write *H* if the feature was part of Harappan civilization, or write *A* if it was a feature of Aryan civilization. Write *B* if it was a feature of both. SS.6.W.4.5

_____ **1.** the development of the caste system

_____ **2.** the use of mud bricks to make buildings

_____ **3.** Farmers grew rice, wheat, and barley.

_____ **4.** the use of the Sanskrit language

_____ **5.** built large cities with paved streets

NGSSS

SS.6.W.4.2 Explain the major belief and practices associated with Hinduism and the social structure of the caste system in ancient India.

SS.6.W.4.4 Explain the teachings of Buddha, the importance of Asoka, and how Buddhism spread in India, Ceylon, and other parts of Asia.

Essential Question
How do religions develop?

Guiding Questions
1. What are the basic beliefs of Hinduism?
2. Why did Buddhism appeal to many people in various parts of Asia?
3. What are the teachings of Jainism?

Terms to Know

Hinduism
one of the oldest religions in the world; main belief: all souls, including many gods, are part of one universal spirit

Brahman
the one, universal spirit worshiped by Hindus

reincarnation
the idea that the soul passes through many different lives

dharma
the law of right living; requires people to perform duties of their caste

karma
the result of the good or evil a person does in his/her lifetime; if you live a good life, you have good karma

Buddhism
a religion founded by Siddhartha Gautama; main belief: inner peace comes from ending desire

nirvana
a state of wisdom achieved after giving up all desires

Jainism
religion of ancient India that emphasizes nonviolence

When Did It Happen?

c. 1900 B.C.
The Harappans begin to leave the Indus Valley

c. 1500 B.C.
Early Hinduism first practiced by the Aryans

c. 599 B.C.
The birth of Siddhartha Gautama, founder of Buddhism

c. 563 B.C.
The birth of Mahavira, founder of Jainism

2000 B.C.   1000 B.C.   500 B.C.   250 B.C.

What Do You Know?

Put a check mark (√) next to each term that you know. For every word that you check, write a short description or definition.

_____ Sanskrit _____

_____ the Vedas _____

_____ *varnas* _____

_____ *guru* _____

_____ the Buddha _____

Origins of Hinduism

Hinduism is one of the oldest religions in the world. Over time, the Aryan religion combined with ideas from other Indian people and Hinduism was formed. Hindus believe in one great spirit called **Brahman.** They also believe that all humans and thousands of gods are each a different part of Brahman. Some very old Hindu writings talk about how each person finds this one spirit.

Hindus believe that a person's soul will eventually rejoin Brahman. Before that can happen, however, a soul must live many lives—even as an animal. The idea of living many lives in different forms, one after another, is called **reincarnation.** According to Hinduism, if people do the duties of their caste, they will get a better next life. They must follow **dharma,** or the law of right living, acting how their caste requires. If they follow dharma, they will have good karma.

Karma is the result of how a person lives. For example, if you live a good life and do your duty, you have good karma and will be reborn into a better life. Eventually, you will reach Brahman. If you have bad karma, you will be reborn into a lower caste or as an animal and will remain in the cycle of reincarnation.

This belief in dharma and karma meant that people had to obey the rules of their caste because that was where they had to stay until the next lifetime. The idea of reincarnation gave them their only hope.

This painting portrays the Buddha (left) and Sujata, a woman who offered him rice and honey.

Rise of Buddhism

Prince Siddhartha Gautama was born about 563 B.C. His father ruled a kingdom near the Himalaya. Siddhartha was wealthy, married, and had a son. Sheltered all his life, one day he went outside the palace and saw that most people were poor and suffering. He asked himself why people suffered. To search for answers, he left his family and lived alone. Legend says that Siddhartha sat under a tree and meditated. Finally, he came to understand the meaning of life. This is called "enlightenment."

PHOTO: Mary Evans Picture Library/Alamy

Think Critically

1. Sequence Fill in the blanks with words from this section.

Hindus believe that the soul goes

through _____ . A person

is born into a _____ .

If they do not follow the

_____ of their caste,

they make bad _____ and

the cycle starts again.

Show Your Skill

2. Identify Cause and Effect According to Hinduism, what causes reincarnation?

_____

_____

_____

_____

_____

_____

_____

_____

Take the Challenge

3. Draw a picture to show the cycle that Hindus believe a person's soul takes to join Brahman.

Siddhartha spent the rest of his life teaching people about his discovery. People called him the Buddha, which means "Enlightened One." His lessons about life and suffering are called **Buddhism.**

The Buddha taught that there was one way to get rid of suffering and find the truth. Everyone should stop wanting fame, money, and worldly things. Then they would reach **nirvana,** a state of wisdom, something like a Hindu finding Brahman. The Buddha said that the only way to stop suffering was to stop desiring things. To do this, people should follow the Eightfold Path—the Buddhist rules for right living. The Buddha believed in reincarnation, but with a difference. He thought that people could stop being reborn if they followed the Eightfold Path.

The Buddha did not agree with the caste system. He taught that all people could reach nirvana. This made Buddhism very popular among the lower castes and the Untouchables. They, too, could stop suffering and find peace.

The Eightfold Path

1. Know and understand the Four Noble Truths.
2. Give up worldly things and do not harm others.
3. Tell the truth, do not gossip, and do not speak badly of others.
4. Do not commit evil acts, such as killing, stealing, or living an unclean life.
5. Do rewarding work.
6. Work for good and oppose evil.
7. Make sure your mind keeps your senses under control.
8. Practice meditation to see the world in a new way.

The Buddha preached his ideas for more than 40 years. When he died, his disciples could not agree about what his message was really about. They split into two groups. One was Theravada Buddhism. *Theravada* means "teachings of the wise men." It says that the Buddha was a great teacher, but not a god. Theravada Buddhism spread south and east. It also became popular in Indochina.

The other kind of Buddhism is *Mahayana* Buddhism. It says that the Buddha is a god who came to save people. Mahayanas believe people can go to heaven if they worship the Buddha. Once they reach heaven, they can follow the Eightfold Path and reach nirvana. Mahayana Buddhists also honor *bodhisattvas.* Bodhisattvas are enlightened people who choose not to go to nirvana even though they could. They keep coming back to earth to help others.

4. Describe In your own words, write a definition for *nirvana*.

_____

_____

_____

_____

_____

5. Interpret Charts How does a Buddhist get to nirvana?

_____

_____

_____

_____

6. Compare and Contrast What is the difference between Theravada Buddhism and Mahayana Buddhism?

_____

_____

_____

_____

_____

_____

7. Contrast Based on what you already know, how is a democracy different from a theocracy?

_____

_____

_____

_____

_____

_____

8. Summarize In your own words, write the meaning of *ahimsa*. Then write an example of a person practicing *ahimsa*.

_____

_____

_____

_____

_____

_____

_____

Mark the Text

9. Underline one difference between Hinduism and Jainism.

Mahayana Buddhism spread north into China, Korea, and Japan. In Tibet it mixed with Hinduism and Tibet's own religions. This mix made a special kind of Mahayana Buddhism. Tibetan *lamas*, or priests, also led the government. This kind of government is called a theocracy.

Today, many Buddhists live in Japan, Korea, Thailand, Cambodia, and Sri Lanka. Very few live in India, where the Buddha first taught.

BUDDHISM	
Theravada Buddhism	**Mahayana Buddhism**
• **The Buddha was a great teacher.** • **The Buddha was not a god.**	• **The Buddha was a god.** • **People who worship the Buddha can go to heaven.**

Jainism

Another religion also came to the people of India at this time. It is called **Jainism.** No one knows exactly where it started. Its main teacher was Mahavira, who lived at about the same time as Siddhartha Buddha. His followers are called Jains after Mahavira's title, "the Jina," or "The Conqueror."

Much of Jainism is like Buddhism. Its followers practice meditation and try to get rid of worldly desire. Their goal is also to stop being reborn and to reach nirvana. Mahavira did not follow the caste system and taught people to give up wealth.

Jainism has one main teaching: Never harm any living thing. The name of this teaching is *ahimsa*. *Ahimsa* means that a person should not kill even insects or worms.

Centuries later, in the early 1900s, an Indian man named Mohandas Gandhi led a movement to free his nation from the rule of the British. Instead of taking up weapons, Gandhi followed the example of *ahimsa*. He and his followers used nonviolent ways of protesting. He told people not to pay taxes or buy British goods. Through peaceful ways, the nation of India gained its independence.

NGSSS Check What are the important beliefs and practices of Hinduism and Buddhism? SS.6.W.4.2

_____

_____

_____

_____

THE MAURYAN EMPIRE

NGSSS

SS.6.W.4.3 Recognize the political and cultural achievements of the Mauryan and Gupta empires.

SS.6.W.4.5 Summarize the important achievements and contributions of ancient Indian civilizations.

Essential Question
What makes a culture unique?

Guiding Questions
1. How did religion affect the development of the Mauryan Empire?
2. Why did the Gupta Empire become powerful?
3. What were the cultural contributions of the Mauryan and Gupta Empires?

Terms to Know

stupa
a special type of building meant to honor the Buddha

pilgrim
a person who travels to places of religious importance

Bhagavad Gita
part of a famous long poem; its story is about the Hindu god Krishna

When Did It Happen?

c. 563 B.C.
The birth of Siddhartha Gautama, founder of Buddhism

c. 321 B.C.
Chandra Gupta Maurya builds a strong army and sets up an empire in northern India

c. 273 B.C.
Ashoka becomes ruler of the Mauryan Empire and brings about a golden age

c. A.D. 330
Samudra Gupta expands the Gupta Empire by force

c. A.D. 700s
The Arabic way of writing numbers begins to spread

500 B.C.   250 B.C.   A.D. 250   A.D. 500   A.D. 700

What Do You Know?

Directions: Write a short definition of each term using your own words.

empire
_____

Sanskrit
_____

Hinduism
_____

Buddhism
_____

Origin of an Empire

India had many small kingdoms. India's princes fought over these kingdoms for years. Then the Persian armies conquered India and made it part of the Persian Empire. More than one hundred years later, Alexander the Great defeated the Persian Empire. He led his army into India, but his soldiers were tired and wanted to go home. Alexander did not want a fight with his soldiers, so he and his army left India.

At that time, Chandra Gupta Maurya took over part of the Ganges River valley. After Alexander left, Chandra Gupta took over almost all of northern India.

In 321 B.C., the Mauryan dynasty began. A dynasty is a group of rulers from the same family. Chandra Gupta set up a well-organized government in the capital city of Pataliputra. To keep control, Chandra Gupta also set up a strong army and a good spy system. He made a postal system for fast communication.

Many historians think that the greatest king of the Mauryan Empire was Chandra Gupta's grandson, Ashoka. Ashoka ruled from about 273 B.C. to 232 B.C. He was a strong military leader who grew to hate war. After one bloody fight, he promised to spend his life making peace. He decided to follow the teachings of Buddha. He built hospitals for people and for animals. He also built new roads with coverings and shade trees so travelers could rest.

Ashoka sent many Buddhists out to teach Buddhism in India and Asia. In India, he had workers carve the Buddha's teaching on pillars, or large, tall stones. He also had workers build thousands of **stupas,** or Buddhist shrines. Unlike most rulers of the time, Ashoka was tolerant of other religions. He allowed Hindus to remain Hindus.

When there is a good road system and a strong ruler, trade is good. Trade was very good under Ashoka. India became the center of a huge trade network. It stretched all the way to the Mediterranean Sea.

The Great Stupa, built during Ashoka's rule, sits atop the Hill of Sanchi, which serves as a center of Buddhism.

PHOTO: Robert Harding Picture Library Ltd/Alamy

Ashoka died in 232 B.C. The kings who followed him were not good leaders. The empire grew weak. These kings made many unwise decisions. They forced merchants to pay heavy taxes. They took the peasants' crops without paying them. The people turned against these rulers. In 183 B.C., the last Mauryan king was killed by one of his own generals. After that, the Mauryan Empire split into small warring kingdoms.

The Gupta Empire

For the next 500 years, India was not united. Then, a prince from the Ganges River valley rose to power. His name was Chandra Gupta, just like the founder of the Mauryan Empire. This Chandra Gupta founded the Gupta dynasty in A.D. 320. He ruled from the old capital city, Pataliputra. When he died, his son Samudra Gupta took over. Samudra Gupta gained new lands for the empire. He also became a patron, or gave money, for people to make art and literature. This brought in a golden age for the Guptas.

Merchants used a network of trade routes to buy and sell. They gained wealth for themselves and the empire. Cities grew along the trade routes and made travel easier.

The Guptas supported Hinduism. They built fine temples and created beautiful works of art to honor the Hindu gods. **Pilgrims**—people who travel to holy places—used the trade routes to get to these popular places. These travelers made the cities rich.

Culture in Ancient India

Artists, builders, scientists, and writers were busy under the Mauryan and Gupta Empires. After Sanskrit developed under the Aryans, the Hindu Vedas were written down. Another kind of popular text was the epic poem. These were long poems about the adventures of brave heroes. The most famous epic poems are the *Mahabharata* and the *Ramayana*.

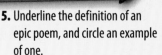
Think Critically

4. Describe Describe in your own words what the Gupta Empire was like.

_____

_____

_____

_____

_____

_____

Mark the Text

5. Underline the definition of an epic poem, and circle an example of one.

In the poem *Ramayana*, Rama and Lakshmana are heroes. Here, Lakshmana is shown speaking with leaders of the Monkey Armies.

Think Critically

6. Infer Why do you think these poems were written down?

_____

_____

_____

_____

_____

Mark the Text

7. Chart List some of the advances of the Indian empires in mathematics, science, and medicine. Write them in the chart.

Think Critically

8. Analyze Choose one advance you wrote in the graphic organizer, and explain why it is important to us today.

_____

_____

_____

_____

The Mahabharata is the longest poem in any language. It was written about 100 B.C. The best-known section of this poem is the **Bhagavad Gita.** The name means "Song of the Lord." The hero in the poem learns from the god Krishna that he should do his duty and follow his dharma, no matter how difficult it is.

Music was important in the religious and social lives of the ancient Indians. Religious poems, such as the *Bhagavad Gita,* were probably sung in group settings. Musical instruments included tambourines, flutes, drums, and lutes (a stringed instrument).

Early Indian art that has survived is mostly religious art made of stone. There are many sculptures of the Buddha. These statues teach different Buddhist messages based on the figure's pose.

Gupta mathematicians were among the first to think about the idea of infinity. Infinity is the idea that space, time, or an amount of something goes on without ending. They invented the concept as a way to show nothingness by using the number zero. The Indian number symbols for 0 through 9 are the same ones we use today. Arab traders brought these "Arabic numerals" to Europe. By about the A.D. 1200s, Europeans were using these numerals, too.

Indian scientists mapped the movements of the planets and stars. They knew that the Earth was round and that it moved around the sun. Metal workers used steel and iron to make tools and weapons.

Gupta doctors set broken bones and performed operations. They invented medical tools and used herbs to treat illness. Indian doctors thought that it was important to find the cause of a disease. A doctor named Shushruta even did plastic surgery.

Amazing Indian Inventions		
Mathematics	Science	Medicine

 NGSSS Check List one accomplishment of each Indian leader. SS.6.W.4.3

Chandra Gupta Maurya

_____

Ashoka

_____

Samudra Gupta

_____

ESSENTIAL QUESTION *How do religions develop?*

Reflect on What It Means . . .

In this chapter, you learned about Hinduism. Use the space below to write down what you learned about Hindu beliefs.

Hinduism teaches that individuals . . .

Hinduism teaches that communities . . .

Keep Going! ➤➤

Hinduism teaches that the world . . .

TAKE THE CHALLENGE

Write a poem about Hinduism that describes its core beliefs, ideas, and teachings. As a class, put your poems together to make one epic poem. Design a cover for the epic poem.

EARLY CHINA

NGSSS

SS.6.G.4.1 Explain how family and ethnic relationships influenced ancient cultures.

ESSENTIAL QUESTIONS *What makes a culture unique? How do new ideas change the way people live? How do governments change?*

Men and women had very different roles in early China. Most women raised children and managed the household. Ban Zhao was unique because she was the first known woman historian in ancient China. She wrote *Lessons for Women* in about A.D. 80.

PHOTO: © Keren Su/China Span/Getty Images

Copyright © by The McGraw-Hill Companies, Inc.

"These three ancient customs epitomize woman's ordinary way of life. . . . let her respect others; let her put others first, herself last. Should she do something good, let her not mention it; should she do something bad let her not deny it. Let her bear disgrace; let her even endure when others speak or do evil to her. . . . When a woman follows such maxims as these then she may be said to humble herself before others."

—FROM *LESSONS FOR WOMEN*

epitomize

Write a short phrase that means the same as *epitomize*.

_____

maxims

What word in the sentence helps you know what *maxims* means?

_____

DBQ BREAKING IT DOWN

Why do you think one of the customs was for women to "bear disgrace" and "endure when others speak or do evil to her"?

_____
_____
_____
_____

What does this excerpt reveal about the life of women in ancient China?

_____
_____
_____
_____

McGraw-Hill
networks
There's More Online!

TEXT: From Pan Chao: Foremost Woman Scholar of China, translated by Nancy Lee Swan (New York: Russell & Russell, 1968, 1932). Reprinted by permission of the East Asian Library and the Gest Collection, Princeton University.

LESSON 1

THE BIRTH OF CHINESE CIVILIZATION

SS.6.W.2.4 Compare the economic, political, social, and religious institutions of ancient river civilizations.

SS.6.W.4.6 Describe the concept of the Mandate of Heaven and its connection to the Zhou and later dynasties.

SS.6.W.4.8 Describe the contributions of classical and post classical China.

Essential Question
What makes a culture unique?

Guiding Questions
1. How have rivers, mountains, and deserts shaped the development of China's civilization?
2. Why did China's Shang rulers become powerful?
3. How did the Zhou claim the right to rule China?

Terms to Know

warlord
a leader who has his own army

aristocrat
a person who belongs to the highest class of society

ancestor
a family member who is no longer living

pictograph
in Chinese writing, a character that stands for an object

ideograph
in Chinese writing, two or more pictographs joined together to express an idea

bureaucracy
officials who carry out government tasks

hereditary
to pass down from parents to children

Mandate of Heaven
the belief that the Chinese king's right to rule came from the gods

Dao
the proper way a king must rule

Where in the World?

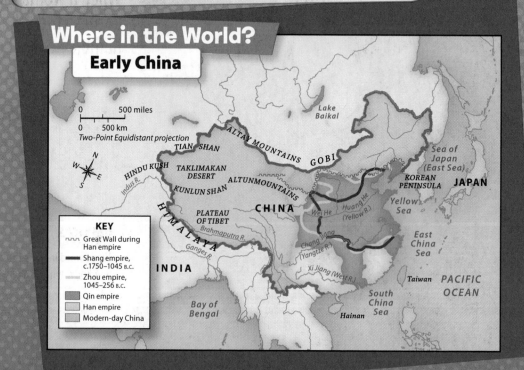

Early China

When Did It Happen?

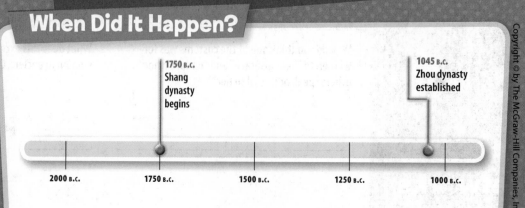

1750 B.C. Shang dynasty begins

1045 B.C. Zhou dynasty established

2000 B.C. | 1750 B.C. | 1500 B.C. | 1250 B.C. | 1000 B.C.

The Land of China

Two powerful rivers have helped to shape Chinese history. The Huang He, or Yellow River, flows across China. As it flows, it carries large amounts of rich soil. The soil spreads along the banks of the river. This makes the land more fertile, or a high quality for farming. Farmers along the Huang He are able to grow more food. However, the Huang He often floods. Millions of people have died because of these floods.

The Chang Jiang, or Yangtze River, is another important waterway in China. Like the Huang He, the Chiang Jiang provides rich soil for farming. It also serves as a way of trade and transportation.

Mountains and deserts cover much of China. They are difficult to cross, making a barrier around China. These natural barriers limited contact between China and other civilizations. The high mountains and vast deserts helped China develop a unique culture. Chinese civilization was different from other civilizations.

Think Critically

1. Explain What are two ways that rivers helped China develop?

_____

_____

_____

_____

_____

_____

Show Your Skill

2. Identify Cause and Effect How did mountains and deserts affect China's culture?

_____

_____

_____

Farmers tend to their rice crops in Shikong. The Yellow River, or Huang He, provides water to irrigate these crops.

3. Underline the name of the first Chinese dynasty.

Show Your Skill

4. Organize List the groups in order, from highest to lowest, in Chinese society.

_____

_____

_____

5. Compare and Contrast What is the difference between a pictograph and an ideograph?

_____

_____

_____

_____

Geographic Feature	Effect on Chinese Civilization
rivers	• provided rich soil for Chinese farmers • many deaths caused by flooding • used as waterways for trade and transportation
mountains	• formed a barrier around the country making it difficult for invaders to enter • made it possible for China to develop a unique culture and civilization
deserts	• like mountains, created a barrier around the country

The First Chinese Dynasty

A dynasty is a line of rulers who belong to the same family. Historians believe the first Chinese dynasty was the Shang. The Shang dynasty began about 1750 B.C. As time passed, Shang kings ruled over more and more land. Warlords helped the Shang kings control the country. A **warlord** is a leader who has his own army.

The king, warlords, and other royal officials were aristocrats. **Aristocrats** are people in the highest class of a society. Their wealth comes from the land they own. Most Chinese people, however, were farmers. They farmed the land owned by aristocrats.

People in Shang China believed in many gods. They believed the gods could bring good or bad fortune. The Chinese also honored their **ancestors,** or long-dead family members.

Writing developed in China during the Shang dynasty. Early Chinese writing used pictographs and ideographs. **Pictographs** are characters that represent objects. **Ideographs** link two or more pictographs to express an idea.

These stone carvings in Guangxi Province have Chinese inscriptions that date back to the Shang dynasty.

The Zhou: China's Longest Dynasty

The Zhou followed the Shang dynasty. The Zhou king led the government. He was helped by a **bureaucracy.** A bureaucracy is a group of selected officials who do different government jobs. Under Zhou rulers, China grew larger. The king divided the country into territories. Each territory was ruled by an aristocrat. When an aristocrat died, his son or another member of his family governed the territory. This means these positions were **hereditary.**

Zhou kings believed that the gods gave them the right to rule to China. This idea is known as the **Mandate of Heaven.** The Mandate said that the king must rule in the proper way. This proper way was known as the **Dao.**

During the Zhou dynasty trade grew. Silk from the Zhou dynasty has been found as far away as Greece. Under the Zhou, new technology helped farmers. The Chinese developed better ways to water their fields, helping farmers grow more food.

The power of the aristocrats grew under the Zhou. Aristocrats began to ignore the king. They took control of their own territory, or states. Aristocrats began to fight each other for power. These battles lasted for nearly 200 years. This time in Chinese history is known as the "Period of the Warring States."

These bronze vessels from the Zhou dynasty may have been used during rituals.

Think Critically

6. Analyze How did changes that took place in China under the Zhou dynasty affect China?

_____

_____

_____

_____

_____

 NGSSS Check Compare and contrast how the Shang and Zhou dynasties ruled China. SS.6.W.2.4

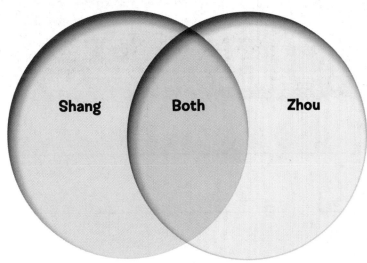

Shang   Both   Zhou

Take the Challenge

7. Draw a diagram to show the concept of the Mandate of Heaven and include labels.

LESSON

2 SOCIETY AND CULTURE IN ANCIENT CHINA

NGSSS

SS.6.G.4.1 Explain how family and ethnic relationships influenced ancient cultures.

SS.6.W.4.7 Explain the basic teachings of Laozi, Confucius, and Han Fei Zi.

SS.6.W.4.8 Describe the contributions of classical and post classical China.

Essential Question
How do new ideas change the way people live?

Guiding Questions
1. How did Chinese thinkers influence society and government?
2. How was early Chinese society organized?

Terms to Know

Confucianism
a system of beliefs based on duty

Daoism
a Chinese philosophy based on living simply

Legalism
a Chinese philosophy based on the importance of laws

social class
a group of people with the same economic and social position

filial piety
the responsibility of children to respect, obey, and care for their parents

When Did It Happen?

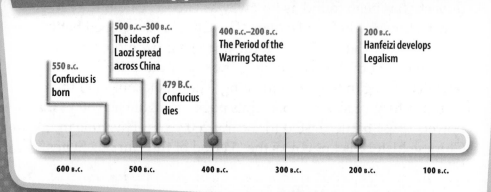

550 B.C. Confucius is born

500 B.C.–300 B.C. The ideas of Laozi spread across China

479 B.C. Confucius dies

400 B.C.–200 B.C. The Period of the Warring States

200 B.C. Hanfeizi develops Legalism

600 B.C.   500 B.C.   400 B.C.   300 B.C.   200 B.C.   100 B.C.

What Do You Know?

Directions: Use the table below to answer the questions based on what you know now in the "Now" column. After the lesson, complete the table by writing the answers in the "Later" column.

	Now	Later
What is Daoism?		
What is Confucianism?		
Who was Laozi?		

Chinese Philosophies

Between 500 B.C. and 200 B.C. Chinese thinkers developed three major philosophies. They were Confucianism, Daoism, and Legalism. The philosophies were different from each other. Each philosophy, however, aimed to create a peaceful society.

	Confucianism	Daoism	Legalism
Founder	Confucius	Laozi	Hanfeizi
Important Ideas	People should put the needs of their family and community first.	People should give up worldly desires in favor of nature and the Dao, the force that guides all things.	Society needs a system of harsh laws and strict punishments.

Confucius believed that all men should be able to serve in the government. This led to a system of examinations to choose government officials. Confucius is honored as a great teacher. After his death, **Confucianism** spread across China.

Like Confucius, Laozi aimed to create a peaceful society. Confucius thought people should work hard to make the world better. Under **Daoism,** however, people turn away from society and towards nature.

Hanfeizi introduced the ideas of **Legalism** during the 200s B.C. He believed that humans are naturally evil. He thought only strict laws and harsh punishment would get people to do what they should do. Many aristocrats supported Legalism. Under Legalism, rulers did not have to think of the wishes of their people.

Mark the Text

1. Circle the names of the founders of each Chinese philosophy. Underline the name of the philosophy each founded. Draw an arrow from the name of the founder to his philosophy.

Think Critically

2. **Infer** Why did aristocrats and kings like Legalism?

_____

_____

_____

_____

Take the Challenge

3. Research and write a short biography of one of the three Chinese philosophers. Provide background information on the philosopher's childhood and any events that may have affected his founding of the philosophy.

Confucius was not an emperor, but his ideas greatly influenced Chinese civilization.

Laozi thought that people should live in harmony with nature.

4. Compare and Contrast How were the social classes alike and different?

_____

_____

_____

_____

_____

_____

_____

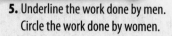

Mark the Text

5. Underline the work done by men. Circle the work done by women.

Think Critically

6. Analyze How important do you think filial piety was to Chinese society? Explain.

_____

_____

_____

_____

Chinese Life

Chinese society was made up of four **social classes.** A social class is a group of all the people in a society with the same economic and social position.

Chinese Society			
Aristocrats	**Farmers**	**Artisans**	**Merchants**
• small number of people • wealthy • owned large plots of land and lived on large estates	• most people • worked on land owned by aristocrats • paid rent in the form of crops • paid taxes • served as soldiers • worked one month a year on public projects, such as roads	• skilled workers who made useful objects • learned skills from fathers and taught them to sons	• shopkeepers and traders • lived in towns • provided goods and services to aristocrats • some wealthy, but not respected because merchants just made money for themselves

The family was the basis of Chinese society. Chinese families practiced filial piety. **Filial piety** is the responsibility children have to respect, obey, and take care of their parents.

Men and women had very different roles in early China. Men grew crops, ran the government, and fought wars. Women raised children and saw to their education. They also managed household affairs and family finances.

 NGSSS Check Complete the chart below with descriptions of the three Chinese philosophies and the founders of each. **SS.6.W.4.7**

Philosophy	Confucianism	Daoism	Legalism
Founder			
Important Ideas			

NGSSS

SS.6.W.4.6 Describe the concept of the Mandate of Heaven and its connection to the Zhou and later dynasties.

SS.6.W.4.8 Describe the contributions of classical and post classical China.

SS.6.W.4.10 Explain the significance of the silk roads and maritime routes across the Indiana Ocean and to the movement of goods and ideas among Asia, East Asia, East Africa and the Mediterranean basin.

3 THE QIN AND THE HAN DYNASTIES

Essential Question
How do governments change?

Guiding Questions
1. How did the Qin Emperor unite China?
2. What improvements did the Chinese make under Han rulers?
3. How did the Silk Road benefit China and the rest of the world?
4. Why did Buddhism become a popular religion in China?

Terms to Know

censor
an official who made sure government workers did their jobs

currency
a type of money

civil service
government work

tenant farmer
a farmer who works land belonging to someone else

acupuncture
medical treatment that uses needles to relieve pain

Where in the World?

Qin and Han Empires, 221 B.C.–A.D. 220

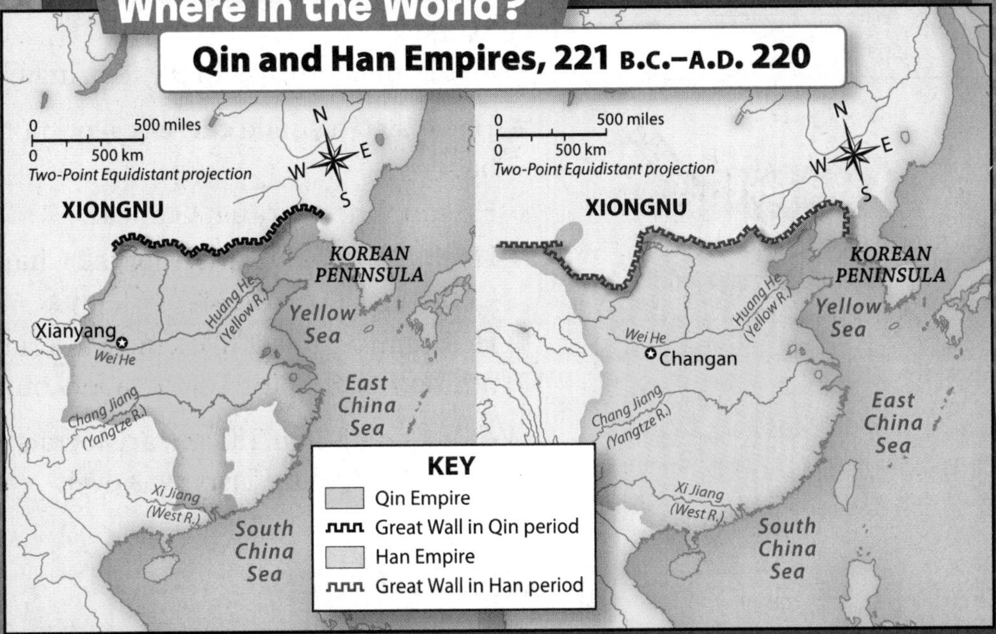

Map 1 (left):
0 — 500 miles
0 — 500 km
Two-Point Equidistant projection
XIONGNU
Xianyang
Wei He
Huang He (Yellow R.)
Chang Jiang (Yangtze R.)
Xi Jiang (West R.)
KOREAN PENINSULA
Yellow Sea
East China Sea
South China Sea

Map 2 (right):
0 — 500 miles
0 — 500 km
Two-Point Equidistant projection
XIONGNU
Wei He
Changan
Huang He (Yellow R.)
Chang Jiang (Yangtze R.)
Xi Jiang (West R.)
KOREAN PENINSULA
Yellow Sea
East China Sea
South China Sea

KEY
- Qin Empire
- Great Wall in Qin period
- Han Empire
- Great Wall in Han period

When Did It Happen?

Read to Learn

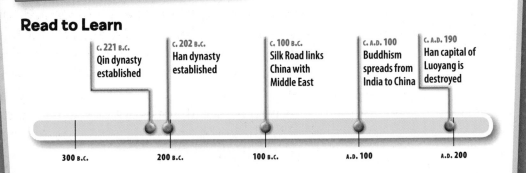

- c. 221 B.C. Qin dynasty established
- c. 202 B.C. Han dynasty established
- c. 100 B.C. Silk Road links China with Middle East
- c. A.D. 100 Buddhism spreads from India to China
- c. A.D. 190 Han capital of Luoyang is destroyed

300 B.C. — 200 B.C. — 100 B.C. — A.D. 100 — A.D. 200

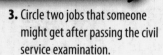
Think Critically

2. **Conclude** Do you think Qin's rule helped to unite the country? Why or why not?

_____

_____

_____

_____

_____

_____

_____

Mark the Text

3. Circle two jobs that someone might get after passing the civil service examination.

netw⊕rks Read Chapter 10 Lesson 3 in your textbook or online.

The Qin Emperor

In 221 B.C., the ruler of the Chinese state Qin took control of the country. The new ruler of China called himself Qin Shihuangdi, which means "the First Qin Emperor." Qin brought many changes to China.

Qin wanted to unify China. He took control of China's provinces. Before then, the provinces were ruled by aristocrats. They passed control to their sons when they died. Now instead, Qin appointed governors.

Qin's rule was harsh. Anyone who disagreed with him was punished or killed. He burned writings that did not agree with him. He appointed **censors** to make sure government officials did their work.

One of Qin Shihuangdi's greatest achievements was starting the construction of what later became known as the Great Wall of China.

Qin did many things to try to bring China together.

- He created a single **currency,** or money, that everyone had to use.
- He simplified written Chinese.
- He built a canal connecting the Chang Jiang in central China to a city in southern China.
- He began a project to connect a series of walls across northern China to keep invaders out.

When Qin died in 210 B.C., aristocrats and farmers revolted. By 206 B.C., the Qin dynasty was over.

Han Rulers

In 202 B.C., a new dynasty was founded in China called the Han dynasty. The Han dynasty would rule China for over 400 years.

The first strong Han emperor was Han Wudi. Han Wudi ruled from 141 B.C. to 87 B.C. Han Wudi wanted educated people to work in the government. He created schools to prepare students for government work, or **civil service.** Civil service tests were a way of choosing educated government workers. The tests for the Chinese civil service were very difficult. Some students who passed the tests got jobs as teachers. Others worked for the government. They won great respect because they were well educated.

PHOTO: Art Archive, The/SuperStock

Copyright © by The McGraw-Hill Companies, Inc.

During the Han dynasty, many farmers become tenant farmers. A **tenant farmer** works on land that belongs to someone else. Most tenant farmers were very poor. As the population grew, the Han empire took in more land. Han armies moved south into Southeast Asia. They went west as far as India.

During this time, ideas, art, literature, and science blossomed. The ideas of Confucius grew in influence. New paintings and sculpture were created. Writers wrote about current events and made copies of old works. New technology helped Chinese farmers produce more food. Waterwheels ground more grain. Silk manufacturing improved. Paper, a Chinese invention, was used to keep records.

Doctors discovered that certain foods prevented illnesses. They learned to treat some illnesses with herbs. Chinese doctors relieved their patients' pain with acupuncture. **Acupuncture** is the practice of inserting thin, short needles into a patient's skin at certain points, to relieve pain.

On the Silk Road

During the Han period, Chinese traders grew rich by transporting expensive goods to other parts of the world. Both sea and land routes led to an exchange of goods and ideas.

In A.D. 139 Han Wudi sent Zhang Qian to explore areas west of China. Zhang returned 13 years later. He told about the people and places he had seen. He told Han Wudi about the strong horses of the West. Han Wudi wanted these horses for his cavalry. To get them, the emperor encouraged trade between China and the West. Chinese merchants traded silk, spices, and other luxury goods. This trade route to the West would later be called the Silk Road.

This silk canvas portrays the transport of ceramics, an export from China, on the Silk Road.

Think Critically

4. List three achievements of the Han dynasty.

_____

_____

_____

Show Your Skill

5. Draw Conclusions Why did Han Wudi encourage trade with the West?

_____

_____

_____

_____

Think Critically

6. Synthesize How did Han Wudi stimulate trade with the West?

_____

_____

_____

_____

_____

_____

_____

_____

PHOTO: DEA / G. DAGLI ORTI/De Agostini Picture Library/Getty Images

Think Critically

7. Explain When Buddhism came to China, how did it travel?

_____

_____

8. Analyze Buddhism appealed to people who felt afraid. Why might Chinese people have felt unsafe at this time?

_____

_____

_____

_____

Take the Challenge

9. With a partner, research the routes of the Silk Road and draw them on a blank map of Asia. Label the map with at least five of the trade goods that people and cultures exchanged.

The Silk Road was a network of trade routes. When it was completed, it stretched from China to the Mediterranean. Travel on the Silk Road was difficult. Traders had to cross high mountains and vast deserts. Robbers and thieves also traveled the roads. Through the Silk Road, China came into contact with other civilizations.

Buddhism Reaches China

The Silk Road also served as a way to spread ideas. Buddhism spread from India to China along the Silk Road. At first, Buddhism attracted few followers.

Han emperors after Han Wudi were weak. Many were dishonest. Farmers and aristocrats rebelled against the Han rulers. In A.D. 190, rebels destroyed the Han capital city, Luoyang. By A.D. 220, civil war divided China. For the next 400 years China was divided into small kingdoms.

The long years of war made many Chinese feel unsafe. Many turned to Buddhism. Buddhist ideas appealed to people dealing with fear. By the 400s, Buddhism had become one of China's major religions.

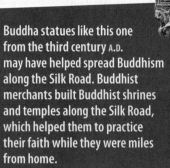
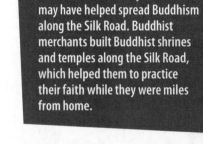

Buddha statues like this one from the third century A.D. may have helped spread Buddhism along the Silk Road. Buddhist merchants built Buddhist shrines and temples along the Silk Road, which helped them to practice their faith while they were miles from home.

NGSSS Check List three difficulties faced by traders on the Silk Road. SS.6.W.4.10

1. _____

2. _____

3. _____

MY REFLECTIONS

ESSENTIAL QUESTION *How do new ideas change the way people live?*

Reflect on What It Means . . .

Three philosophies were born in ancient China that spread throughout the world through trade on the Silk Road. Buddhism was the most popular. Today, Buddhism is one of the major world religions. It is mainly practiced in Asia but has followers around the globe.

Based on what you learned in the chapter about Buddhism and Buddhist beliefs and ideas, think about how Buddhism views the individual, the community, and the world. In the space below, write a simple explanation of Buddhist beliefs in general, and then details for each group.

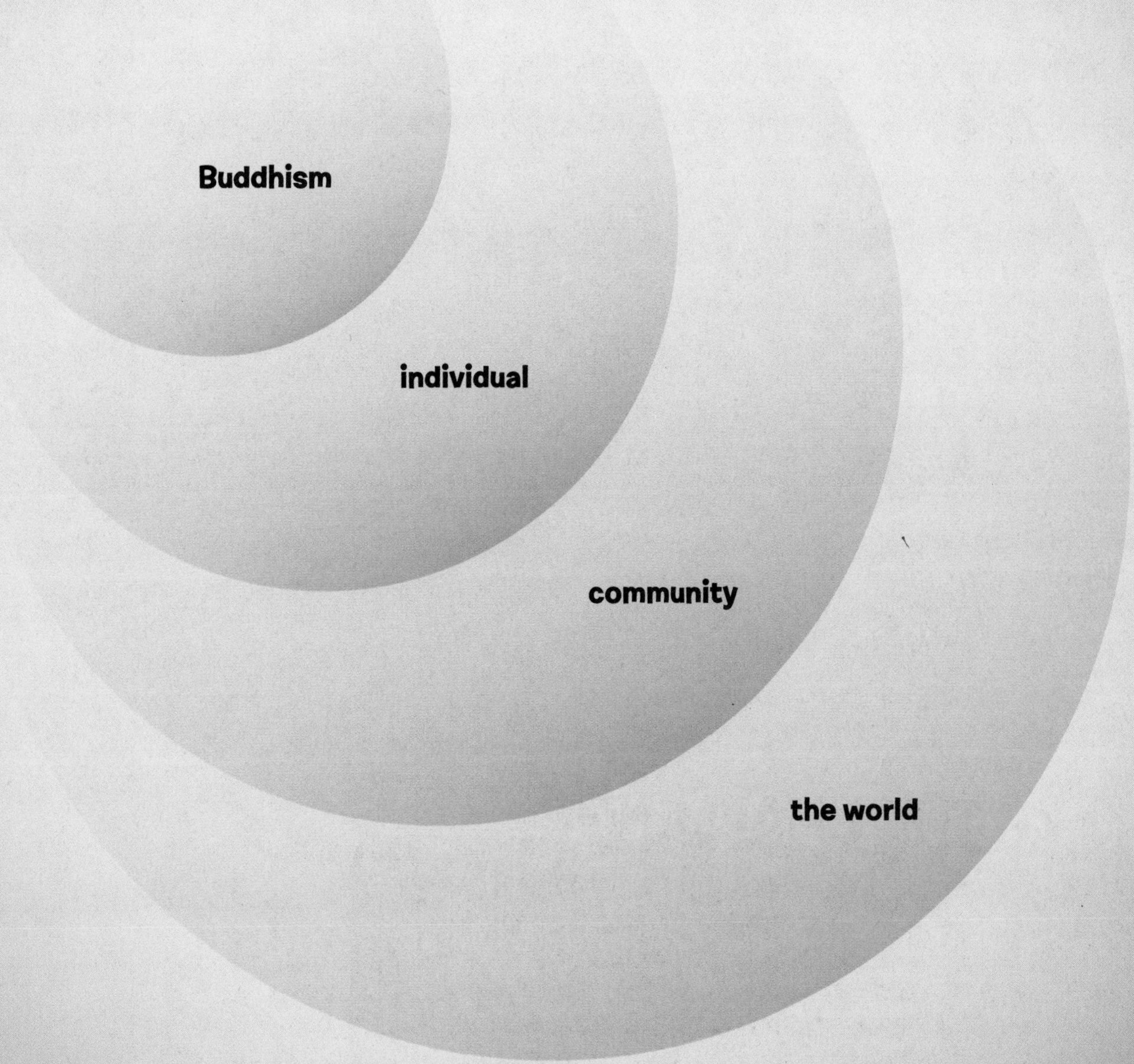

Buddhism

individual

community

the world

Keep Going! ⇒

In the space below, use what you learned in this chapter to illustrate a scene from ancient China after the arrival of Buddhism.

TAKE THE CHALLENGE

With your classmates, on a map of the world or a globe in the classroom or online, map out the different countries where Buddhism is practiced. You may use print or online references to help you. Mark each country where Buddhism is practiced. Make connections between those locations and how Buddhism traveled from different areas. Look at waterways and the old routes of the Silk Road. Discuss how trade and physical geography influence the movement of ideas around the world.

ROME: REPUBLIC TO EMPIRE

NGSSS

SS.6.W.3.8 Determine the impact of significant figures associated with ancient Rome.

SS.6.W.3.11 Explain the transition from Roman Republic to empire and Imperial Rome, and compare Roman life and culture under each one.

SS.6.W.3.12 Explain the causes for the growth and longevity of the Roman Empire.

ESSENTIAL QUESTIONS *How does geography influence the way people live? How do governments change? Why does conflict develop? What are the characteristics of a leader?*

The Deeds of the Divine Augustus were written in A.D. 14. Roman emperor Caesar Augustus wrote them and intended them to be read after his death. Here is an excerpt from the document:

"I extended the borders of all the provinces of the Roman people which neighbored nations not subject to our rule. I restored peace to the provinces of Gaul and Spain, likewise Germany. . . . I brought peace to the Alps from the region which I near the Adriatic Sea to the Tuscan, with no unjust war waged against any nation."

CAESAR AUGUSTUS

extended the borders

What does Augustus mean by *extending the borders*?

_____

_____

_____

unjust

Write another word (synonym) for *unjust* below.

_____

DBQ BREAKING IT DOWN

Do you think that the point Augustus is trying to make is that he waged war to bring peace? Explain.

_____

_____

_____

_____

What might make a war a "just" war? Explain.

_____

_____

_____

McGraw-Hill
networks™
There's More Online!

1

THE FOUNDING OF ROME

NGSSS

SS.6.G.2.1 Explain how major physical characteristics, natural resources, climate, and absolute and relative locations have influenced settlement, interactions, and the economies of ancient civilizations of the world.

SS.6.G.2.2 Differentiate between continents, regions, countries, and cities in order to understand the complexities of regions created by civilizations.

SS.6.W.3.8 Determine the impact of significant figures associated with ancient Rome.

Essential Question
How does geography influence the way people live?

Guiding Questions
1. What effect did geography have on the rise of Roman civilization?
2. How did Rome become a great power?

Terms to Know

republic
a form of government in which citizens elect their leaders

legion
a small group of Roman soldiers

Where in the World?

Early Rome

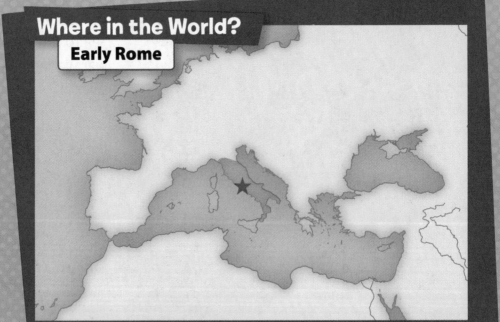

When Did It Happen?

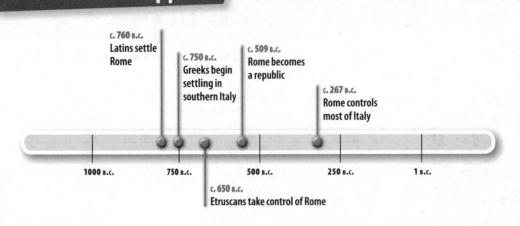

c. 760 B.C.
Latins settle Rome

c. 750 B.C.
Greeks begin settling in southern Italy

c. 509 B.C.
Rome becomes a republic

c. 267 B.C.
Rome controls most of Italy

1000 B.C.   750 B.C.   500 B.C.   250 B.C.   1 B.C.

c. 650 B.C.
Etruscans take control of Rome

The Beginning of Rome

Italy is a peninsula in the Mediterranean Sea. It is shaped like a boot. The heel points toward Greece. The toe points toward the island of Sicily.

The Alps cross the top of Italy and separate it from the rest of Europe. The Apennines Mountains run down Italy, from north to south. These mountains could be crossed easily, helping to link people from different parts of early Italy. They could trade ideas and goods with each other. Italy has a mild climate, rich soil, and large, flat plains that make good farmland.

Historians do not know much about the first people in Italy. People in Europe crossed the Alps between 2000 B.C. and 1000 B.C. These people included the Latins. Historians think that a group of Latins tended herds and grew crops on Rome's hills. Their community developed into Rome. The people who founded Rome became known as the Romans.

Rome was built along the Tiber River, which was used for fresh water and transportation. In addition, Rome was built 15 miles up the river from the Mediterranean Sea. This meant that pirates could not attack the city. Rome was built on seven hills. The hills also protected the city from attackers. Rome's location made it a good trading post.

Roman history does not just involve the Latins. Around 800 B.C., the Greeks and the Etruscans came to Italy. The Greeks built many colonies in Italy between 750 B.C. and 500 B.C. They taught the Romans to grow olives and grapes and to use the Greek alphabet. Romans also copied Greek sculpture and other art forms.

The Etruscans were from the area north of Rome. Many Etruscans were rich miners and traders. Others were devoted to art. They painted pictures and created jewelry, tools, and weapons. When the Etruscans came, Rome was a village with straw huts. That changed, however, after 650 B.C. when the Etruscans conquered Rome. They taught the Romans to build roads, buildings, temples, streets, and public squares.

The Etruscans introduced togas and short cloaks. A toga is like a sheet wrapped around your body, with one end thrown over your shoulder. Most important, the Etruscans showed the Romans how an army could be more effective. Later, the Romans copied the Etruscan army model and conquered an empire.

Mark the Text

1. Underline the physical features that helped make Rome prosperous.

Show Your Skill

2. **Make a Connection** The Roman way of life was influenced by Latin, Greek, and Etruscan civilizations. How do other cultures influence your daily life?

_____

_____

_____

_____

_____

_____

Think Critically

3. **Infer** Why do you think the Romans used the Greek alphabet?

_____

_____

_____

_____

_____

_____

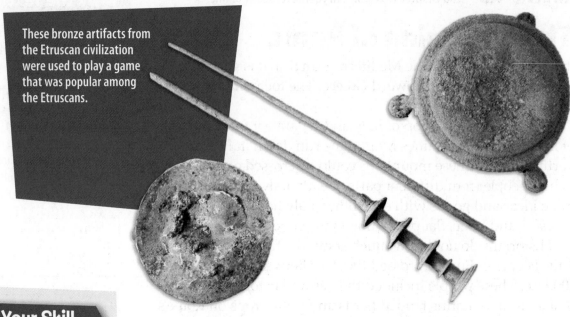

These bronze artifacts from the Etruscan civilization were used to play a game that was popular among the Etruscans.

PHOTO: David Lees/CORBIS

Show Your Skill

4. Identify Cause and Effect
Why did the Romans rebel against the Etruscans?

_____

_____

_____

_____

Think Critically

5. Contrast How did the Romans rule differently from the Etruscans?

_____

_____

_____

_____

_____

Becoming a Republic

The Etruscans ruled Rome for more than 100 years. The ruling family was named the Tarquins. The Romans benefited from Etruscan rule in many ways, but they got tired of Etruscan rulers. As a result, in 509 B.C., the Romans rebelled and set up a **republic.** A republic is a form of government in which leaders are elected.

Rome was still a small city when it became a republic. It had enemies all around it. Over the next 200 years, Rome fought many wars. By 267 B.C., the Romans had acquired, or taken over, the Greek colonies in what is now known as Italy. By 267 B.C., the Romans ruled almost all of the Italian peninsula.

The Romans were skilled soldiers. At the beginning of the republic, every male citizen who owned land had to join the army. Men who ran away, or deserted, were killed. This turned Romans into fighters who did not give up easily.

The Romans also thought of better ways to organize their army. For example, at first the Romans marched next to each other. They held their shields together to block enemy arrows and spears. This way of fighting was slow. Then, the generals divided their armies into smaller groups called **legions.** Each legion had about 6,000 men. Legions were broken into even smaller groups of 60 or 120 men. These small groups could move very quickly in battle.

Roman soldiers wore a plumed helmet, sandals, and a belt as part of their uniform.

Roman soldiers used a short sword called a gladius and a spear called a pilum. Each group also had a standard. A standard was a tall pole with a symbol on top—sometimes an eagle or other animal. One soldier would hold up the standard so others could see it. This helped the group stay together during battle.

The Romans were also smart planners. They built military towns everywhere they conquered. Then they built roads to these towns. Soon their armies could travel quickly across the land.

The Romans let some of the people they conquered become full citizens. They could vote and be in the government. They were also treated the same as other citizens by law.

The Romans made other people allies. Allies could run their own towns, but they had to pay taxes to Rome. Allies also had to fight in Rome's armies. The Romans let the allies know that if they were loyal, they might become citizens.

The Romans treated the people they conquered well. They stressed that people who are treated well do not rebel. If an area did rebel, Rome squashed it. As a result, the Roman republic grew stronger.

 NGSSS Check How did other civilizations influence the Romans? SS.6.G.2.1

_____

_____

Show Your Skill

6. Draw Conclusions How do you think the people conquered by the Romans felt about their new rulers?

_____

_____

_____

_____

Take the Challenge

7. In a small group, write a short skit about Rome after it became a republic. Perform the skit for the class.

SS.6.W.3.9 Explain the impact of the Punic Wars on the development of the Roman Empire.

SS.6.W.3.10 Describe the government of the Roman Republic and its contribution to the development of democratic principles (separation of powers, rule of law, representative government, civic duty).

SS.6.W.3.16 Compare life in the Roman Republic for patricians, plebeians, women, children, and slaves.

SS.6.C.1.2 Identify how the government of the Roman Republic contributed to the development of democratic principles (separation of powers, rule of law, representative government, civic duty).

LESSON 2 · ROME AS A REPUBLIC

Essential Question
How do governments change?

Guiding Questions
1. How did conflict between classes change Rome's government?
2. How did Rome conquer the Mediterranean region?

Terms to Know

patrician
a member of the ruling class

plebeian
ordinary citizen

consul
a head of the government

veto
to reject or say no to

praetor
government official who interprets the law and serves as a judge

tribune
an elected official who serves to protect the rights of ordinary citizens

dictator
a ruler with total control over a country

civic duty
the idea that people have a duty to help their country

Where in the World?

The Roman Republic

When Did It Happen?

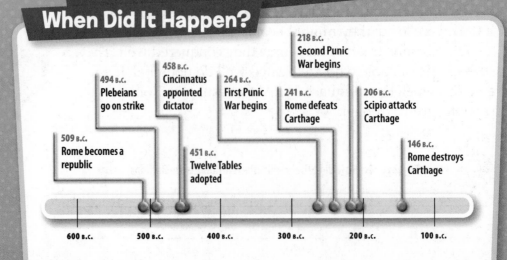

509 B.C.
Rome becomes a republic

494 B.C.
Plebeians go on strike

458 B.C.
Cincinnatus appointed dictator

451 B.C.
Twelve Tables adopted

264 B.C.
First Punic War begins

241 B.C.
Rome defeats Carthage

218 B.C.
Second Punic War begins

206 B.C.
Scipio attacks Carthage

146 B.C.
Rome destroys Carthage

600 B.C.   500 B.C.   400 B.C.   300 B.C.   200 B.C.   100 B.C.

Governing Rome

There were two main social classes in early Rome: **patrician** and **plebeian.** Patricians were wealthy landowners. They were nobles who held government offices. However, most people were plebeians—shopkeepers, artisans, and small farmers. Patricians and plebeians could not marry each other.

All patrician and plebeian men were citizens and had the right to vote. They had to pay taxes and join the army, but only patricians could be in the government.

The Roman government was designed to stop one part from getting too strong. The top government leaders were two **consuls** who served for one year. One consul headed the army. The other headed the rest of the government. If one consul made a bad decision, the other consul could **veto** it. This means they could reject the other person's decision.

Mark the Text

1. **Chart** Circle the two groups responsible for making laws.

Show Your Skill

2. **Make a Connection** What is one difference between the Roman government and the U.S. government?

_____

_____

_____

_____

_____

3. Do you think that the term that Senators served was valid? Why or why not?

_____

_____

_____

_____

_____

Rome's Republican Government			
Consul	Senate	Assembly of Centuries	Praetors
Head of military	Made laws	Made laws	Judges
Head of government	Advised consuls	Elected consuls	Interpreted laws
	Planned buildings		Led armies

The government of the Roman Republic also included **praetors** (or judges), tax collectors, and builders. Unlike judges in the United States today, Roman praetors could lead armies and help run the government.

Rome had two major legislative bodies, or groups that made laws. They were the Senate and the Assembly of Centuries. The 300 senators served for life. At first, they only advised the consuls. By the 200s B.C., the Senate passed laws and directed building programs. The Assembly of Centuries elected the consuls and praetors.

At first, only patrician men could be senators, assembly members, or consuls. Since the plebeians fought in the army and paid taxes, just like the patricians, they wanted equal rights.

Show Your Skill

4. Identify Cause and Effect
How did the Council of Plebs change things for the plebeians?

_____

_____

_____

_____

_____

Think Critically

5. Summarize What did dictators do in the early Roman Republic?

_____

_____

_____

_____

_____

_____

_____

As a result, in 494 B.C., the plebeians went on strike. They would not join the army. Many left Rome and set up their own government. The patricians were scared that the republic would collapse. In 474 B.C., the plebeians were given the right to set up the Council of Plebs and elect **tribunes.** The tribunes told the government what the plebeians thought about issues. The tribunes could also veto government decisions.

Soon, plebeians were allowed to become consuls. They were also allowed to marry patricians. In 287 B.C., the Council of Plebs could pass laws for all Romans. However, a few wealthy families still held most of the real power.

The Roman Republic included **dictators.** Today, a dictator is a cruel ruler who controls everything. In early Rome, the dictators were elected by the Senate when there was an emergency. As soon as the emergency ended, the dictator quit.

About 460 B.C., the Roman army was attacked. The Senators elected a farmer named Cincinnatus to be dictator. Cincinnatus had been a respected Roman consul. He was known for his loyalty to Rome. Cincinnatus gathered an army to help Rome. He and his army defeated the enemy quickly. Afterward, he went home to his farm. Cincinnatus was famous for doing his **civic duty** by serving his government when he was needed.

At first, Rome's laws were not written down. Plebeians thought that the judges agreed with the rich people too often. The plebeians demanded that the laws be written down. That way, everyone could know the laws and make sure the judges followed them.

In 451 B.C., the first code of laws was written down. The laws were called the Twelve Tables. They were based on the idea that all citizens should be treated equally under the law. All future Roman laws were based on the Twelve Tables.

Cincinnatus (left) was just a farmer, but the Senate elected him to serve as dictator. After he led his army to victory, he retired to his farm.

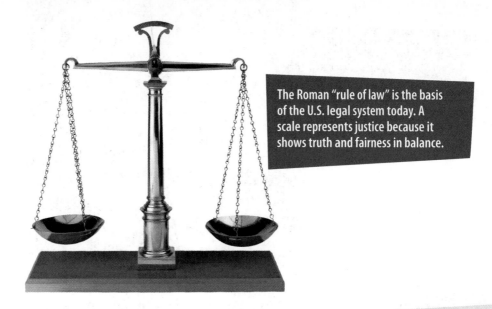

The Roman "rule of law" is the basis of the U.S. legal system today. A scale represents justice because it shows truth and fairness in balance.

The Twelve Tables were only for Roman citizens. When Rome began taking over other nations, they needed laws to protect people who were not citizens. They made a new set of laws called the Law of Nations.

The Law of Nations listed principles, or ideas, for justice. These ideas for justice were for everyone. We still use some of these ideas today. For example, the Law of Nations said that people are innocent until they are proven guilty. The Law of Nations said that judges had to study evidence before making decisions.

Rome's legal system assumed that the law should treat everyone equally. This is called "the rule of law." Many rich people did not like the rule of law. They were used to having special privileges. In fact, many rich people were not used to obeying the law at all. The rule of law made the rich respect the rights of the poor.

The Punic Wars

The Romans ruled most of Italy by 267 B.C. Rome wanted to control the trade routes, but so did an empire called Carthage.

Carthage was located on the coast of North Africa. It was the largest and richest city in the western Mediterranean. Carthage was built around 800 B.C. by the Phoenicians, who were skilled sailors and traders. Carthage soon became a great trading empire.

In 264 B.C., the conflict between Rome and Carthage intensified, or grew stronger. Rome and Carthage both wanted to rule the island of Sicily. Carthage already had colonies on Sicily.

Carthage was a sea power. In response, Rome built a navy. The Romans added one new thing, an innovation, to their navy ships. It was a bridge that could move. This allowed Roman soldiers to climb onto enemy ships quickly.

Show Your Skill

6. Draw Conclusions Why do you think rich Romans did not like the rule of law? How do you think poor Romans felt about it?

_____

_____

_____

_____

_____

_____

Take the Challenge

7. You are a news correspondent traveling with the Roman army during the First Punic War. Write a list of questions that you will pose to Roman soldiers.

Hannibal and his army were a mighty force. They crossed the Alps to fight the Roman army during the Second Punic War.

PHOTO: Look and Learn / The Bridgeman Art Library International

Copyright © by The McGraw-Hill Companies, Inc.

8. Sequence List the major events of the Punic Wars in chronological order.

_____

_____

_____

_____

_____

_____

_____

_____

_____

_____

_____

Show Your Skill

9. Identify Cause and Effect
What happened to Carthage after the Third Punic War?

_____

_____

_____

The First Punic War was fought between Rome and Carthage. This war lasted 20 years until Rome won in 241 B.C. Carthage had to leave Sicily and pay a huge fine to the Romans.

Carthage then conquered southern Spain. The Romans helped the people there rebel. In 218 B.C., Carthage sent their great general, Hannibal, to attack Rome. These events led to the Second Punic War.

Hannibal assembled about 46,000 men, horses, and several dozen elephants. He landed in Spain and marched them across the Alps and into Italy. Hannibal's army reached Italy in 216 B.C. They beat the Romans at Cannae and began raiding Italy. In response, the Roman general Scipio attacked Carthage in 206 B.C. Finally, Scipio's army beat Hannibal's forces. Carthage gave Spain to Rome. Carthage also had to give up its navy and pay another huge fine. Rome now ruled the western Mediterranean region.

Carthage was no longer a military power, but it was still a rich trading center. In 146 B.C., Roman soldiers burned the city to stop Carthage from getting stronger again. This led to the Third Punic War. After it was defeated for a third time, Carthage became a Roman province, or regional district. Many people in Carthage were enslaved.

In the 140s B.C., Rome conquered all of Greece. Rome also acquired, or got, its first province in Asia. Romans began to call the Mediterranean Sea *mare nostrum*, which means "our sea."

 NGSSS Check How was Rome's government set up? SS.6.W.3.10

_____

_____

_____

_____

LESSON

3 THE END OF THE REPUBLIC

NGSSS

SS.6.W.3.8 Determine the impact of significant figures associated with ancient Rome.

SS.6.W.3.11 Explain the transition from Roman Republic to empire and Imperial Rome, and compare Roman life and culture under each one.

Essential Question
Why does conflict develop?

Guiding Questions
1. What factors led to the decline of the Roman Republic?
2. How did Julius Caesar rise to power in Rome?
3. How did Rome become an empire?

Terms to Know

latifundia
large farming estates

triumvirate
three rulers who share power

Where in the World?
The Roman Empire

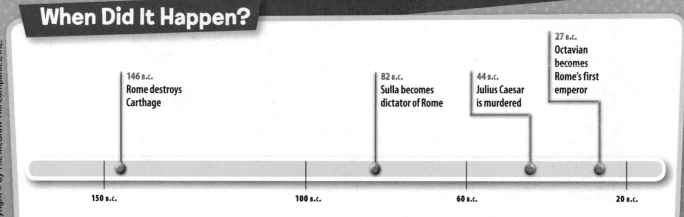

When Did It Happen?

146 B.C.
Rome destroys Carthage

82 B.C.
Sulla becomes dictator of Rome

44 B.C.
Julius Caesar is murdered

27 B.C.
Octavian becomes Rome's first emperor

150 B.C.   100 B.C.   60 B.C.   20 B.C.

Mark the Text ✏

1. Underline the meaning of *latifundia*.

Show Your Skill

2. Make Inferences Why did Marius make changes to the army?

_____

_____

_____

Think Critically

3. Defend Do you think it was fair that the Gracchus brothers were killed? Why or why not?

_____

_____

_____

Problems in the Republic

Even though Rome's armies were doing well, Rome had problems at home. By 100 B.C., the plebeian farmers were in trouble. Many could not work on their farms because they were in the army. Others watched Hannibal ruin their small farms.

At the same time, rich Romans were buying land. They formed large farming estates called **latifundia.** Enslaved people from Carthage worked the land. They were not paid any wages. As a result, the rich charged less for their crops than the plebeian farmers did. This caused the plebeian farmers to go out of business.

Many farmers sold their farms and went to the cities for work. Because enslaved people also did most of the work in the cities, jobs were hard to find. Pay was low. The plebeians became angry.

Roman politicians feared that the plebeians might riot. They gave the poor free food and shows, called "bread and circuses."

Two brothers—Tiberius and Gaius Gracchus—thought the poor should get their farms back. They asked the Senate to take some land from the rich and return it to the poor. Many Senators did not want to give up any of their land. In 133 B.C., some Senators killed Tiberius. Twelve years later, they killed Gaius.

In 107 B.C., a military leader named Marius became consul. Until then, only men who owned property served in the military. They did not get paid. Marius changed that. He paid the poor who had no land to serve as soldiers. He also promised to give his soldiers land.

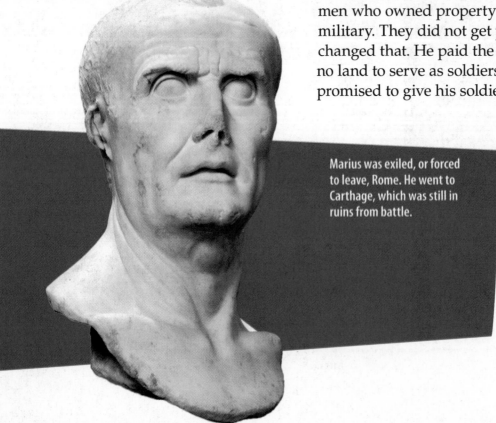

Marius was exiled, or forced to leave, Rome. He went to Carthage, which was still in ruins from battle.

By paying the soldiers, Marius made them professional fighters. The soldiers, however, no longer felt loyalty to Rome. They felt loyalty to the general who paid them. Having a loyal army gave a general power. Generals soon became powerful politicians. The generals wanted to keep their soldiers loyal. They worked to pass laws that gave the soldiers land. In 82 B.C., General Sulla forced Marius and other generals from Rome. He made himself dictator.

Over the next three years, Sulla made the Council of Plebs weaker and the Senate stronger. Then he retired. Sulla had shown other generals how to use their armies to grab political power. For the next 50 years, civil war tore Rome apart.

The Rise of Julius Caesar

By 60 B.C., three men emerged as the most powerful in Rome. They were three generals: Crassus, Pompey, and Julius Caesar. The three formed the First Triumvirate. A **triumvirate** is a political partnership of three people.

Each member of the triumvirate had a military command. Pompey led in Spain. Crassus led in Syria. Caesar led in Gaul. Caesar became a hero to Rome's lower classes. But the Senators thought that he was too popular. When Crassus was killed in 53 B.C., the senators gave Pompey complete control of Rome. Four years later, they ordered Caesar to give up his army. Caesar didn't want to obey the Senate. He knew his rivals might kill him. If he did not obey, then he knew he was starting a civil war against Rome.

Caesar kept his army and marched 5,000 soldiers into Italy. Pompey tried to stop Caesar. Caesar's forces drove Pompey's army out of Italy and into Greece. Then, in 48 B.C., Caesar's army destroyed Pompey's army completely. After that, the Senate named Caesar dictator of Rome, but just for one year.

Julius Caesar was made dictator of Rome in 46 B.C. and later crowned himself dictator for life.

Think Critically

4. Summarize Below are some people who lived when the Roman Republic was ending. List one accomplishment for each of them.

Marius

_____

_____

_____

_____

_____

Sulla

_____

_____

_____

_____

_____

_____

_____

Julius Caesar

_____

_____

_____

_____

_____

_____

_____

_____

_____

_____

6. Summarize What happened at the Battle of Actium?

_____

_____

_____

_____

_____

7. Evaluate At first, did Octavian's government reflect Cicero's ideas? Explain.

_____

_____

_____

_____

In 44 B.C., Caesar made himself dictator for life. He also filled the Senate with people who supported him. Caesar knew many reforms were needed. He freed men in Rome's territories. He started new colonies so that farmers and soldiers would have land. He forced patricians to hire free workers.

Caesar also created the Julian calendar. It had 12 months, 365 days, and a leap year. It was used in Europe until A.D. 1582. It was very close to our calendar today.

Caesar's supporters thought he was a strong leader who brought peace to Rome. His enemies thought that he wanted to be king. In Shakespeare's famous play *Julius Caesar*, Caesar was told to "beware the Ides of March" (March 15), but he did not. On March 15, 44 B.C., his enemies stabbed him to death. The enemies who were implicated in Caesar's death were led by Cassius and Brutus. Brutus had been Caesar's friend.

From Republic to Empire

After Caesar was killed, another civil war broke out. Octavian, Antony, and Lepidus won the civil war. Octavian was Caesar's grandnephew. Antony and Lepidus had been Caesar's best generals. In 43 B.C., they formed the Second Triumvirate.

Soon Octavian, Antony, and Lepidus were fighting with each other. Octavian forced Lepidus to retire. Then, Octavian and Antony divided the Roman world. Octavian took the west and Antony the east. While he was in the east, Antony fell in love with Cleopatra. She was an Egyptian queen. They made an alliance, agreeing to help each other. Octavian thought they wanted to take over Rome. He declared war against Antony and Cleopatra.

In 31 B.C., the forces of Antony and Cleopatra fought Octavian's forces at the Battle of Actium. Actium is off the west coast of Greece. Octavian's forces crushed Antony and Cleopatra's army and navy. Antony and Cleopatra returned to Egypt and later killed themselves. Their deaths ended Rome's civil war. The Roman Republic died with them. Octavian was 32 years old, and he became the sole, or only, ruler of the Roman world. He decided to build a different kind of government—the Roman Empire.

Octavian knew that many people wanted a republic. They wanted to be able to vote for their leaders. Cicero agreed. Cicero was a Roman writer, political leader, and speaker. Many people read Cicero's books and heard him speak. Cicero supported Octavian. He thought that Octavian would rebuild the republic.

Cicero died before Octavian rose to power. Octavian said he supported a republic. However, Octavian knew that the republic was too weak to solve Rome's problems. He decided to keep most of the power for himself. The Senate agreed, knowing Octavian had a strong and loyal army.

Octavian took the title *Augustus. Augustus* means "the majestic one." After that, all the Romans called him Caesar Augustus.

Show Your Skill

8. Interpret Diagrams How did Julius Caesar's death eventually lead to Octavian becoming emperor of Rome?

_____

_____

_____

_____

_____

_____

Caesar's death

↓

Civil War

↓

Second Triumvirate

↓

Battle of Actium

↓

Antony and Cleopatra die

↓

Octavian becomes emperor

Take the Challenge

9. What if Cleopatra and Antony had not killed themselves after the Battle of Actium? What if they had taken over Rome? Write a new ending.

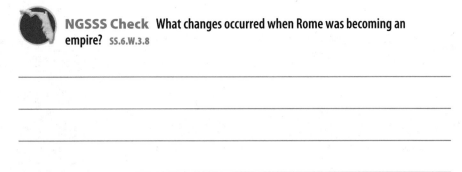

NGSSS Check What changes occurred when Rome was becoming an empire? **SS.6.W.3.8**

_____

_____

_____

_____

4 ROME BUILDS AN EMPIRE

NGSSS

SS.6.W.3.8 Determine the impact of significant figures associated with ancient Rome.

SS.6.W.3.11 Explain the transition from Roman Republic to empire and Imperial Rome, and compare Roman life and culture under each one.

SS.6.W.3.12 Explain the causes for the growth and longevity of the Roman Empire.

Essential Question

What are the characteristics of a leader?

Guiding Questions

1. How did Augustus create a new age of prosperity for Rome?
2. How did the Roman Empire become rich and prosperous?

Terms to Know

Pax Romana
Roman peace; a long period of peace and prosperity in Roman history

proconsul
Roman governor

Where in the World?

Rome: A.D. 200

When Did It Happen?

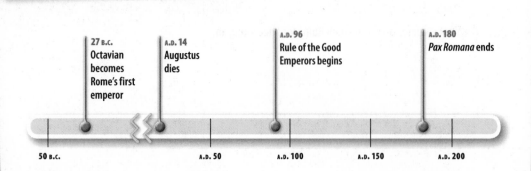

27 B.C.
Octavian becomes Rome's first emperor

A.D. 14
Augustus dies

A.D. 96
Rule of the Good Emperors begins

A.D. 180
Pax Romana ends

50 B.C.   A.D. 50   A.D. 100   A.D. 150   A.D. 200

The Rule of Augustus

For hundreds of years, there had been fighting in the area around the Mediterranean Sea. Augustus (formerly called Octavian) ended the fighting. He took control of the whole area. That brought **Pax Romana,** or the "Roman peace." This peace lasted about 200 years.

Augustus wanted to make the empire strong and safe. He made a professional army of about 150,000 Roman citizens. Augustus also made the Praetorian Guard, which had about 9,000 men. These men were specially picked to guard the emperor.

Augustus wanted Rome's borders to be easier to defend. He set the empire's borders along natural boundaries. The empire's northern and eastern boundaries were along rivers. The Atlantic Ocean was the western boundary. The southern boundary was the Sahara.

At the same time, Augustus built beautiful buildings out of marble. Augustus also distributed, or handed out, grain from Africa to the poor. He knew that well-fed people do not rebel as much as hungry people.

At that time, more than 50 million people lived in the Roman Empire. The Empire was divided into provinces. Augustus appointed a **proconsul,** or governor, for each province. He visited the provinces often to inspect the proconsuls' work.

He changed the tax laws and made tax collectors government workers. This stopped them from taking some of the taxes for themselves. He also made a set of laws for free men who were not citizens. This meant that Roman laws protected everyone. Many of these free men later became citizens.

Octavian, or Caesar Augustus, had political ties to Rome, as his great-uncle was Julius Caesar.

Mark the Text

1. Underline how long the *Pax Romana* lasted.

Think Critically

2. **Infer** Why do you think Augustus divided the empire into provinces?

_____

_____

_____

_____

_____

3. **Analyze** How were there free men in Rome who were not citizens?

_____

_____

_____

_____

4. Identify the Main Idea What did all five of the Good Emperors build?

_____

_____

_____

_____

Mark the Text ✏

5. Underline the two disasters that struck while Titus ruled Rome.

Take the Challenge

6. Choose one of the Five Good Emperors to research. Write 10 facts about him and his contributions to Rome on blank index cards. Write the emperor's name on the other side of the card. Work with two other students who researched different emperors and play a game to guess which fact describes the correct emperor.

Augustus ruled for almost 40 years. He died in A.D. 14. A relative named Tiberius was his successor. This means he became emperor after Augustus. The next three emperors—Caligula, Claudius, and Nero—were also relatives. They are called the Julio-Claudian emperors.

Not all of them were good rulers. Tiberius and Claudius were capable—they ruled well. In contrast, Caligula and Nero were very cruel. Caligula had people killed, wasted a lot of money, and even made his horse a consul. Eventually, the Praetorian Guard killed him and made Claudius emperor. Nero also killed many people, including his mother and two wives. He finally killed himself.

The Roman Peace

A general named Vespasian restored peace. He also began building the Colosseum, a huge stadium in the middle of Rome. Vespasian stopped several rebellions. In addition, in A.D. 70 his son, Titus, led an army that defeated the Jews. The Romans destroyed the Jewish temple in Jerusalem.

After Vespasian died, Titus ruled. Two disasters struck when Titus ruled. First, the volcano Mount Vesuvius erupted and buried the city of Pompeii. Second, a large fire burned Rome.

After Titus, Vespasian's other son, Domitian, ruled. Both of Vespasian's sons helped Rome to grow.

From A.D. 96 to A.D. 180, a series of "good emperors" came to power. They were Nerva, Trajan, Hadrian, Antoninus Pius, and Marcus Aurelius. During their rule, trade grew and people enjoyed a better life.

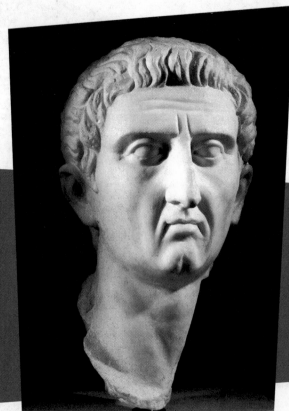

The first of the "Five Good Emperors" was Nerva, who served for only about 16 months before his death.

The Five Good Emperors ruled wisely. Trajan gave money to the poor. Hadrian made the laws easier to understand. Antoninus Pius passed laws to help orphans. All five built roads, bridges, monuments, harbors, and aqueducts. An aqueduct is a channel that carries water for long distances.

The empire was biggest in size when Trajan ruled. It spread from the Mediterranean to Britain and Mesopotamia. This made the empire too big to rule well. Hadrian pulled troops out of Mesopotamia. He made the empire's boundaries at the Rhine and the Danube Rivers stronger. Hadrian also built Hadrian's Wall in northern Britain to stop the Picts and Scots from attacking. The Picts and Scots were warrior tribes in Britain.

In the A.D. 100s, the Roman Empire was one of the greatest empires in history. It had 3.5 million square miles (9.06 million square km) of land. The empire held together because people thought of themselves as Romans. Even if they spoke different languages, they had the same laws and rulers. They had many of the same customs, too. Soldiers and government workers brought Roman culture to different parts of the empire. In addition, the Romans gave many people the rights of being a citizen. In A.D. 212, every free man was made a Roman citizen.

Agriculture was the most important part of the empire's economy. Farmers in Italy, Gaul (France), and Spain grew grapes and olives. Making wine and olive oil became big business. Farmers in Britain and Egypt grew grains.

There was industry with potters, weavers, and jewelers. Some cities became centers for making glass, bronze, and brass.

Emperor Hadrian was fascinated by Greek civilization. His interest in travel resulted in numerous journeys throughout the empire.

Think Critically

7. Infer What was the most important part of Rome's economy? Why?

_____

_____

_____

Summarizing

8. What did all people throughout the Roman Empire share?

_____

_____

_____

Think Critically

9. Explain List three products that traders brought into Rome's ports.

_____

_____

_____

_____

Antoninus Pius and Marcus Aurelius were the last two "good emperors." Pius initiated some important social reforms, while Aurelius introduced economic and government reforms.

Traders came from all over the world to ports in Italy. They brought silk from China, spices from India, tin from Britain, lead from Spain, and iron from Gaul.

The Roman Empire had a good transportation system. This helped grow trade. During the *Pax Romana*, the empire had 50,000 miles (80,467 km) of roads. The Roman navy kept pirates off the Mediterranean Sea. This made it safer for ships to bring goods in and out of the empire's ports.

By A.D. 100, everyone in the empire used a common currency, or money. This made it easy to trade. It meant that a merchant in Greece could sell to a person in Italy or Egypt.

The Romans also made a system of weights and measures. People knew how much they were selling and buying. This made trade easier, too.

Shopkeepers and merchants lived well during this time, and so did skilled workers who made things. Rich Romans made bigger fortunes. However, most people in the cities and on the farms were still poor. Many other people were still enslaved.

NGSSS Check Why did the Roman Empire last so long? Give reasons to support your answer. SS.6.W.3.12

_____

_____

_____

_____

ESSENTIAL QUESTION *What are the characteristics of a leader?*

Reflect on What It Means . . .

Ancient Rome grew from a republic to an empire in about 500 years. During the rule of Augustus, Rome experienced the *Pax Romana,* which lasted for about 200 years. Then Rome became an empire and went on to have other good emperors. Think about the characteristics that make a great leader in your community and in our world today.

My Community

Research a leader in your community whom you respect. Write down the characteristics that you list about him or her. Include that person's major contributions to the community. Glue or tape a picture of the leader next to what you wrote.

The World

Research a leader in the world whom you respect. Write down the characteristics that you list about him or her. Include that person's major contributions to the world. Glue or tape a picture of the leader next to what you wrote.

Keep Going! ➤➤

To Me

Write down the characteristics that you have or want to have to make you a great leader. Include any contributions that you have made or want to make to your community or world. Glue or tape a picture of yourself next to what you wrote.

TAKE THE CHALLENGE

Write five questions that you would like to ask the community or world leader that you chose. Then, with a partner, take turns role-playing the interviewer and the leader. You may need to do additional research to find out how the leader might respond to your questions.

ROMAN CIVILIZATION

NGSSS

SS.6.W.3.14 Describe the key achievements and contributions of Roman civilization.

ESSENTIAL QUESTIONS *What makes a culture unique? Why do civilizations rise and fall?*

Horace was a Roman poet who lived and wrote during the time of Augustus Caesar, the first Roman emperor. This excerpt is translated from *The Works of Horace.*

" It is not enough that poems be beautiful; let them be tender and affecting, and bear away the soul of the auditor [wherever] they please."

HORACE

auditor

Auditor has multiple meanings. Using context clues, what do you think it means?

_____

_____

bear away the soul

Horace thinks that poetry should transport the imagination of a listener to a new place in their minds. What poem or song has had that effect on you?

DBQ BREAKING IT DOWN

Why does Horace think that poems need to do more than be beautiful? What is their real purpose, according to him?

_____

_____

_____

McGraw-Hill
networks™
The eNetworks online!

PHOTO: PRISMA ARCHIVO/Alamy

1 THE ROMAN WAY OF LIFE

NGSSS

SS.6.W.3.14 Describe the key achievements and contributions of Roman civilization.

SS.6.W.3.16 Compare life in the Roman Republic for patricians, plebeians, women, children, and slaves.

Essential Question
What makes a culture unique?

Guiding Questions
1. What was daily life like for the Romans?
2. How did the Greeks influence Roman culture?

Terms to Know

gladiator
a person who fought people and animals for public entertainment

satire
writing that pokes fun at human weaknesses

ode
poem that expresses strong emotions about life

vault
a curved ceiling

anatomy
the body's structure

Where in the World?

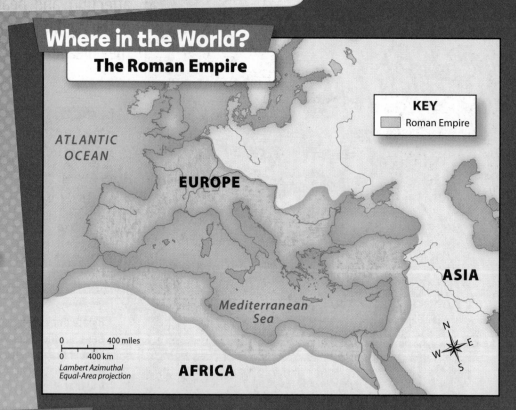

The Roman Empire

When Did It Happen?

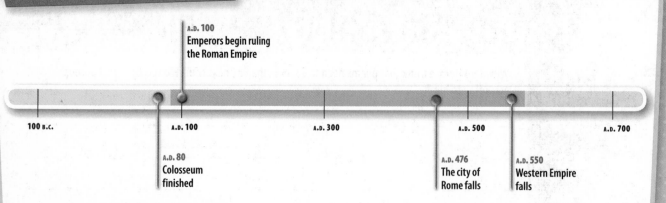

A.D. 100
Emperors begin ruling the Roman Empire

A.D. 80
Colosseum finished

A.D. 476
The city of Rome falls

A.D. 550
Western Empire falls

Daily Life

Many Romans lived in big cities that were centers of business, culture, and government. Rome was one of the largest and most carefully planned cities in the ancient world. It had a public square called the Forum. Romans shopped, conducted business, played games, and visited with friends in this area. Temples and other public buildings surrounded the Forum.

Wealthy people lived in big houses built around courtyards. Most Romans were poor and did unskilled labor. They lived in apartment buildings. Those neighborhoods were crowded, noisy, and dirty.

Politicians offered free entertainment and food to get the support of the poor. People watched chariots race. They also watched **gladiators** fight. Gladiators fought each other or even wild animals to entertain the crowds.

Roman Men

- Heads of household
- Responsible for their children's education
- Responsible for the family business
- Could work outside the home
- Could own property

Roman Women

- Not full citizens
- Had strong influence on their families
- Did the housework
- Could work in the family's business
- Few worked outside their homes

Roman families were large and included relatives and enslaved servants. Fathers had complete control over their families. They could even sell their children into slavery. Children of wealthy families received an education. Sons went to school to learn reading, writing, math, and rhetoric, or public speaking. Children of poor families could not afford to go to school. Many poor people learned only enough reading, writing, and math to help them conduct business.

Wives of wealthy, powerful men had more freedom than those who were less fortunate. They could own land. They could hire enslaved people to do their housework, so they had free time to study art and literature, and go out for entertainment. Women with little money generally had to work and take care of their households.

Think Critically

1. Explain What did politicians do to make people like them?

_____

_____

_____

Show Your Skill

2. Compare and Contrast How was the life of upper-class women alike and different from the life of women in other classes?

_____

_____

_____

_____

_____

_____

_____

Mark the Text

3. Underline the phrase that explains why wives of wealthy men had time for studying art and for entertainment.

5. Compare and Contrast How were satires different from odes?

_____

_____

_____

_____

The use of enslaved persons in Rome became more common as the empire grew larger. Most enslaved people were prisoners of war. They worked in homes and on farms. They also helped build roads, bridges, and buildings.

Romans believed that gods and spirits controlled all parts of life. Greek gods and goddesses were popular in Rome, but the Romans gave them new names. The Roman Senate declared that the emperors were gods. The Romans worshiped their gods by praying and offering food to them.

Romans borrowed ideas such as Stoicism from the Greeks and changed them to fit their culture. For Greeks, Stoicism meant finding happiness through reason. For the Romans, it meant living in a practical way. Roman Stoics urged people to do their civic duty and participate in government. These ideas are still important to us today.

Science and Art

The Romans used many features of Greek writing, art, and architecture, but changed them to fit Roman style. Like the Greeks, Roman artists created statues. Greek statues showed perfect and beautiful people. Roman statues, on the other hand, showed people that looked more realistic.

Greeks	Romans
believed in gods and goddesses	gave Greek gods and goddesses new names
Stoicism taught people to find happiness through reason.	Stoicism taught people to do their duties as citizens and participate in government.
Statues made people look perfect and beautiful.	Realistic statues showed details like warts and wrinkles.
Writers honored their gods and praised their generals' successes.	Writers wrote comedies about their gods' mistakes. Writers also wrote about the failures of their generals.

Some Roman writers based their work on Greek models. The Roman poet Virgil borrowed some of the ideas for his poem the _Aeneid_ from the Greek poem called the _Odyssey_. The poet Horace based his **satires** and **odes** on Greek works. Satires poke fun at human weakness, like comedians do today. He also wrote odes, which are poems that express strong emotions about life.

The Romans were not the first builders of aqueducts, but theirs are probably the most famous. This ancient Roman aqueduct still stands in present-day Segovia, Spain.

Other Romans wrote plays about the gods. Unlike the Greek plays, however, Roman plays showed that the gods sometimes made mistakes.

Romans added new ideas and style to Greek architecture, too. Architecture is the art of making structures, such as buildings. The Romans built with concrete and added arches, or curved supports. By putting many arches together, they could form a **vault,** or curved ceiling. Curved ceilings created beautiful domes to build large, open rooms.

Romans also learned science from the Greeks. They read books written by a Greek doctor named Galen. Galen studied **anatomy** to learn about the body's structure. Doctors today still study anatomy to help people live better lives.

Roman engineers built practical things such as bridges, buildings, and roads. Roman roads connected the city of Rome to every part of the empire. The road system allowed soldiers to travel quickly. Many other people traveled along the roads and their ideas spread to the people they met. Traders used the roads so trade grew. The Romans also built aqueducts that carried fresh water into the cities.

The Romans influenced future generations in many ways. A number of Roman aqueducts are still standing. Concrete and other elements of Roman architecture are still used today. Latin, the language of the Romans, also influenced others. Until about A.D. 1500, Latin was the official language of European government, trade, and learning. It became the basis of many modern languages, such as Italian, French, and Spanish.

 NGSSS Check List three things the Romans borrowed from the Greeks and then adapted to meet their needs. SS.6.W.3.14

_____

_____

Show Your Skill

7. Make a Connection Where are arches and domes used today?

_____

_____

_____

8. Identify the Main Idea What was the relationship between Greek and Roman ideas?

_____

_____

_____

Mark the Text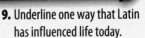

9. Underline one way that Latin has influenced life today.

2 ROME'S DECLINE

NGSSS

SS.6.W.3.15 Explain the reasons for the gradual decline of the Western Roman Empire after the Pax Romana.

Essential Question

Why do civilizations rise and fall?

Guiding Questions

1. What problems led to Rome's decline?
2. What effect did Germanic invaders have on the Roman Empire?
3. What are the key achievements and contributions of Roman civilization?

Terms to Know

reforms
political changes to bring about improvement

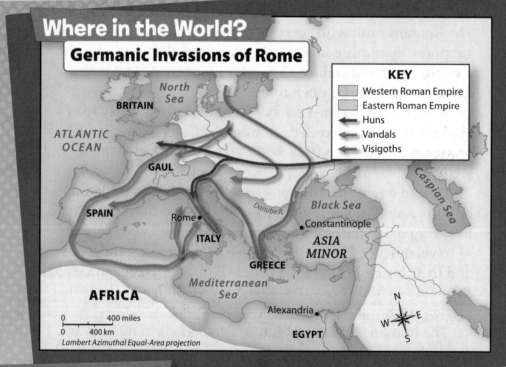

Where in the World?

Germanic Invasions of Rome

KEY
- Western Roman Empire
- Eastern Roman Empire
- → Huns
- → Vandals
- → Visigoths

North Sea
BRITAIN
ATLANTIC OCEAN
GAUL
SPAIN
Rome
ITALY
Danube R.
GREECE
Black Sea
Constantinople
ASIA MINOR
Caspian Sea
Mediterranean Sea
AFRICA
Alexandria
EGYPT

0   400 miles
0   400 km
Lambert Azimuthal Equal-Area projection

When Did It Happen?

The Roman Empire declines

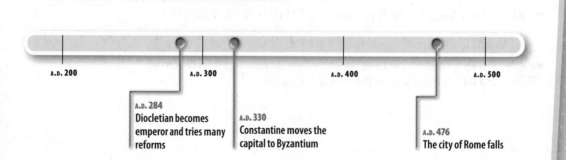

A.D. 200   A.D. 300   A.D. 400   A.D. 500

A.D. 284
Diocletian becomes emperor and tries many reforms

A.D. 330
Constantine moves the capital to Byzantium

A.D. 476
The city of Rome falls

A Troubled Empire

The peace of the *Pax Romana* was followed by a century of confusion and violence. The Roman government grew weak and the army grew strong and independent. The legions of the army fought each other to put new emperors on the throne. Rome had 22 emperors in a period of 50 years.

This period of civil war caused great suffering. Attacks on farms meant ruined crops and that meant less food. People grew hungry and sick.

The Roman economy suffered, too. People lost their jobs. Many Romans stopped paying taxes. The government tried to fix the economy by making more and more new coins. These new coins had less value, so it cost more to buy goods. This is called inflation. Inflation happens when prices go up and money is worth less and less. To get what they needed, people began to barter. Instead of using money, they traded one product or service for another.

As Rome struggled, Germanic tribes began to attack the empire. The Romans built walls around their cities for protection. The Roman government hired Germanic soldiers for the Roman army, but these soldiers felt no loyalty to Rome.

Diocletian became emperor in A.D. 284. He tried to strengthen the empire by making many **reforms,** or changes to make things better. Diocletian was too weak to make people obey his new laws so his reforms did not work.

Copyright © by The McGraw-Hill Companies, Inc.

Diocletian's Reforms	Reasons
built forts on borders	for defense
split empire's rule among 4 emperors	to make it easier to rule
set prices and wages	to stop inflation
ordered workers to keep their jobs until they died	to improve productivity
made officials responsible for local taxes	to make sure taxes were paid

Show Your Skill

1. Compare and Contrast Is there a difference between bartering and trading?

_____

_____

_____

_____

Mark the Text

2. Chart Circle the three reforms that Diocletian made to help Rome's economy.

Show Your Skill

3. Identify Cause and Effect Why did Diocletian's reforms fail?

_____

_____

_____

_____

Think Critically

6. Analyze Why do historians consider A.D. 476 an important date?

_____

_____

_____

The Fall of Rome

The next emperor was Constantine. He tried to make Diocletian's reforms work so the empire would grow strong again. Constantine made the military stronger. Nothing seemed to help Rome improve. In A.D. 330, he moved the capital from Rome to Byzantium in the east. Then he changed the name of the new capital to Constantinople. That name lasted many years. Today the city is known as Istanbul. Constantine's reforms helped the empire, but not enough. The western part kept getting worse.

In A.D. 337, Constantine died. People began fighting all over the empire. The next emperor, Theodosius, stopped this trouble. He knew that the empire had grown too big to rule. When Theodosius died, he left a will that instructed the Romans to divide their empire. When the Romans divided the empire, they also divided the army. The western half of the empire was now too weak to stop invaders.

In the A.D. 300s and A.D. 400s, many Germanic tribes took over Roman land. Some wanted better land for raising crops and farm animals. A tribe called the Visigoths feared another tribe, the Huns. The Visigoths asked Rome for protection. Later, the Romans treated the Visigoths badly so the tribe fought back. The Visigoths captured Rome in A.D. 419.

Then the Vandals invaded the Western Roman Empire. They burned buildings and took valuable things. When the Huns attacked, the Vandals helped the Romans drive them out. Some of the Vandals earned jobs in the government and the army. In A.D. 476, a Germanic general named Odoacer overthrew the emperor. He took control of Rome. This was the end of the Western Roman Empire.

The Fall of Rome

Constantine moves capital from Rome to Byzantium, A.D. 330 → Constantine dies, A.D. 337 → Roman Empire and Roman army are divided, A.D. 395 → Germanic tribes take Roman lands, A.D. 300s–400s → Visigoths capture Rome, A.D. 419 → Odoacer overthrows Roman emperor, A.D. 476

Rome's Legacies

How have Roman ideas influenced our lives today? We still read Roman literature. Modern buildings use Roman arches, domes, and concrete.

We share Roman ideas about justice and the law. Like the Romans, we believe that everyone is equal under the law and that a person is innocent until proven guilty. We also believe that judges should decide court cases fairly.

Our government, too, is similar to the Roman republic. In a republic, citizens elect their leaders. As in Rome, our republic works best when citizens get involved.

The Romans also influenced how we speak. Latin shaped many European languages. Many English words have Latin roots. We use the Latin alphabet. Doctors, lawyers, and scientists use Latin phrases in their work. All plant and animal species have Latin names.

One of the world's major religions, Christianity, began in the Roman Empire. It spread with the help of the Roman road system. When Roman emperors adopted Christianity in the A.D. 300s, they also helped spread the new religion.

The first road that the Romans built was the *Via Appia*, which started in Rome and ended in southern Italy.

 NGSSS Check Connect the boxes with arrows in the correct historical order. Hint: The letters are not in order. SS.6.W.3.15

Mark the Text

7. Highlight the Roman ideas that tell how the language of the Romans influenced languages used today.

Take the Challenge

8. With a partner, research words with Latin roots. See how many you can find!

a. **Diocletian and Constantine make changes.**

b. **Foreign tribes move into the empire.**

1. **START Rome's government weakens.**

e. **Empire divides, making each army smaller.**

f. **Visigoths defeat Roman legions and capture Rome.**

The Roman Empire falls! END

c. **Emperor overthrown.**

d. **Vandals invade, taking valuables and burning buildings.**

CHAPTER 12 MY REFLECTIONS

ESSENTIAL QUESTION ***Why do civilizations rise and fall?***

Reflect on What It Means . . .

Ancient Roman civilization came to an end when Rome fell in A.D. 476. However, the legacies that Rome left behind continue to remind us of this great civilization. Use what you learned in this chapter as well as what you can observe around you. What evidence of Roman civilization influences your life, your community, and the world today? List or draw examples in each column of the chart below.

Me	My Community	The World

TAKE THE CHALLENGE

Write a different ending to the fall of Roman civilization. You may decide that it should have continued or had fallen in a different way. Share your ending with the class.

THE RISE OF CHRISTIANITY

NGSSS

SS.6.W.3.13 Identify key figures and the basic beliefs of early Christianity and how these beliefs impacted the Roman Empire.

ESSENTIAL QUESTIONS *What are the characteristics of a leader? How do religions develop?*

Paul was an apostle. He spread Christian teachings through Judaea and Galilee. In this excerpt from Romans in the New Testament of the Christian Bible, Paul writes:

"I hope to visit you while passing through and to have you assist me on my journey there, after I have enjoyed your company for a while. Now, however, I am on my way to Jerusalem in the service of the saints there. For Macedonia and Achaia were pleased to make a contribution for the poor among the saints in Jerusalem."

ROMANS 15:24–26

journey

Do you think that Paul is referring to a trip or something else?

_____

_____

_____

PHOTO: SuperStock/Getty Images

S·PAVLVS·

DBQ BREAKING IT DOWN

Whom is Paul speaking to in these verses from the Bible? What is his purpose?

_____

_____

McGraw-Hill
networks™
There's More Online!

LESSON 1

EARLY CHRISTIANITY

NGSSS

SS.6.W.3.13 Identify key figures and the basic beliefs of early Christianity and how these beliefs impacted the Roman Empire.

Essential Question
What are the characteristics of a leader?

Guiding Questions
1. How did the Jews respond to Roman rule?
2. Why were the life and death of Jesus of Nazareth important to his followers?
3. How did early Christianity spread throughout the Roman Empire?

Terms to Know

parables
short stories that help people understand difficult ideas

resurrection
coming back from the dead

apostle
a Christian leader who spread the message of Jesus

salvation
the act of being saved from the effects of wrongdoing

Where in the World?

The Mediterranean Region

When Did It Happen?

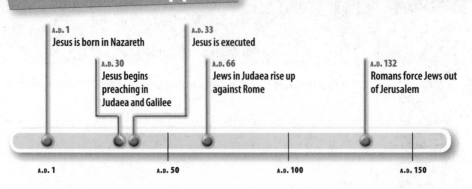

A.D. 1 Jesus is born in Nazareth

A.D. 30 Jesus begins preaching in Judaea and Galilee

A.D. 33 Jesus is executed

A.D. 66 Jews in Judaea rise up against Rome

A.D. 132 Romans force Jews out of Jerusalem

A.D. 1   A.D. 50   A.D. 100   A.D. 150

Judaism and Rome

The Roman Empire allowed Jews to practice their religion. However, in Judaea and Galilee, the Romans made life very difficult for Jews. The Romans replaced the Jewish king with a Roman governor. Many Jews hoped a leader would come along to free them from Roman rule.

The Jews who lived in Judaea and Galilee had different ways of dealing with the Romans. Some Jews simply avoided the Romans as best they could. Other Jews tried to get along with the Romans. Still others set up their own communities where they could practice their beliefs without Roman interference.

One group of Jews wanted to fight the Romans in order to win their freedom. These Jews were called Zealots. In A.D. 66 they rose up against the Romans. Four years later, the Zealots took over an ancient mountain fort called Masada. For about two years, the Zealots held off a powerful Roman army. Eventually the Romans defeated the Zealots.

As a result of the rebellion, the Romans burned down the Jewish temple in Jerusalem. The Romans also killed thousands of Jews. In A.D. 132 the Jews once again rose up against the Roman rulers. Once again they were defeated. This time the Romans drove the Jews out of Jerusalem and told them they could never return. The Jews continued to practice their religion. They established communities in other parts of the world. By A.D. 700 there were Jews living in Spain and Central Asia. In later centuries, they settled in Europe and the Americas.

Show Your Skill

1. Identify Cause and Effect
What did the Romans do to the Jews after the Jews rebelled?

_____

_____

_____

_____

Think Critically

2. Explain Who were the Zealots?

_____

_____

_____

Take the Challenge

3. Research to learn more about Masada. Write a short essay that explains how the Zealots were able to hold off the Roman army.

The Masada fortress sits atop a rock cliff. It overlooks the Judaean Desert and Dead Sea.

PHOTO: Sylvester Adams/Photodisc/Getty Images

Copyright © by The McGraw-Hill Companies, Inc.

Show Your Skill

5. Make Inferences Why do you think Jesus traveled to Jerusalem when there was already so much tension between the Romans and the Jews?

_____

_____

_____

Think Critically

6. Analyze Why did some Jews not support Jesus and his teachings?

_____

_____

_____

Jesus of Nazareth

Jesus was born in the small town of Nazareth in Galilee. In about A.D. 30 he began to preach in Galilee and Judaea. He traveled with a group of close followers called disciples. Jesus was born and raised in a Jewish family. His teachings drew upon his understanding of the Jewish religion. Jesus often taught using **parables,** short stories that made his ideas easier to understand. He taught that people should love God and that God loved people the way a father loves his children.

This painting from the nineteenth century depicts Jesus teaching on the seashore.

Jesus also preached that God was coming soon to rule the world. For this reason, Jesus wanted people to do more than follow the laws of their religion. He told them they must also love one another just as God loved them. His message did not go against the Jewish religion. Instead, it upheld the main beliefs of this religion. It also gave people a new way of practicing their religion.

Not everyone agreed with Jesus. The Romans saw him as a threat to their power and the system of government they had set up. This was because more and more people began to believe in what Jesus was saying. The more his influence grew, the more dangerous he became in the eyes of Roman rulers.

On the Jewish holy day of Passover, Jesus traveled with his disciples to the city of Jerusalem. By this time, there was much tension between the Jews and the Romans. Many Jews refused to worship Roman gods or to treat the Roman emperor like a god. The Romans feared that this growing tension could lead to an uprising. When Jesus and his disciples entered Jerusalem, a large crowd greeted him. By now he had become very popular, even though some Jews did not support him.

Jesus celebrated the Passover meal with his disciples. This event has come to be known as the Last Supper. After the meal, leaders in Jerusalem arrested Jesus. By arresting him, they thought they would keep the tension in the city from boiling over. Jesus was accused of disloyalty to the Roman government. He was sentenced to death by crucifixion. This meant he would be hung from a wooden cross until he died.

According to Christian belief, three days after Jesus died, he rose from the dead and appeared to some of his followers. The disciples of Jesus still thought of themselves as Jews. However, the message of his **resurrection,** or coming back from the dead, led to the birth of Christianity.

Who Were the Apostles?

The **apostles** were early Christian leaders who spread the teachings of Jesus after his death. They traveled through Judaea and Galilee and spoke mainly to other Jews. Later they went to other parts of the Mediterranean region. They taught both Jews and non-Jews. People who accepted these teachings and believed in Jesus came to be known as Christians.

Early Christians met in people's homes. They prayed and studied the Hebrew Bible. These gatherings were the first churches. Two of the most influential leaders of the early Christian church were Peter and Paul. Peter was one of the 12 disciples of Jesus. Before becoming a disciple, he had been a fisher in Galilee. According to Christian tradition, after Jesus died, Peter went to Rome and set up a Christian church.

Paul was an educated Jew. At first, he tried to stop Christianity from spreading. Then one day, according to Christian writings, Paul saw a great light and heard the voice of Jesus. This happened while he was traveling to the city of Damascus in Syria. The experience changed his mind about the new religion. Paul became a Christian and spent the rest of his life spreading the message of Jesus.

Christianity grew out of the Jewish religion. Both religions believe in the God of Israel and draw their teachings from the Hebrew Bible. However, many Christian beliefs are different from Jewish teachings. For example, Christians believe that Jesus is the Son of God. Jews do not. Many Christians also believe that God exists as three persons—Father, Son, and Holy Spirit. The three persons of God are known as the Trinity. Another important difference is the belief in **salvation.** Christians believe that people who accept Jesus will be saved from the consequences of their wrongdoing. After they die, they will go to heaven and one day be resurrected the way Jesus was.

NGSSS Check Who were two early Christian leaders, and how did they help spread Christian teachings? SS.6.W.3.13

_____

_____

_____

Mark the Text

7. Underline the term that explains what led to the birth of Christianity.

Think Critically

8. **Explain** What happened to Paul that made him become a Christian?

_____

_____

_____

_____

_____

Show Your Skill

9. **Compare and Contrast** How are Judaism and Christianity alike and different?

_____

_____

_____

_____

_____

_____

_____

_____

NGSSS

SS.6.W.3.13 Identify key figures and the basic beliefs of early Christianity and how these beliefs impacted the Roman Empire.

Essential Question
How do religions develop?

Guiding Questions
1. How did Christianity change over time?
2. How did early Christians organize their church and explain their beliefs?

Terms to Know

martyr
someone who is willing to die rather than give up his or her beliefs

hierarchy
an organization with different levels of authority

clergy
church officials

doctrine
official church teaching

gospel
an account of the life and teaching of Jesus

pope
a special title for the bishop of Rome, who is the head of the Roman Catholic Church

laity
regular church members

When Did It Happen?

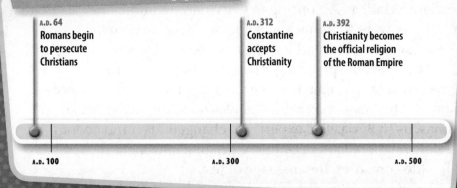

A.D. 64
Romans begin to persecute Christians

A.D. 312
Constantine accepts Christianity

A.D. 392
Christianity becomes the official religion of the Roman Empire

A.D. 100   A.D. 300   A.D. 500

What Do You Know?

Directions: Write your answers to the questions based on what you know now in the "Now" column. After the lesson, complete the "Later" column.

	Now	Later
Why do you think the Romans punished people who became Christians?		
How were Christians able to pass on the teachings of Jesus after his death?		

Christianity and the Empire

The first followers of Jesus brought his teachings to Jews and non-Jews in the Mediterranean region. From there Christianity spread throughout the Roman Empire. This happened for many reasons. Rome established law and order in the lands it controlled. It also created a network of roads that made long-distance travel fairly safe and easy. The people who lived under Roman rule spoke either Latin or Greek. This meant that Christians generally had little trouble sharing their ideas.

Another important reason for the spread of Christianity was its appeal. The old Roman religion, with its many gods, had nothing to offer people whose lives were hard. Christianity, however, promised a better life after death. It gave people hope, something the Roman religion could never do. Many people who became Christians could also enjoy a more secure life. This was because Christian communities took care of their members instead of leaving them on their own.

For about three centuries after the death of Jesus, the Romans tried to stop Christianity from spreading. They treated Christians in ways that were similar to how they treated Jews in Judaea. Rome saw the new religion as a dangerous threat to its empire. Christians refused to worship the emperor as a god. They did not believe in Roman gods and criticized Roman games and festivals that honored these gods. Christians also refused to serve in the Roman army and were against warfare as a way to solve problems. For these and other reasons, the Romans accused Christians of being traitors and outlaws. Christians were arrested, beaten, and sometimes killed. Some Christians became **martyrs,** people who were willing to give up their lives rather than their beliefs.

Christians were persecuted by the Romans and by other groups. In this painting, Christians are hiding from the Huns.

Show Your Skill

1. **Make Inferences** Why did Christianity appeal to many people more than the old Roman religion did?

_____

_____

_____

_____

Mark the Text

2. Underline the definition of *martyrs*.

Think Critically

3. **Summarize** Why did the Romans mistreat Christians?

_____

_____

_____

_____

4. Identify the Main Idea List three things that show how Constantine supported Christianity.

_____

_____

_____

_____

_____

_____

Mark the Text

5. Diagram Circle the most powerful leaders of the early Christian church.

Think Critically

6. Explain Who made up the clergy in the early Christian church?

_____

_____

In the early A.D. 300s the emperor Diocletian made one last attempt to destroy Christianity. He failed because Christianity had grown too strong. In A.D. 312 there was a major turning point in the history of the new religion. Emperor Constantine converted to Christianity because the night before an important battle, Constantine had a life-changing dream. In his dream he saw a flaming cross in the sky. The next day he had his soldiers paint the symbol of the cross on their shields. After his army won the battle, Constantine was convinced the Christian God had helped him.

During his reign as emperor, Constantine did many things to support Christianity. He built churches in Jerusalem and Rome. He also let Christians serve in the military and work in the government. Under his rule, they no longer had to pay taxes and could receive government aid. In A.D. 313 he issued the Edict of Milan. This important decree gave religious freedom to all religions in the empire, including Christianity.

In A.D. 392 the emperor Theodosius outlawed Greek and Roman religions. At the same time, he made Christianity the official religion of the Roman Empire.

Organizing the Church

The early Christian church had to become better organized in order to unite its many followers. It also had to make sure that Christian communities shared similar beliefs and practices. Early church leaders used the Roman Empire as a model. The empire was ruled by a **hierarchy** of officials. A hierarchy is an organization with different levels of authority.

Hierarchy of the Early Christian Church

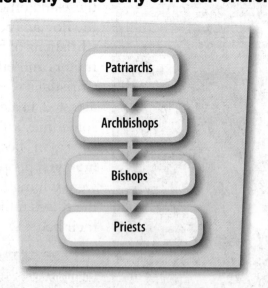

St. Augustine, Florida, was named for the Christian saint by the same name. This painting of St. Augustine is from the fifteenth century.

Church officials came to be known as the **clergy.** By A.D. 300 the clergy consisted of priests, bishops, and archbishops. In this hierarchy, archbishops had the most authority. Priests had the least power. The five most powerful archbishops were each in charge of an entire city. These leaders were called patriarchs. The **laity** were regular church members.

The bishops decided the true teachings of the Church. Accepted teachings became **doctrine.** Teachings that the bishops rejected were heresies. They went against the Christian faith.

Church leaders also had to preserve stories about Jesus and the writings of the apostles. By A.D. 300 there were four accepted accounts of the life and teachings of Jesus. Christians believed four apostles of Jesus wrote these accounts, or **gospels.** The word *gospel* means "good news." The New Testament includes all four gospels and the writings of early Christians. The Old Testament is the Greek version of the Jewish sacred writings. The Christian Bible consists of the Old Testament and the New Testament.

Two of the most influential early Christian writers were Paul and Augustine. Paul's writings are part of the New Testament. Augustine is one of the Church Fathers. These writers and thinkers played an important role in explaining and defining the teachings of Christianity.

As the Church grew, the bishop of Rome came to believe he had authority over all the other bishops. By A.D. 600, the bishop of Rome had the title of **pope.** *Pope* is from a Latin word that means "father." Christians in the western part of the Roman Empire accepted the pope as the head of all the churches. These Christians spoke Latin. Their churches formed the Roman Catholic branch of Christianity.

Christians in the eastern part of the empire spoke Greek. They did not believe the pope had authority over them. Their churches became the Eastern Orthodox Church.

 NGSSS Check How did early Christians explain their beliefs and teachings?
SS.6.W.3.13

_____

_____

Think Critically

7. Analyze The four gospels were written after the death of Jesus. How do you think people were able to remember what Jesus did and said before the gospels were written?

_____

_____

_____

Show Your Skill

8. Compare and Contrast What were some differences between Christians in the eastern and western parts of the Roman Empire?

_____

_____

_____

_____

_____

_____

ESSENTIAL QUESTION *How do religions develop?*

Reflect on What It Means . . .

Ideas about Christianity spread across the Roman Empire as teachers traveled to different cities to share their beliefs. Use what you learned in this chapter to predict what message the apostles or early church leaders would deliver to each of the following. Use 20 words or fewer for each message.

To an Individual

To a Community Leader

To a World Leader

TAKE THE CHALLENGE

Research one of the parables that Jesus taught. Think about how that parable translates to life today. Write about or draw a picture to explain or illustrate the parable.

THE AMERICAS

NGSSS

SS.6.W.2.10 Compare the emergence of advanced civilizations in Meso and South America with the four early river valley civilizations.

ESSENTIAL QUESTIONS *How does geography affect the way people live? What makes a culture unique?*

The Maya used the natural resources in their environment as they rose to become a great Mesoamerican civilization:

"Settling near rivers, lakes, and swamps, they learned to maximize the thin soil's productivity. They cleared the forest for maize, squash, and other crops by slashing and burning, much as today's Maya do, then re-enriched the land by alternating crops and letting fields lie fallow [unplanted]. As populations grew, they adopted more intensive methods of cultivation — composting, terracing, irrigation."

FROM *THE MAYA: GLORY AND RUIN*

productivity

Why would the Maya want the soil to have high productivity? Use the word *yield* in your response.

_____

_____

_____

cultivation

What caused the Maya to use "more intensive methods of cultivation"?

_____

DBQ BREAKING IT DOWN

Based on the description of the Maya's productivity in this excerpt, why do you think the title of the article is about the glory and ruin of the Maya? What do you think happened to the Maya?

_____

_____

McGraw-Hill
networks™
There's More Online!

TEXT: "The Maya: Glory and Ruin" by Guy Gugliotta, pp 68-109. National Geographic Magazine August 2007. Copyright © 2007 National Geographic Society. All rights reserved.

THE FIRST AMERICANS

NGSSS

SS.6.W.2.10 Compare the emergence of advanced civilizations in Meso and South America with the four early river valley civilizations.

Essential Question

How does geography affect the way people live?

Guiding Questions

1. How did geography shape the ways people settled in the Americas?
2. How did prehistoric people reach the Americas and form settlements?
3. How did farming make civilization possible in the Americas?
4. Why did a large number of civilizations develop in North America?

Terms to Know

isthmus
a narrow piece of land that connects two larger areas of land

maize
corn

Where in the World?

The Americas

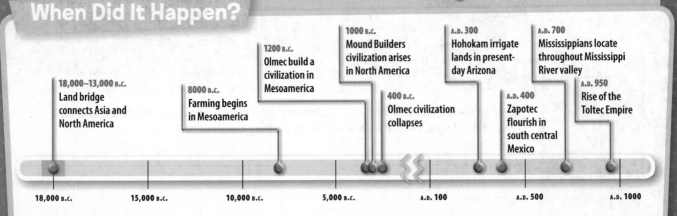

ARCTIC OCEAN

NORTH PACIFIC OCEAN

Gulf of Mexico

NORTH ATLANTIC OCEAN

Caribbean Sea

SOUTH PACIFIC OCEAN

SOUTH ATLANTIC OCEAN

When Did It Happen?

18,000–13,000 B.C.
Land bridge connects Asia and North America

8000 B.C.
Farming begins in Mesoamerica

1200 B.C.
Olmec build a civilization in Mesoamerica

1000 B.C.
Mound Builders civilization arises in North America

400 B.C.
Olmec civilization collapses

A.D. 300
Hohokam irrigate lands in present-day Arizona

A.D. 400
Zapotec flourish in south central Mexico

A.D. 700
Mississippians locate throughout Mississippi River valley

A.D. 950
Rise of the Toltec Empire

18,000 B.C.   15,000 B.C.   10,000 B.C.   5,000 B.C.   A.D. 100   A.D. 500   A.D. 1000

netw⚬rks Read Chapter 14 Lesson 1 in your textbook or online.

Geography of the Americas

The Americas is a vast region. It includes North America, Central America, South America, and the Caribbean. Central America is an isthmus. An **isthmus** is a narrow piece of land that connects two larger areas of land. Central America connects North America and South America.

The Americas have many different geographic features. Mountain chains run along the western side of North and South America. The Rocky Mountains are in western North America. The Andes range stretches along the Pacific coast of South America. Both North America and South America also have large areas of plains.

The Mississippi is the longest river in North America. It begins in Minnesota and empties into the Gulf of Mexico. The Amazon is South America's longest river. It starts in the Andes and flows into the Atlantic Ocean.

Settling the Americas

About 15,000 to 20,000 years ago, ocean levels were low. A thin strip of land linked Asia and North America. Some scientists think that early people walked across this land bridge from Asia into North America. Other scientists believe the first people came to America by boat.

The first Americans were hunters and gatherers, moving from place to place looking for food. They used what they found for food, clothing, and shelter.

Farming began in Mesoamerica around 9,000 to 10,000 years ago. Mesoamerica is the land from central Mexico to Costa Rica in Central America. The land in Mesoamerica was rich. The climate was mild. Crops grew well there. Early people grew squash, peppers, potatoes, and beans. Later, they grew **maize,** or corn. Maize became the major crop of the area.

Mark the Text

1. Circle the names of the major mountain ranges and rivers in North America and South America.

Show Your Skill

2. **Identify the Main Idea** What are two ways early people could have come to North America?

_____

_____

_____

_____

Mark the Text

3. Underline the two reasons why farming was successful in Mesoamerica.

Potatoes, squash, and corn were important crops in Mesoamerica and still are today.

4. Compare and Contrast
What were some of the similarities among the Mesoamerican civilizations?

_____

_____

_____

_____

Think Critically

5. Infer What could cause a civilization to decline?

_____

_____

_____

_____

Mark the Text

6. Circle the location where the Chavín lived.

First American Cultures

The Olmec civilization might be the oldest in Mesoamerica. It began about 1200 B.C. and lasted about 800 years. The Olmec civilization was based on farming and trade. The people built cities with pyramids and stone monuments. After the Olmec, other civilizations based on agriculture grew powerful. One group built Teotihuacán, a city of over 100,000 people. Teotihuacán was one of the first planned cities in the Americas. As many as 200,000 people lived there. Temples and palaces lined its streets.

Another group, the Zapotec, built Monte Albán. Monte Albán was a large city with stone temples, monuments, and tombs. The Zapotec also developed a writing system. Over time, Zapotec cities were abandoned. Historians are not sure why the Zapotec declined. Some people think that the Zapotec might have experienced a long period of time without rainfall, known as a drought. Others think that overpopulation or revolts might have brought an end to the Zapotec.

The Maya civilization began in the rain forests of Mexico. From there, the Maya spread deeper into southern Mexico and Central America.

Along the Pacific coast in South America, different civilizations also developed. One of these civilizations was found along the coastal areas of present-day Peru and Ecuador. The Chavín emerged around 900 B.C. They built many religious structures. They used stones from the region to build a temple. The temple was surrounded by pyramids, along with monuments in the shape of the Chavín's gods. The Chavín, however, did not create an empire. They declined around 200 B.C.

The ruins of Monte Albán are located in present-day Oaxaca, Mexico. The capital city was once home to a thriving civilization.

Early Cultures in North America

Many groups of people in North America learned how to farm from the people of Mesoamerica. As farming spread across North America, new civilizations developed.

The Hohokam lived in the desert of the American Southwest. They dug irrigation canals to bring river water to their fields. They grew corn, cotton, beans, and squash.

The Anasazi also lived in the Southwest. They collected water that ran off cliffs and used irrigation canals to bring water to their fields. The Anasazi built stone buildings called pueblos. They also built dwellings in the walls of cliffs. Both the Anasazi and Hohokam civilizations faded in the early A.D. 1000s. A lack of rain caused their crops to die. Settlements broke up. People formed smaller communities.

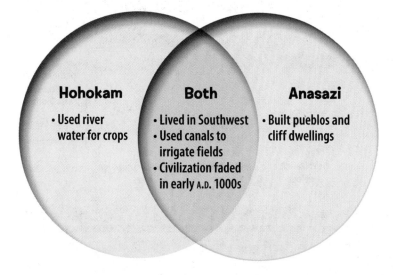

Hohokam
- Used river water for crops

Both
- Lived in Southwest
- Used canals to irrigate fields
- Civilization faded in early A.D. 1000s

Anasazi
- Built pueblos and cliff dwellings

East of the Mississippi River, another civilization arose—the Mound Builders. The Mound Builders built huge mounds of earth. These mounds were used as tombs or for ceremonies. Mound Builders were mostly hunters and gatherers. They did practice some farming and grew corn. This civilization began around 1000 B.C. It ended around A.D. 400.

By A.D. 700 the Mississippians arose. The Mississippians were farmers. Some Mississippian cities had over 10,000 people. Mississippians also built mounds. Their civilization collapsed during the A.D. 1200s. Historians are not sure why. Perhaps there was too little food or another group attacked them.

NGSSS Check As in Mesopotamia, Egypt, India, and China, what economic activity was important to the early cultures of the Americas? SS.6.W.2.10

Think Critically

7. Analyze What made it possible for new civilizations to develop in North America?

_____

_____

_____

Show Your Skill

8. Compare and Contrast
Complete these sentences about the Mound Builders and the Mississippians.

Like the Mound Builders, the Mississippians also

_____ _____.

Unlike the Mississippians, who were farmers, the Mound Builders were mostly

_____ and _____.

Take the Challenge

9. Choose a Mesoamerican civilization. Design a monument that shows an important event or a cultural aspect of the civilization. Think about what was most important to their civilization.

NGSSS

SS.6.E.3.2 Categorize products that were traded among civilizations, and give examples of barriers to trade of those products.

SS.6.G.3.1 Explain how the physical landscape has affected the development of agriculture and industry in the ancient world.

Essential Question

What makes a culture unique?

Guiding Questions

1. How did the Maya live in the rain forests of Mesoamerica?
2. What were the societies of North American peoples like?

Terms to Know

sinkholes
areas where the soil has collapsed into a hollow or depression

hogans
square, wooden homes built by the Navajo

When Did It Happen?

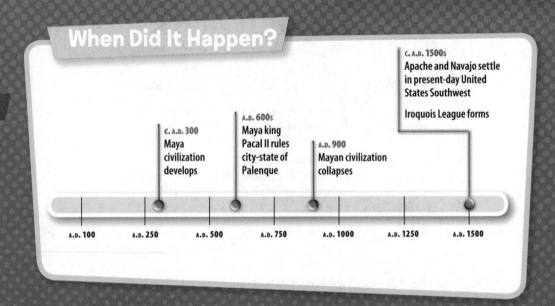

c. A.D. 300
Maya civilization develops

A.D. 600s
Maya king Pacal II rules city-state of Palenque

A.D. 900
Mayan civilization collapses

c. A.D. 1500s
Apache and Navajo settle in present-day United States Southwest

Iroquois League forms

A.D. 100   A.D. 250   A.D. 500   A.D. 750   A.D. 1000   A.D. 1250   A.D. 1500

What Do You Know?

Directions: Write your answers to the questions based on what you know before you study in the "Now" column. After this lesson, complete the "Later" column.

	Now	Later
Where did the Maya establish their empire?		
How did early Americans in North America adapt to their environment?		

The Maya

Around A.D. 300, the Maya developed a civilization in southern Mexico and Central America. They settled in an area of swampy forests. The swamps gave the Maya a source of fresh water. The Maya also used sinkholes for water. **Sinkholes** are areas where the land has fallen and formed a hollow. The Maya used the sinkholes to reach water underground.

The Maya planted corn and built cities. They set up more than 50 city-states. The Maya city-states shared a similar culture. Their governments were alike too, and they traded with each other. The city-states, however, often fought each other for territory.

Each Maya city-state was ruled by a king. The Maya believed that the king descended from the sun god, Kinich Ahau. The king was expected to serve the Maya people. Pacal II is considered to be the greatest Maya king. Pacal II ruled the city-state of Palenque during the A.D. 600s. He had many structures built during his reign. These structures are considered to be some of the best examples of Maya architecture ever created.

Each Maya city-state had a similar class system. At the top of the class system was the king. The king ruled with the help of nobles and priests. The class below them included farmers, artisans, and hunters. This class paid the taxes in the city-state and built the large Maya structures.

Mark the Text

1. Underline the two ways in which the Maya got fresh water.

Think Critically

2. **Infer** In a Maya city-state, who had to pay taxes? Why?

_____

_____

_____

_____

_____

Mark the Text

3. Circle the sentence that describes the Maya belief about gods.

Caracol was an important regional capital of the Maya Empire. It is located in present-day Belize.

Show Your Skill

4. Make a Connection What do you think future historians will say was our greatest achievement? Explain.

_____

_____

_____

_____

_____

Mark the Text

5. Underline the mathematical concept that the Maya developed.

Take the Challenge

6. Create an alphabet using recognizable shapes and symbols. Then, create a word or phrase using the symbols. Give a partner the word or phrase, along with your alphabet, so that he or she can decode it.

Religion was very important in Maya city-states. The Maya believed that gods controlled the events that occurred on Earth. Priests would conduct ceremonies in order to please the gods. Sometimes these ceremonies involved the sacrifice of human beings. When drought threatened to destroy Maya crops, priests would offer gifts to the god Chac, the god of rain.

Maya women often played an important role in the city-states. For example, in the city-state of Calakmul, at least two women ruled as queens. Sometimes, royal Maya women would marry into other royal families in different city-states. This practice increased the trade between the city-states. It also helped create alliances between them. Alliances are agreements between people or states to work together.

Maya priests believed that their gods revealed their plans through the movements of the sun, moon, and stars. As a result, priests studied the sky so that they could predict events on Earth. Their observations helped them learn about astronomy.

Priests created calendars by writing down when certain astronomical events occurred, such as eclipses. These calendars were then used to schedule religious events. Maya priests also referred to calendars to identify dates for planting and harvesting crops.

The Maya had two calendars. One calendar included 260 days and was used to mark religious events. Another calendar included 365 days and was used for noting events related to the change of seasons and agriculture.

In addition to astronomy, the Maya developed a system of mathematics. They created a method for counting based on 20. The Maya also used the concept of zero.

The Maya invented a written language based on hieroglyphics. They used this written language to record numbers and dates. The Maya hieroglyphics consisted of recognizable shapes and symbols. These shapes and symbols included plants, animals, and human faces showing emotion. The Maya carved these shapes and symbols on stone monuments.

Although the Maya civilization was strong and prosperous, it collapsed around A.D. 900. Historians, however, do not know why the civilization collapsed. Some historical evidence shows that warfare between different city-states increased during this

Maya Achievements

- Understood astronomy
- Developed calendars
- Developed a system of mathematics
- Used the concept of zero
- Invented a written language

time. Also, erosion and the overuse of soil might have caused a decrease in the amount of food that was produced. This drop in food production would have led to increased diseases and starvation.

Decline of Maya Civilization

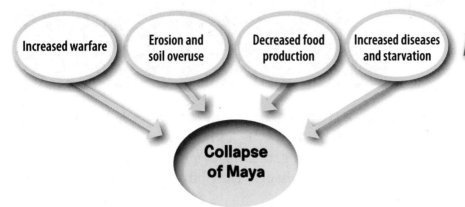

North American Peoples

By A.D. 1500 many different groups of Native Americans lived in North America. Throughout North America, people adapted to the environments they lived in.

The Inuit settled just south of the Arctic Circle, where the land was harsh, cold, and treeless. The Inuit built homes from stone and blocks of earth. When they traveled, they made shelters from blocks of hard-packed snow, called igloos. They hunted seals, walruses, and polar bears. They used the oil from seals and whales for lamps.

Many different groups of Native Americans lived along the Pacific coast. The climate was mild. It was not difficult to find food. People could fish and build houses from the tall trees. In the southern deserts, other groups gathered roots and seeds.

The Hopi, the Acoma, and the Zuni lived in the Southwest. They built homes from adobe. Adobe are bricks made from dried mud. They built canals to bring water to their fields. Major crops were corn, beans, squash, and melons.

Types of Native American Buildings

Igloos   ⟶ Far North homes made of pressed snow
Pueblos ⟶ Southwestern homes made of adobe, or sun-dried bricks
Hogans ⟶ Southwestern homes made of wood
Tepees ⟶ Great Plains tents made from animal skins

Mark the Text

7. Circle the reason why Maya food production might have decreased around A.D. 900.

Think Critically

8. **Explain** How did the Inuit use the resources of their environment to survive?

_____

_____

_____

_____

_____

Mark the Text

9. Underline the name of the group that lived near the Arctic Circle. Circle the names of the groups that dominated the Southwest.

Native Americans living on the Great Plains were nomads. The buffalo they hunted provided food as well as hides and bones for tools.

PHOTO: David David Gallery/Superstock/Getty Images

In the A.D. 1500s the Apache and Navajo settled in the Southwest. At first, the Apache and the Navajo did not farm. They were hunters and gatherers. Later, the Navajo began to farm. They settled in villages. They built square wooden homes called **hogans.**

Native Americans on the Great Plains were nomads. They stayed in villages for only one or two growing seasons. They lived in tepees, tents made from animal skins. They grew corn, beans, and squash. Women did most of the gardening. Men hunted antelope, deer, and buffalo. Plains people used every part of the buffalo.

The Eastern Woodlands was the land east of the Mississippi River. The woodlands were covered by thick forests. Native people of the Eastern Woodlands farmed and hunted. Some Native Americans in the Eastern Woodlands formed governments that linked several groups. The Iroquois League, for example, included five different Native American groups.

Before the League was set up, the groups fought with each other. The League brought peace. The League also created a constitution. A constitution is a plan of government. This was the first constitution written in what would become the United States.

Show Your Skill

10. Compare and Contrast How did the people in the Great Plains and Eastern Woodlands use the resources of their environment in similar and different ways?

_____

_____

_____

_____

_____

_____

_____

_____

Think Critically

11. Analyze Why do you think the Iroquois League is important?

_____

_____

_____

_____

_____

_____

 NGSSS Check Complete the following sentences. SS.6.G.3.1

1. Sinkholes and _____ provided freshwater for the Maya.

2. By studying the movements of the moon and stars, the Maya were able to create a _____ in order to know when to plant and harvest crops.

3. The Inuit could not farm due to the harsh climate near the Arctic Circle. Instead, they hunted _____.

4. North American peoples took advantage of the _____ _____ where they lived to build their homes.

Copyright © by The McGraw-Hill Companies, Inc.

CHAPTER 14

MY REFLECTIONS

ESSENTIAL QUESTION *How does geography affect the way people live?*

Reflect on What It Means . . .

You have learned how several groups of Native Americans lived between 8000 B.C. and A.D. 1500. Some of these groups had to contend with harsh environments. Others had abundant natural resources and an ideal climate. Think about the geographic factors that influenced these groups. Now think about how geography affects how you and people in your community live and how people in a specific location in the world live. Complete the chart below.

	In My Community	In ___________ (write the name of a place in the world)
Climate		
Clothing		
Food		
Sports		
Homes		

Keep Going!

TAKE THE CHALLENGE

You're on assignment for a travel magazine to go to the place in the world that you selected and featured in the chart on page 219. Write a list of questions below that you will ask the people who live there about how geography affects the way they live. Make sure that you write questions for children and adults. You may want to ask different questions for people who have lived there all their lives and for people who maybe have only lived there for a short time.

CHAPTER 15
IMPERIAL CHINA

NGSSS

SS.6.W.4.10 Explain the significance of the silk roads and maritime routes across the Indian Ocean and to the movement of goods and ideas among Asia, East Asia, East Africa and the Mediterranean basin.

ESSENTIAL QUESTIONS *How does geography influence the way people live? How do new ideas change the way people live? What are the characteristics of a leader?*

In his book, *The Travels of Marco Polo*, the famous world tourist wrote vivid descriptions about what he saw. If you had read this excerpt back in the 1400s when the book was published, would it have drawn you to China?

"Nanghin is a very noble province towards the west. The people... live by trade and manufactures. They have silk and great abundance, and they weave many fine tissues of silk and gold. They have all sorts of corn and victuals very cheap, for the province is a most productive one. Game also is abundant, and lions are found there. The merchants are great and opulent, and the Emperor draws a large revenue from them, in the shape of duties on the goods which they buy and sell."

MARCO POLO

victuals

The Latin word *victus* means "nourishment." What do you think *victuals* means?

_____

_____

opulent

What is an antonym (opposite word) for *opulent*?

_____

_____

DBQ BREAKING IT DOWN

What probably attracted readers the most in this excerpt? Why do you think Marco Polo describes in detail the abundance and wealth of the merchants and emperor of Nanghin?

_____

_____

McGraw-Hill
netw⚙rks™
There's More Online!

PHOTO: Imagno/Hulton Archive/Getty Images

CHINA REUNITES

 NGSSS

SS.6.W.4.4 Explain the teachings of Buddha, the importance of Asoka, and how Buddhism spread in India, Ceylon, and other parts of Asia.

SS.6.W.4.7 Explain the basic teachings of Laozi, Confucius, and Han Fei Zi.

SS.6.W.4.9 Identify key figures from classical and post-classical China.

Essential Question

How does geography influence the way people live?

Guiding Questions

1. How did imperial China rebuild its empire after years of war?
2. Why did Buddhism become popular in Tang China?
3. How did Confucian ideas shape China's government?

Terms to Know

neo-Confucianism a new understanding of Confucianism that included some Daoist and Buddhist beliefs

Where in the World?

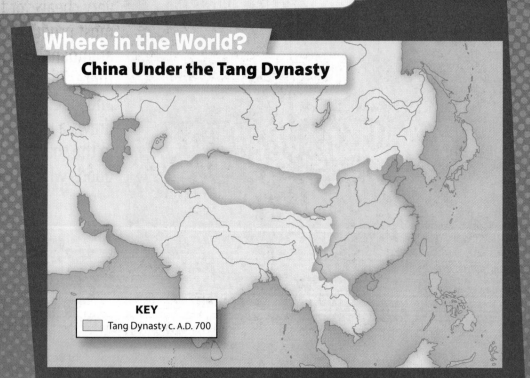

China Under the Tang Dynasty

KEY

Tang Dynasty c. A.D. 700

When Did It Happen?

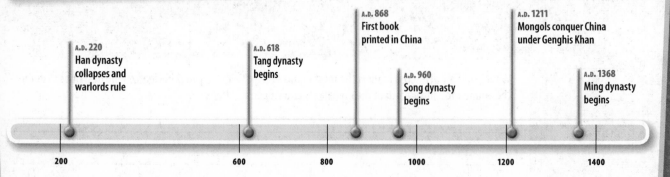

A.D. 220 Han dynasty collapses and warlords rule

A.D. 618 Tang dynasty begins

A.D. 868 First book printed in China

A.D. 960 Song dynasty begins

A.D. 1211 Mongols conquer China under Genghis Khan

A.D. 1368 Ming dynasty begins

200   600   800   1000   1200   1400

China Rebuilds Its Empire

China's Han empire ended in A.D. 220. China had no government for the next 300 years. Chinese warlords—military leaders who ran these kingdoms—fought with each other. China finally unified again in A.D. 581. Wendi, a general, made himself emperor. He won many battles and brought China back together. He founded a new line of rulers called the Sui.

After Wendi died, his son Yangdi took his place as emperor. Yangdi took on many large building projects. He rebuilt the Great Wall. Yangdi's biggest job was building the Grand Canal. These waterways connected the Chang Jiang (Yangtze River) and Huang He (Yellow River). The Grand Canal was a major shipping route. It was used to ship products between northern and southern China, helping to make China's economy stronger.

Yangdi rebuilt China, but he also made life very hard for the Chinese people. He made farmers work on the Great Wall and the Grand Canal. The people also had to pay for these projects with high taxes. The farmers became so angry that they killed Yangdi and took control of the government. When Yangdi died, the Sui dynasty ended.

In A.D. 618, one of Yangdi's generals made himself emperor. He took over China and set up a new dynasty called the Tang. This dynasty lasted much longer than the Sui. It was in power for about 300 years. The Tang capital of Changan was a very big and beautiful city. About one million people lived there.

Tang rulers made a number of reforms, or changes, to make China's government stronger. The most powerful Tang emperor was Taizong. He went back to using special tests called civil service examinations for choosing government officials. Government officials could not use family connections to get them jobs. Taizong also gave land to farmers and brought order to the countryside.

Improvements and Reforms	
Sui	Tang
• brought back law and order • built Grand Canal • helped China's economy grow	• brought back civil service examination • gave land to farmers • brought order to the countryside • made the military stronger

During the late A.D. 600s, a woman named Wu became the only woman in Chinese history to rule the country on her own. As a strong leader, Empress Wu made the government bigger. She also made the military stronger.

Show Your Skill

1. Identify Cause and Effect
What effects did the reforms that the Tang rulers introduced have on China?

_____

_____

_____

_____

_____

_____

Think Critically

2. Compare How were the Sui, Tang, and Song rulers similar?

_____

_____

_____

_____

_____

_____

_____

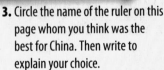

Mark the Text

3. Circle the name of the ruler on this page whom you think was the best for China. Then write to explain your choice.

_____

_____

_____

Think Critically

5. **Sequence** What events led to the end of the Tang dynasty?

_____

_____

_____

_____

_____

Show Your Skill

6. **Draw Conclusions** Why was Buddhism first accepted and then ended by Tang rulers?

_____

_____

_____

_____

_____

_____

China grew strong again in Asia under the Tang. It also gained control of a larger area. Tang armies took control of the Silk Road in Tibet, an important trade route, but in the mid- A.D. 700s, the Tang dynasty began to have problems. A new group of wandering people took control of central Asia and the Silk Road. China's economy became weak. Chinese farmers and people in Tibet also rose up against the government. All of these events weakened the Tang. The dynasty ended in A.D. 907.

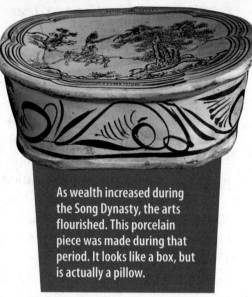

As wealth increased during the Song Dynasty, the arts flourished. This porcelain piece was made during that period. It looks like a box, but is actually a pillow.

Military leaders ruled China for the next fifty years. Then a general named Song made himself emperor in A.D. 960. The Song dynasty ruled from A.D. 960 to A.D. 1279. This was a time of great wealth and rich culture, but Song rulers did not have enough soldiers to control their large empire. Nomads took over land in northern China. The Song moved their capital south to the city of Hangzhou for safety.

Buddhism in China

Traders and missionaries from India had brought Buddhism to China in about A.D. 150. At the same time, the Han dynasty was very weak. A short time later, China broke apart. A civil war started. Many people suffered greatly. People died from the war and from a lack of food and housing. Buddhism taught that people could escape their suffering. Many Chinese who were looking for peace and comfort became Buddhists.

Early Tang rulers were not Buddhists, but they allowed people to practice Buddhism in China. They also allowed people to build Buddhist temples. Many Chinese Buddhists became monks and nuns. They lived in places called monasteries, or religious communities where people pray and worship. Buddhist nuns and monks ran schools. They also provided rooms and food for travelers. Buddhist monks served as bankers and gave medical care.

Some Chinese officials did not like Buddhism. Many thought it was wrong for the monasteries to accept money. Others thought that monks and nuns did not encourage respect for families because they did not marry. In the early A.D. 800s, people in the Tang government feared that Buddhism was gaining too much power. They saw Buddhism as an enemy of Chinese traditions. In A.D. 845, the Tang destroyed many Buddhist monasteries and temples.

Path of Buddhism in China

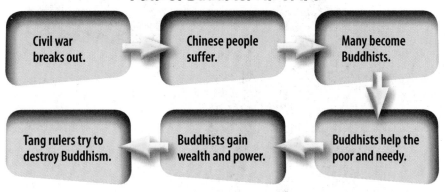

Korea broke free from China when the Han dynasty fell. For hundreds of years after A.D. 220, Korea was divided into three separate kingdoms. In the A.D. 300s, Chinese Buddhists brought their religion to Korea. In about A.D. 660, however, the Koreans came together to form one country. The new government supported Buddhism. Buddhism grew even stronger in Korea and spread to the islands of Japan.

Revival of Confucian Ideas

Confucius and his followers believed that a good government depended on wise leaders. The Tang dynasty supported a kind of new Confucianism, or Neo-Confucianism. Unlike Buddhism, it taught that life in this world was just as important as life in the next one. Followers of Confucius thought it was important to be active in their communities and to help others. Neo-Confucianism became more than a list of rules for being good. It became a religion. People who followed the teachings would find peace.

The new Confucianism also helped to make the government stronger. Tang and Song rulers gave special tests to people who wanted to work for the government. These tests were called civil service examinations. In the past, jobs had been given to people because of their wealth, family, or friends. Now the government hired people based on their knowledge and ability to think. People taking the tests had to show how much they knew about Confucian writings. To pass, they had to write with style and understanding.

8. Identify Cause and Effect How did the civil wars affect the people of China?

_____

_____

_____

_____

Think Critically

9. Infer Where in Asia do you think Buddhism is practiced today? Why?

_____

_____

_____

_____

_____

_____

_____

_____

10. Explain What is the new Confucianism?

_____

_____

_____

_____

_____

_____

11. Make a Connection What do people today spend years of training to learn?

_____

_____

_____

_____

_____

_____

_____

_____

12. Make a list of the kinds of questions you think might have been on the civil service exam.

The teachings of Confucius (pictured here) were somewhat transformed under the Tang dynasty. Neo-Confucianism, or New Confucianism was later revived in the 20th century in China.

The tests were supposed to be fair, yet only men could take the tests, and only rich people had enough money to help their sons study for the tests. It was very hard to pass the tests. It took years of study. Even with all of their work, only one out of every five men passed. Those who failed could get jobs teaching, but they could never get a government job.

NGSSS Check List three ways that the Sui dynasty rebuilt its empire after years of war. SS.6.W.4.9

1. _____

2. _____

3. _____

List four ways that the Tang dynasty improved China. SS.6.W.4.9

4. _____

5. _____

6. _____

7. _____

CHINESE SOCIETY

NGSSS

SS.6.E.3.1 Identify examples of mediums of exchange (currencies) used for trade (barter) for each civilization, and explain why international trade requires a system for a medium of exchange between trading both inside and among various regions.

SS.6.G.2.5 Interpret how geographic boundaries invite or limit interaction with other regions and cultures.

SS.6.W.4.8 Describe the contributions of classical and post-classical China.

Essential Question
How do new ideas change the way people live?

Guiding Questions
1. How did China's economy change under the Tang and Song dynasties?
2. How did new inventions change China's society?
3. Why were the Tang and Song dynasties a golden age of literature and the arts?

Terms to Know

porcelain
a ceramic made of fine clay baked at extremely hot temperatures

calligraphy
the use of ink and brush to draw Chinese characters

When Did It Happen?

A.D. 618
Tang rulers take power

A.D. 868
Chinese make first printed book

A.D. 1150
Chinese sailors begin using the compass

A.D. 600   A.D. 800   A.D. 1000   A.D. 1200

What Do You Know?

Directions: Put a check mark (✓) next to each true statement. When you finish the lesson, come back to check your answers.

_____ 1. Tang rulers made Chinese government stronger.

_____ 2. Tang rulers did not allow people to practice Buddhism.

_____ 3. China grew weaker under the Song rulers.

_____ 4. New Confucianism taught that people should care about this life as much as the next one.

_____ 5. People who wanted to work for the Chinese government had to pass difficult tests.

Show Your Skill

1. Identify Cause and Effect
What was the cause of China's economic problems in the A.D. 200s?

_____

_____

_____

_____

Think Critically

2. Explain Was the Tang dynasty a good time to be a farmer? Why?

_____

_____

_____

_____

_____

_____

_____

Mark the Text

3. Underline the improvements that helped Chinese traders.

Economic Growth

China's economy suffered when the Han dynasty ended in the A.D. 200s. When the fighting started, cities were ruined, and farms were burned. People had little food and few goods to trade. Under the Tang dynasty, these problems were solved.

The Tang rulers took power in A.D. 618. They brought peace to the countryside and gave more land to farmers. This allowed farmers to improve ways of watering and growing crops. They also grew new kinds of rice. Because farmers produced more food, the number of people in China grew. People moved to new areas, too. For example, farmers moved south where they could grow even more rice.

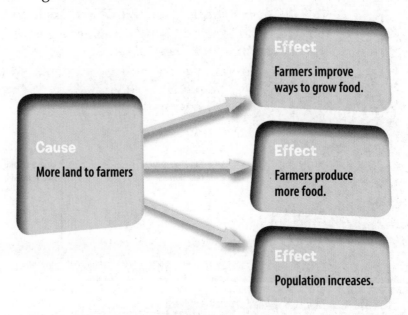

Cause
More land to farmers

Effect
Farmers improve ways to grow food.

Effect
Farmers produce more food.

Effect
Population increases.

Tang rulers also built roads and waterways, which made travel inside and outside of China easier. Merchants could now trade with people in other parts of Asia. The Silk Road was under Tang control, so trade increased. They traded silk fabric, tea, steel, paper, and porcelain. **Porcelain** is a kind of pottery made of fine clay and baked at high temperatures. For these Chinese products, other countries traded gold, silver, precious stones, and fine woods. Other trade routes connected China with central Asia, India, and Southwest Asia. The Tang also opened new ports on China's coast to help trade.

Technological Advances

During the Tang and Song dynasties, people made new inventions that changed life in China. These discoveries would soon spread to other parts of the world. For a long time, people burned wood to keep warm and cook food. Eventually, many trees were cut down and wood was hard to get. The Chinese then learned that coal could be burned to heat things. When they heated coal to make iron in a furnace, the melted iron mixed with carbon from the coal. It became a new, stronger metal known as steel. The Chinese made strong armor, swords, and helmets for their army with steel. They also made stoves, farm tools, drills, chains, nails, and sewing needles from steel. These changes made the army stronger and helped workers do more work.

The Chinese also found a new way to print books. Before this, people had to copy books by hand. This made books costly, so few books were made. The Chinese began printing in the A.D. 600s. They cut the characters of an entire page onto a block of wood. Then they put ink on the wood block. They placed paper on top of the inked block to print a page. Cutting a block took a long time. Once it was cut though, it could be used again and again to make more pages.

Soon the Chinese began printing books. The first known printed book is from about A.D. 868. Printing made it easier to make books. More books made it easier to spread ideas and information throughout China. In the A.D. 1000s, a Chinese printer named Pi Sheng made a new way to print. He used movable type. This meant that each character—instead of each page—was a separate piece of wood. These pieces could be moved around to make sentences. Pieces could be used again and again. Printing also led to another Chinese invention— paper money. With paper money, which is light and easy to carry, merchants helped the economy grow.

The Chinese made gunpowder for use in weapons and fireworks. One weapon was the fire lance. It was like an early gun. It helped make the Chinese army a strong force. The Chinese also built large ships with sails and rudders for steering. At about A.D. 1150, Chinese sailors also began using the magnetic compass to help them find their way. The magnetic compass let ships sail farther from land.

Chinese Inventions That Changed the World	
• steel	• gunpowder
• printing	• ships with rudders
• movable type	• compasses

4. Make Inferences How did steel help China's army?

_____

_____

_____

_____

_____

Think Critically

5. Evaluate What was the most important Chinese invention? Why?

_____

_____

_____

_____

_____

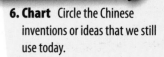

Mark the Text

6. Chart Circle the Chinese inventions or ideas that we still use today.

Emperor Hui-tsung of the Song dynasty painted this "Five Colored Parakeet on the Branch of a Blossoming Apricot Tree" on silk.

Literature and the Arts

The years of the Tang and Song dynasties were the best for Chinese culture. That is why those years are called "a golden age." Printing helped spread Chinese ideas and art. Chinese rulers supported art and literature. They invited artists and poets to live and work in the capital city of Chang'an (CHANG AHN).

The Tang dynasty was the great age of poetry in China. Some Tang poets wrote about the beauty of nature, the changing seasons, and the joy of friendship. Other poets wrote about the shortness of life. Li Bo was one of the most popular Tang poets. He often wrote about nature.

Another favorite Tang poet was Du Fu. He was poor and lived a hard life as a government worker. Civil war in China made life hard and food difficult to find. Du Fu almost died of hunger. These experiences helped him see the suffering of people. Du Fu's poems were serious. He often wrote about the unfairness of life for the poor and the wastefulness of war.

During the Song dynasty, Chinese artists painted large nature scenes called landscapes. These artists didn't try to make their pictures look exactly like what they were painting. Instead, they tried to show the power of the mountains and lakes. They wanted to show the idea that people may live in nature, but they can't control it. As a result, people appeared to be small in the paintings, much smaller than the nature around them. Chinese painters often wrote poetry on their works. They used a brush and ink to write beautiful characters called **calligraphy.**

During the Tang period, Chinese artisans, or skilled workers, made very fine porcelain. Because porcelain comes from China, people around the world call it by the name "china." Porcelain can be made into plates, cups, figurines, and vases. Knowledge of the process for making porcelain spread to other parts of the world. It did not reach Europe until the A.D. 1700s.

 NGSSS Check How did life in China improve under the Tang and Song dynasties? SS.6.W.4.8

_____

_____

PHOTO: Burstein Collection/CORBIS

Show Your Skill

7. Identify the Main Idea What contribution did Pi Sheng make to Chinese culture?

_____

_____

_____

_____

_____

_____

Think Critically

8. Summarize What is a golden age?

_____

_____

_____

_____

SS.6.W.4.9 Identify key figures from classical and post classical China.

SS.6.W.4.10 Explain the significance of the silk roads and maritime routes across the Indian Ocean and to the movement of goods and ideas among Asia, East Asia, East Africa and the Mediterranean basin.

SS.6.W.4.11 Explain the rise and expansion of the Mongol Empire and its effects on peoples of Asia and Europe including the achievements of Genghis and Kublai Khan.

SS.6.W.4.12 Identify the causes and effects of Chinese isolation and the decision to limit foreign trade in the 15th century.

LESSON

3

THE MONGOLS IN CHINA

Essential Question
What are the characteristics of a leader?

Guiding Questions
1. **Why were the Mongols able to build a vast empire so quickly?**
2. **How did the Mongols rule the Chinese?**

Terms to Know

steppe
wide, rolling, grassy plain

terror
violent acts that are meant to promote fear in people

Where in the World?

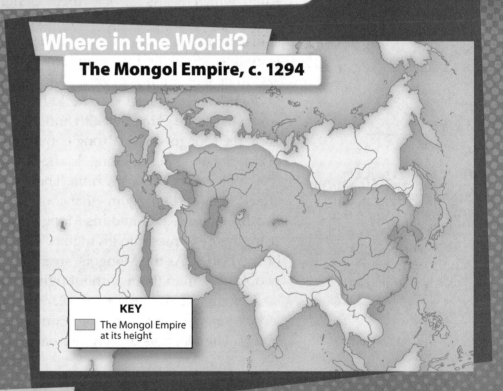

The Mongol Empire, c. 1294

KEY

☐ The Mongol Empire at its height

When Did It Happen?

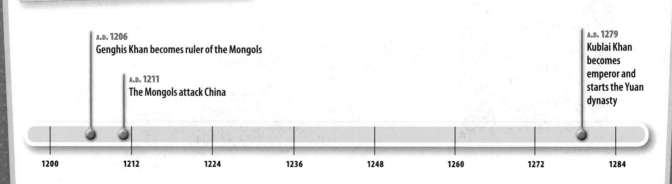

A.D. 1206
Genghis Khan becomes ruler of the Mongols

A.D. 1211
The Mongols attack China

A.D. 1279
Kublai Khan becomes emperor and starts the Yuan dynasty

| 1200 | 1212 | 1224 | 1236 | 1248 | 1260 | 1272 | 1284 |

Show Your Skill

1. Identify Cause and Effect
How did the geography of the steppes affect the way the Mongols lived?

_____

_____

_____

_____

2. Identify Cause and Effect
How did the Mongols' use of terror affect their enemies?

_____

_____

_____

_____

_____

Take the Challenge

3. Write a letter to Genghis Khan asking him to stop the terror that he is causing in China. Make an appeal and offer an alternative strategy for him to follow.

Mongol Expansion

The Mongols lived in an area north of China called Mongolia. They lived in clans, or groups of loosely related families. The Mongols raised cattle, sheep, goats, and horses. They moved as the animals fed on Mongolia's great **steppes,** or wide, rolling, grassy lands. Mongolia's steppes stretch from the Black Sea to northern China. The Mongols could ride horses very well. Also, they could fight very well. They could shoot arrows at enemies from far away while riding toward them. Then they attacked with spears and swords.

Mongol leaders came together in A.D. 1206 in the Gobi, a desert covering parts of Mongolia and China. At that meeting, they elected a young warrior named Temujin to be Genghis Khan, which means "strong ruler." Genghis Khan organized the Mongols into a strong army and chose leaders for their skills, not for their family ties. With these changes, Mongols were the most skilled fighting force in the world. Their goal was to take over lands beyond Mongolia.

Genghis Khan started to build his empire. Each time he won a battle, he gained wealth and new soldiers for his army. Soon the Mongols were strong enough to attack larger groups of people. In A.D. 1211, Mongols attacked China. In three years, they took all of northern China. Then they moved west to attack cities and kingdoms that controlled parts of the Silk Road. Genghis Khan and his Mongol fighters used **terror** to scare their enemies into giving up. They attacked, robbed, and burned cities. As the Mongols' strength became known, many people gave in to them without fighting.

Genghis Khan died in A.D. 1227. His four sons split up the large Mongol Empire. The sons continued to make the empire bigger. The Mongols moved into parts of eastern and central

The Mongols placed high value on their horses, which they used in war. Here, Genghis Khan is portrayed riding with a bow and arrow.

PHOTO: Sergio Momo/Getty Images

Europe. They also took over much of Southwest Asia. The Mongols brought all of these lands together under their rule. At its height, the empire reached from the Pacific Ocean in the east to eastern Europe in the west. It reached from Siberia in the north to the Himalaya in the south. It was the largest land empire ever.

The Mongols brought peace to their lands. Peace was good for trade, and this helped the Mongols. The Mongols now had control of many of Asia's trade routes. They gained great wealth by taxing the goods that were traded. The Mongols had great respect for the cultures they now ruled. Sometimes they took on the beliefs and customs of the people. For example, the Mongols in Southwest Asia accepted Islam. The Mongols also learned from the Chinese. They learned about gunpowder and the fire lance. With these new weapons, their enemies were even more afraid of the Mongols.

Mark the Text

4. Underline the description of how large the Mongol empire was.

Think Critically

5. **Summarize** What technological advances did the Mongols learn from the Chinese?

_____

_____

_____

_____

6. **Analyze** How did Kublai Khan change Chinese government?

_____

_____

_____

_____

_____

_____

_____

_____

_____

The Mongols

War
- skilled horsemen
- skilled fighters
- used terror
- adopted gunpowder and fire lance

Peace
- largest land empire
- respected cultures they ruled
- protected trade

Mongol Conquest of China

In A.D. 1260, Genghis Khan's grandson, Kublai Khan, became ruler. Kublai Khan took over more and more of China. In A.D. 1264 Kublai moved his capital from Karakorum in Mongolia to Khanbaliq in northern China. Today the city of Beijing stands in the same place.

In A.D. 1279 Kublai Khan made himself China's new emperor and started the Yuan dynasty. *Yuan* means "beginning." This name showed that the Mongols wanted to rule China for a long time, but the Yuan dynasty lasted for only about 100 years.

As emperor, Kublai Khan stopped giving the civil service examinations for government jobs. He let non-Chinese work in the government. He also let many Chinese keep their jobs. The Mongols and Chinese were different in many ways. The Mongols had their own language, laws, and customs. The two groups lived separately and did not mix.

Think Critically

8. **Explain** Why did China grow wealthy under the Mongol rulers?

_____

_____

_____

_____

_____

Show Your Skill

9. **Identify Cause and Effect** Who was Marco Polo? How did news of his travels affect people in Europe?

_____

_____

_____

_____

_____

_____

_____

Many Mongols were Buddhists, but they did accept other religions. For example, Kublai Khan allowed people to practice their faiths and share them with others.

China reached its greatest wealth and power under Mongol rule. Its wealth drew people from other countries to China. They came on the Silk Road. China's capital city was admired for its wide streets, beautiful palaces, and nice homes.

One person who came to China was Marco Polo. He was from Italy. Kublai Khan liked the stories Polo told about his travels. For many years, Kublai Khan sent Polo on trips to learn things. When Polo finally went back to Europe, he wrote a book about his travels. His stories of China amazed Europeans.

The Mongols ruled a large empire, covering land between the Pacific Ocean and eastern Europe. This made China wealthy from trade. The Chinese traded tea, silk, and porcelain for silver, spices, carpets, and cotton from Europe and other parts of Asia. Europeans and Muslims traded and took Chinese steel, gunpowder, and the compass back to their homes.

The Mongols made China's empire larger. They took over Vietnam and northern Korea. The Mongols forced the Koreans to build warships. The Mongols tried to use these ships to take over Japan.

After the end of Mongol rule, the Ming dynasty came to power in China. During the early 1400s, the Ming rulers sent voyages of exploration to South Asia and East Africa. These voyages were led by Zheng He, a Chinese Muslim. Chinese officials later persuaded the emperor to stop the voyages. The officials felt the voyages were too expensive and posed a threat to traditional Chinese culture. As a result, China became more isolated. Its overseas trade declined.

This porcelain jar is from the Ming dynasty.

 NGSSS Check How did the Mongols rule the Chinese? SS.6.W.4.11

_____

_____

ESSENTIAL QUESTION *How do new ideas change the way people live?*

Reflect on What It Means . . .

You have learned about how the Mongol conquest of China brought peace and economic prosperity. The Mongols also often picked up aspects of the cultures of the people they conquered. They picked up some of their beliefs and customs. Think about how the Mongol's control of China affected individuals who were living there and their communities, and how the effects of the conquest affected the world.

The Mongols' Conquest of China

Individuals	Communities	The World

Keep Going!

TAKE THE CHALLENGE

You are a conquest correspondent traveling with the Mongols on the Silk Road as they make their way through China. Write an article below about what you observe. Include in your feature how the conquest affects China's economy, its people, and its culture. You may want to point out new inventions and technology, interesting trade goods, and customs and traditions that you see on your travels.

NGSSS Inventory Test

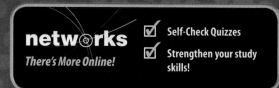

The state of Florida uses tests to measure your knowledge in different subject areas. The tests that you take will vary from year to year. However, the skills you need to perform well on standardized tests apply to every subject.

✓ Be Prepared

To do your best on test days, you need to take care of yourself beforehand. Try to get plenty of sleep for several nights before the test. Make sure to eat a good breakfast and lunch on test day. Then, be ready to do your best!

✓ What to Expect

The questions on your end-of-course tests will be multiple choice. Each question will be followed by four answer choices. Your job is to decide which of the four is the best possible answer.

Sometimes you absolutely know the answer to a question and the right answer leaps out at you. Other times you have to analyze the options and eliminate ones you know are wrong in order to zero in on the right answer.

✓ Pace Yourself

When you take an end-of-course test, it is important to pace yourself. If you work too quickly, you will be more likely to make mistakes. Instead, read each question and all of the answer choices carefully. If there's a question you can't answer, skip it and answer the next question. When you are done with the test, you can go back and reread those questions you did not understand.

✓ Read Every Word

Pay extra attention to every word in the questions. Just a word or two can change the meaning of the question.

✓ Make Your Best Guess

Make sure you go back and answer every question before submitting your test. Any question left blank will be marked wrong, so it's better to make your best guess. Remember to use the process of elimination to narrow the possibilities. Then make your guess from the remaining choices.

✓ Check Your Work

After you finish the test, go back to the beginning and check your work.

Directions: Circle the best answer.

1 Hunter-gatherers

   A   developed societies after the Bronze Age.

   B   were nomads.

   C   lived in small farming settlements.

   D   sought permanent shelter in caves.

 SS.6.W.2.1 Compare the lifestyles of hunter-gatherers with those of settlers of early agricultural communities.

2 In ancient Egypt, three benefits to living near the Nile River were

   A   boat racing, religious ceremonies, and fishing.

   B   fishing, support for animals, and fertile soil from flooding.

   C   fertile soil from flooding, warfare transportation, and religious ceremonies.

   D   support for animals, fishing, and boat racing.

 SS.6.G.2.1 Explain how major physical characteristics, natural resources, climate, and absolute and relative locations have influenced settlement, interactions, and the economies of ancient civilizations of the world.

3 What were the achievements of Ramses II?

   A   As a reformer, he introduced a new religion

   B   He rebuilt the empire and constructed major temples.

   C   He gained great wealth for the empire through trade and tribute.

   D   As a ruler of Upper Egypt, he overtook Lower Egypt and united the kingdoms.

 SS.6.W.2.6 Determine the contributions of key figures from ancient Egypt.

4 Both Athens and Sparta

   F   allowed women to serve in the military.

   G   were run as democracies.

   H   focused on building a strong military.

   J   provided boys with an education.

 SS.6.W.3.3 Compare life in Athens and Sparta (government and the status of citizens, women and children, foreigners, helots.)

5 According to the Hebrew Bible, David

   A   led the Israelites out of Egypt.

   B   wrote many proverbs.

   C   united the Twelve Tribes while he was king.

   D   was told by God to settle in Canaan.

 SS.6.W.2.9 Identify key figures and basic beliefs of the Israelites and determine how these beliefs compared with those of others in the geographic area.

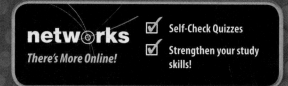

6 How was Athenian direct democracy different from the representative democracy we practice in the United States?

F Athenian citizens voted for officials to make laws on their behalf.

G Athenian citizens gathered at mass meetings and voted on laws.

H The council made laws for all the people.

J The Athenian law-making body met only once a year.

 SS. 6.C.1.1 Identify democratic concepts developed in ancient Greece that served as a foundation for American constitutional democracy.

7 Which statement below is true of Emperor Ashoka?

F He was a strong military leader.

G He became a Buddhist but allowed his subjects to continue practicing Hinduism.

H He ruled India during its golden age of mathematics.

J He founded the Mauryan empire.

 SS.6.W.4.4 Explain the teachings of Buddha, the importance of Asoka, and how Buddhism spread in India, Ceylon, and other parts of Asia.

8 Hindus believe in one great spirit known as

A Brahman.

B Nirvana.

C Jesus Christ.

D Dharma.

 SS.6.W.4.2 Explain the major beliefs and practices associated with Hinduism and the socials structure of the caste system in ancient India.

9 What did Gupta mathematicians invent?

A early forms of computers

B the zero

C long division

D geometry

 SS.6.W.4.5 Summarize the important achievements and contributions of ancient Indian civilization.

10 How was Chinese civilization along the Huang He similar to ancient Egypt?

A Both developed in a river valley that flooded the land and made it rich.

B Both experienced constant invasions by surrounding nations.

C Both developed a writing system based on hieroglyphics.

D Both built a large bureaucracy to rule the kingdom.

 SS.6.W.2.4 Compare the economic, political, social, and religious institutions of ancient river civilizations.

11 The Silk Road was important to China because it

F allowed China to learn about better ways of governing.

G brought China into contact with other civilizations.

H taught the Chinese how to follow Western customs.

J created a new maritime route.

 SS.6.W.4.10 Explain the significance of the silk roads and maritime routes across the Indian Ocean to the movement of goods and ideas among Asia, East Africa, and the Mediterranean Basin.

12 In the early days of the Roman Republic, the patricians

A were nobles who served as the top government officials.

B were farmers who could serve in the Senate.

C made up the largest group in society and had fewer rights that others.

D owned all the land and made laws for all the people.

 SS.6.W.3.16 Compare life in the Roman Republic for patricians, plebeians, women, children, and slaves.

13 What Roman legal principle did Americans adopt?

F People are innocent until proven guilty.

G All accused criminals have the right to a lawyer.

H All citizens must vote in elections.

J Accused criminals must convince the judge of their innocence.

 SS.6.C.1.2 Identify how the government of the Roman Republic contributed to the development of democratic principles (separation of powers, rule of law, representative government, civic duty).

14 How does the Latin language live on in the English language?

A Judges and lawyers speak Latin in court.

B Every person has a Latin name.

C The English alphabet is the same as the Latin alphabet.

D Many English words come from Latin.

 SS.6.W.3.17 Explain the spread and influence of the Latin language on Western Civilization.

15 Which early Christian leader was known for traveling extensively, preaching, and writing important letters?

A Peter

B Luke

C Matthew

D Paul

 SS.6.W.3.13 Identify key figures and the basic beliefs of early Christianity and how these beliefs impacted the Roman Empire.

NGSSS Inventory Test

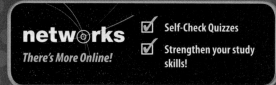

16 Christianity became legal in the Roman Empire after

A Jesus's crucifixion and the teaching of the Apostles.

B Julius Caesar made it the official state religion.

C Nero became emperor.

D Constantine converted to Christianity and issued the Edict of Milan.

 SS.6.W.3.13 Identify key figures and the basic beliefs of early Christianity and how these beliefs impacted the Roman Empire.

17 Trade throughout the Roman Empire was made easier because

F horses were captured in war and traded to others.

G a common currency was used.

H Roman law regulated trade.

J aqueducts brought fresh water to the cities.

 SS.6.E.3.1 Identify examples of mediums of exchange (currencies) used for trade (barter) for each civilization, and explain why international trade requires a system for a medium of exchange between trading both inside and among various regions.

18 The Eastern Roman Empire was able to avoid many Germanic invasions because

A it was protected by the Spartans.

B the Western Roman Empire had more wealth.

C the Mediterranean Sea and Black Sea offered protection from invaders.

D Theodosius moved the capital to Constantinople.

 SS.6.W.3.15 Explain the reasons for the gradual decline of the Western Roman Empire after the Pax Romana.

19 Mesoamericans began forming more complex societies because they

A learned to make iron tools.

B discovered fire.

C could grow corn and other crops well.

D developed a written language.

 SS.6.W.2.10 Compare the emergence of advanced civilizations in Meso and South America with the four early river valley civilizations.

20 In what ways did Paleolithic and Neolithic people differ?

F Paleolithic hunters did not use tools, but Neolithic hunters did.

G Paleolithic people created forms of art, but Neolithic people did not.

H Paleolithic people did not domesticate animals, but Neolithic people did.

J Paleolithic men and women did the same jobs, but Neolithic men and women did different jobs.

 SS.6.W.2.1 Compare the lifestyles of hunter-gatherers with those of settlers of early agricultural communities.

Copyright © by The McGraw-Hill Companies, Inc.

 21 To grow crops in a hot, dry climate Mesopotamian farmers

A used buckets to carry the water from the river to the fields.

B prayed to the gods to bring the annual floods.

C dug deep wells to find the water under the earth.

D built irrigation waterways and ditches to bring water from rivers to their fields.

SS.6.G.2.1 Explain how major physical characteristics, natural resources, climate, and absolute and relative locations have influenced settlement, interactions, and the economies of ancient civilizations of the world.

 22 How were the Mauryan and Gupta empires alike?

F They had Hindu rulers.

G They tried to change the caste system.

H They ruled from Pataliputra.

J They conquered northern and central India.

SS.6.W.4.3 Recognize the political and cultural achievements of the Mauryan and Gupta empires.

 23 Qin Shihuangdi unified China by

A making everyone follow the same religion.

B building a road and a huge canal.

C building the Great Wall.

D closing the Silk Road.

SS.6.W.4.9 Identify key figures from classical and post-classical China.

 24 What change did new Confucianism bring to the Song dynasty?

F Chinese rulers were convinced to ban Buddhism.

G New Confucian officials introduced the idea of a merit system.

H New Confucianism became the dynasty's official philosophy.

J Scholar-officials lost their place in Chinese society.

SS.6.W.4.8 Describe the contributions of classical and post classical China.

 25 Why did early civilizations develop in Mesoamerica?

A Long rainy seasons provided water for people and crops.

B The land had rich, volcanic soil and a mild climate.

C The dense forests protected people from the harsh sunlight.

D Groups were able to fish in the Indian Ocean.

SS.6.G.2.1 Explain how major physical characteristics, natural resources, climate, and absolute and relative locations have influenced settlement, interactions, and the economies of ancient civilizations of the world.